People and Land

Theology in the Age of Empire

Series Editor: Jione Havea

In these five volumes, an international collective of theologians interrogate Christianity's involvement with empires past and present, trouble its normative teachings and practices whenever they sustain and profit from empire, and rekindle the insights and energies within the Christian movement that militate against empire's rapacity.

Titles in the Series

Religion and Power, edited by Jione Havea
Scripture and Resistance, edited by Jione Havea
People and Land, edited by Jione Havea

Forthcoming

Vulnerability and Resilience, edited by Jione Havea
Mission and Context, edited by Jione Havea

People and Land

Decolonizing Theologies

Jione Havea

LEXINGTON BOOKS/FORTRESS ACADEMIC
Lanham • Boulder • New York • London

Published by Lexington Books/Fortress Academic
Lexington Books is an imprint of The Rowman & Littlefield Publishing Group, Inc.
4501 Forbes Boulevard, Suite 200, Lanham, Maryland 20706
www.rowman.com

6 Tinworth Street, London SE11 5AL

British Library Cataloguing in Publication Information Available

Library of Congress Cataloging-in-Publication Data

Names: Havea, Jione, 1965- editor.
Title: People and land : decolonizing theologies / edited by Jione Havea.
Description: Lanham : Lexington Books/Fortress Academic, 2019. | Series: Theology in the age of empire | Includes bibliographical references and index. | Summary: "Empires rise and expand by taking lands and resources and by enslaving the bodies and minds of people. Even in this modern era, the territories, geographies, and peoples of a number of lands continue to be divided, occupied, harvested, and marketed. The legacy of slavery and the scapegoating of people persists in many lands, and religious institutions have been co-opted to own land, to gather people, to define proper behavior, to mete out salvation, and to be silent. The contributors to People and Land, writing from under the shadows of various empires-from and in between Africa, Asia, the Americas, the Caribbean, and Oceania-refuse to be silent. They give voice to multiple causes: to assess and transform the usual business of theology and hermeneutics; to expose and challenge the logics and delusions of coloniality; to tally and demand restitution of stolen, commodified and capitalized lands; to account for the capitalizing (touristy) and forced movements of people; and to scripturalize the undeniable ecological crises and our responsibilities to the whole life system (watershed). This book is a protest against the claims of political and religious empires over land, people, earth, minds, and the future"-- Provided by publisher.
Identifiers: LCCN 2019039987 (print) | LCCN 2019039988 (ebook) | ISBN 9781978703605 (cloth) | ISBN 9781978703612 (ebook) ISBN 9781978703629 (pbk)
Subjects: LCSH: Land tenure--Religious aspects--Christianity. | Postcolonial theology.
Classification: LCC BR115.L23 P46 2019 (print) | LCC BR115.L23 (ebook) | DDC 230/.046--dc23
LC record available at https://lccn.loc.gov/2019039987 LC ebook record available at https://lccn.loc.gov/2019039988

∞™ The paper used in this publication meets the minimum requirements of American National Standard for Information Sciences Permanence of Paper for Printed Library Materials, ANSI/NISO Z39.48-1992.

This book was made possible
through the kind contribution
of the Council for World Mission

Praise for *People and Land*

"*People and Land* deftly enacts and provides models for counter-imperializing, by refocusing the gaze from plural vantages, as contributors—across multiple contexts from Pasifika and Australia to the Middle East and Asia, from Jamaica to Africa—unpick threads of repetition and mutation that serve to re-instantiate imperialist violence. Offering creative resistance, strategies of liberation, and workable hope, this accessible collection should be on the curricula and in the libraries not only of scholars of postcolonial theologies and hermeneutics but also in what were once considered mainstream studies. *People and Land* is a sharp, critical, and thoroughly readable assembly of essays that should inspire change not only at the level of scholarship but also and especially in sociopolitical religious practice."
—**Anne Elvey**, University of Divinity and Monash University

"In the shadows of the neoliberal development narrative that denies the inextricable relationship of land, people, and life, we have a volume that advocates for a new story based on relationality and justice."
—**Upolu Lumā Vaai**, Pacific Theological College

"Deeply rooted in the ground from which life and thought emerges, the theologies in this collection bear the character and groans of peoples and of their lands. Here are authentically located theologies! Reading this collection exposes theology in a vacuum as chicanery."
—**Lily Fetalsana Apura**, Silliman University

"Persuaded that the land and the peoples, especially the indigenous people in various postcolonial contexts, are intricately bound together and fully aware of the adverse repercussions of empire and its persistent harmful death-dealing legacies on the previously colonized people and their lands, the authors in this brilliant volume mock, unsettle, and challenge empire and empire-driven theologies, ideologies, and biblical hermeneutics in their commitment to producing a justice-conscious, transformative, liberating product. Profound and unapologetically prophetic! This book is a must read for all justice-seeking persons whose vision is to pull down the ruthless strongholds of empire.

Probing, provoking, and prophesying. Profound, prophetic, and pro-marginalized people and lands."
—**Madipoane Masenya (Ngwan'a Mphahlele)**, University of South Africa

"Brilliant! This volume is more than another book relating to Empire hermeneutics. This volume has a voice that needs to be heard, a voice that needs to challenge the churches, and a voice that needs to confront the consciences of social and political leaders across the globe for what has been done to motherlands.

The chapters reflect the consciences of authors from the original Promised Land of Palestine to the dispossessed lands of Australia and the mutilated islands of the Pacific. The abuse of motherlands across the face of Earth is exposed as a series of vicious crimes by numerous 'empires'—crimes that demand more than theological reflection.

Ultimately, land is revealed to be alive and the source of life, reflecting the colors of life and calling for restorative justice for all the cruelties and pain inflicted. Land is depicted as the suffering soul of the planet, a soul that needs to be saved by more than mission theology."
—**Norman Habel**, Flinders University

"*People and Land: Decolonizing Theologies* is a collection of thoughtful and provocative essays. It incisively connects seemingly disparate dots—forced migration, modern tourism, war, exploitation, and climate crisis, to name a few—to challenge the 'color-blind' Eurocentric theological and hermeneutical underpinnings of imperial and ecclesial structures that have perpetuated coloniality from antiquity to the present day. By raising up voices of thought leaders and community activists from the Global South, contributors to this volume present alternative interpretations of scriptures and traditions that reframe the crises of our time and elucidate pathways toward healing and emancipation of motherlands and their dismembered communities, nonhuman and human alike."
—**Lauress Wilkins Lawrence**, Wisdom Commentary Series (Liturgical Press) Editorial Board

Contents

Part II: Dispossessions and Responsibilities

Foreword

Collin I. Cowan

Christianity conceives of God in relationship to land and people. The Bible opens with creation accounts in which land and people come forth in partnership, and God moves in mutual communion with both. God's creation is first imagined in joy as a blessing, but this blessing is swindled when rival claims and ways of peoplehood stir up violence, murder, and division.

Christian faith at times claims a colonizing attitude to land and people (Josh. 1:13); at other times it embraces people separated from their land (Jer. 29:4–7) and affirms God's claim upon the whole earth—upon all lands and peoples (Ps. 24). We find in Jesus, whose early years were spent as a refugee (Matt. 2:13–15), a savior who lived as a stranger among indigenous people who were displaced from their land (John 1:11). His life, death, and resurrection forged a covenant for all peoples and all lands (Matt. 28:19) and stirred up a movement in which Jew and Gentile, male and female, slave and free, were called into citizenship in the New Heaven and New Earth (Gal. 3:28; Eph. 2:19).

In this collection of essays, the authors explore the inextricable interconnections of land and people for faith and life and advocate the pursuit of justice and peace in the shadows of empire. They collectively invite us to consider what our mission is in the midst of empire's destruction of the earth and denial of right to land and life, as well as encourage us to dismantle the global empire by proudly asserting our diverse personhood according to our contexts and lands. This volume will inspire readers to confront the superpowers that target the oceans and lands, minerals and resources, peoples and cultures to build their strongholds; as well as prompt readers to expose and subvert agendas that disadvantage the majority of the earth's population and further erode the already vulnerable environment.

Council for World Mission (CWM) supported and endorses this work, mindful of its history in the occupation of lands and peoples. Our complicity with colonization and enslavement is clear from our history in the London Missionary Society, and it is our desire to dismantle and transform their legacies through the current vision and spirit of CWM's mission in the context of empire. CWM began as a movement which brought the good news of Jesus Christ to new peoples and lands who would contextualize the gospel and create churches and movements as their context led. That quickly gave way to a desire to colonize and replicate European models of life and faith while occupying the hearts, minds, souls, and resources of lands and peoples. The task of dismantling this heritage still stirs up people and lands in 2019 and in CWM's work and program, especially when we live in a climate catastrophe that is driving many people from their lands and threatens all land and people.

Collin I. Cowan
General Secretary, CWM
July 13, 2019

Preface

D. S. Yatawara, a Sri Lankan street artist, explained that "mother land" (the artwork printed on the cover of this book) is about Sri Lanka, referring to his homeland and to his people. Bared. Parched. Vulnerable. Yet embracing. Shielding. Surviving, plus a host of other qualities that befit a "mother land" that has received the fallen bodies of its people, animals, and plants, as a consequence of colonial abuse, persisting poverty, civil war, religious violence, and social and political instability. At the heart of "mother land" is a clinging, dismembered child.

Drawing upon Yatawara's work, the essays in this collection respond to "mother land" situations across time and space. Following Jione Havea's opening essay, which invites theological and hermeneutical engagement with colors and demands respect for the cursed subjects in texts and societies, the essays are divided into two parts. The first part contains essays that deal with texts and traditions of "Promises and Losses" with respect to the subjects of land and people. And the second part ("Dispossessions and Responsibilities") contains essays that narrate dispossessions (Yatawara's dismembered child) in different parts of the world and the responsibilities that those narratives put before readers.

Steed Vernyl Davidson opens the first part with a study of how Eden, as part of a biblical concept, and paradise, as an add-on to the biblical notion, circulate within tourism discourse. The search for the Garden of Eden and the modern quest to exploit the benefits of the tropics are different expressions of European imperialism. These different elements are held together through the transmission of ideas, practices, and structures that stretch as far back as primeval times and enter into modern times through repetition but also through mutations. The ideas, practices, and structures represent a Eurocentric perspective that maps on to Genesis 2–3 and its interpretations various forms of exoticization of what constitutes paradise. Davidson interrogates aspects of this exoticization in the tourism industry.

Gemma Tulud Cruz focuses on how wars, conflicts, and broader development processes force millions of people to move across borders every year. Cruz explores the double-edged experience, especially in relation to empire, of people who are forced to move in the age of migration. She begins with a brief survey of contemporary global migration followed by a discussion around the forced migrants' experience of land and, in particular, empire. This is followed by a critical description of migrants' subversions of empire and a brief conclusion. While forced migrants' experience of empire is fraught with oppression, migrants do not get completely swallowed up, nor utterly defeated, by empire. They fight back in strategic and creative ways in their struggle for bare or better life.

Santiago Slabodsky explores the interrelations between theology and coloniality—the patterns of domination developed during colonialism that have transcended that historical period. Slabodsky surveys the theological formulations of empty land and the consequences that these colonial narratives have had in the usurpation of (historical) colonized territories. He goes beyond the perception of theology as either legitimizing or protesting against empire and identifies how both the conservative and liberal formulations have been accomplices in these processes of dispossession. Slabodsky concludes by demanding that we question theology by delinking it from both hateful theologies of "Just War" and naïve theologies of "Just Love."

Mitri Raheb analyzes three cases relating to the State of Israel's settlement in the West Bank and East Jerusalem: a debate at the UN Security Council, the interaction between religion and state in the Arab world, and the powerful influence of Christian Zionists. With liberationist motivations, Raheb draws three theological conclusions: human rights are connected with divine rights, the cross is a critique of state and religious terror, and the healthy form of spirituality and theology urgently needed today in the case of Israel-Palestine is one that embraces diversity and celebrates it as strength.

Sifiso Mpofu explores the land question from a theological perspective, with special reference to the Zimbabwean context. Land is not a mere commodity, but an essential element for the realization of social benefits and human rights. Land is a source of livelihood and is central to citizens' economic rights. Biblically, land is linked to peoples' identities, their social needs, and their cultural rights. In this context, it is important to investigate the varied issues around the land question among many indigenous communities. Mpofu concludes with a synopsis of the theology of the land in an environment where religion has tended to be a pivotal center for informing communities.

Part I flows from the heritages of "lost paradise," "promised land," and "empty land" toward "spirituality of liberation" and "covenant responsibility." In light of Yatawara's work, the essays in part I, together challenge cultures of coloniality and seek emancipation and accountability for the "mother land." The essays in part II add ecological and contextual narratives of dispossession and extend calls for responsibility.

Kuzipa Nalwamba explains that landlessness in Southern Africa has historically served as a tool for oppression and exclusion of the powerless. The divide between the wealthy and the poor in many parts of Southern Africa stems from injustices that pertain to landownership. Nalwamba problematizes the mixed legacy that the church inhabits as landowner in postcolonial Southern Africa. First, she explores church landownership as a legacy of the imperial colonial project. As such, the church does not share in the powerlessness of its landless members because that heritage locates the landowning churches on the side of dispossessing power. Second, Nalwamba proposes that from a relational ontology founded on African cultural and intellectual infrastructure ensues a life-giving hermeneutic that confronts church landownership based on the internal logic of empire. Third, Nalwamba concludes with an outline of theologically grounded actions that could potentially engender a life-giving alternative to the underlying assumptions of church landownership in imperial mode.

Garnett Roper examines the resurgence of empire in the Caribbean. The longing for empire on both sides of the North Atlantic coincides with the depleting of the economic and social options for the majority of people in the Caribbean. Critical to this reality is the inequitable distribution of land. The high homicide rates in places like Montego Bay, Jamaica, relate to the overpopulation of landless people in squatter settlements. While the empire may have reconfigured itself, the circumstances of the majority population have not changed much. Roper explores public policy options for development, liberation, and selfhood, and proposes platforms for the renewal of the Jamaican society in the interest of its people.

Nāsili Vaka'uta shows how empires are founded on delusions—that is, idiosyncratic beliefs, doctrines, or ideologies invented, maintained, and/or propagated despite being contradicted by reality or reason. Imperial delusions inspired the most violent forms of injustice pertaining to people and land in colonized contexts. People (especially non-European natives) had been, and still are, subjected to dehumanizing measures—like racism, religious violence, ethnic cleansing, and cultural deracination—because imperial expansion operated upon the delusion that people with certain skin color, belief, ethnicity, and culture are inferior and less human. As such, they do not deserve to own land, have access to resources, or be free with the right to self-determination. Vaka'uta makes particular reference to the impact of imperial delusions on the people and land in Oceania.

Jude Lal Fernando challenges the traditional claim that one's deepest yearning is for God ("My soul is thirsting for God"). In Asia, particularly arising from places that have been militarized, people's yearning is for land. The deepest yearning for land can be understood by adopting hermeneutical tools that can form a theology that resists the empire. Fernando develops such a theology, focusing on faith-related activism in the islands of Jeju, Okinawa, and Sri Lanka (particularly among the Eelam Tamils). Peoples' yearning for land is their collective resistance against imperial peace. The empire seeks peace through a permanent state of war, which is aimed at destroying and/or absorbing the subjugated people physically and mentally into its imperial complex; the resistance of Asian islanders is for a peace with an alternative relationship to land.

George Zachariah evaluates ecological activism and discourses from the perspective of subaltern social movements. Dominant environmentalism remains apolitical and feel-goody, incapable to disrupt the power of the empire and its conquest of life. Informed by Dalit feminist hermeneutics, Zachariah rereads the story of Hagar with the life story of Soni Sori, an Adivasi woman activist from India, and her struggle to protect and nurture the watershed. This contrapuntal event invites disrupting the regime of truth that comes from locations of power and privilege and rediscovering meaning in the struggles of subaltern earth and its children.

Barbara Rossing draws courage from early Christian responses to the Roman Empire's avaricious conquests of lands and peoples. Apocalyptic scriptures give us tools for resisting the totalizing narratives of empires and for subverting those narratives with a countervision for healing. Rossing presents Emperor Trajan's column as exemplifying the Roman narrative of conquest that John critiques in the book of Revelation. The iconography of Trajan's column—including the conquest of Romania's forests—furnishes visual insights on how John constructed his counternarrative against Rome's idolatrous economy. For Rossing, visual reimagining of the tree of life (Rev 22:2) can help us envision worldhealing today.

The essays in part II juxtapose current and ancient "dispossessions" of people, land, and earth, with a common hope that, going back to Yatawara's street wisdom, the "heart" of the "mother land" is still alive and could be nourished (symbolized by the exposed breast) into meaningful life. Such a hope rises through the cracked skin of the land, and in the leaves of this collection, to be our responsibility.

Chapter One

The Land Has Colors

Jione Havea

Native proverbs and wisdom sayings from Pasifika (Pacific Islands, Oceania) affirm that the land has *mana* (dignity, presence, energy), eyes (so it can see and cry), voices (so it has will and intelligence, and it could be heard, ignored, or silenced), teeth (so it can bite), and other human-like features and images.[1] While native artists present the land in different shades of four main colors—black (for fertile land), red (as on the Indigenous Australian flag), brown (for exposed land), and gray (for barren land)—there is, as far as i know,[2] no native Pasifika proverb or wisdom saying that sees or suggests the colors of the land. This lack is telling given that we have sayings about the colors of the sky, the ocean, and the underworld, and because we first see colors before we could see structures and details.

There could be several explanations for the lack of native portrayals of the colors of the land: the land contains all the colors, so it is absurd to limit to only a few colors; the land is at one with native people, so the colors of the land are worn on native bodies; artworks are part of oral cultures,[3] so there is no need for words (proverbs, sayings) about the colors of the land; or simply, that the land has lost its colors. This last explanation puts this reflection in the realm of children's imaginations.[4] My aim, however, is not to restore the colors of the land—for even though the land may change colors, it is never colorless. Rather, this reflection is an invitation: that the intersection of *people and land* is an opportunity to reflect on the difference (that their) colors make. People have colors. The land too has many colors, including black (a color rarely included in children's color charts or blocks). Texts too have colors, and so do interpreters, theologies and theologians, and deities.[5] One might physically be color-blind but, as the participative black theologian Anthony G. Reddie repeatedly challenges us, that is not justification for being hermeneutically or theologically color blind.[6] Even if God is color-blind, there is no excuse for not seeing the colors on bodies (of people and land) and texts, teachings and ideologies. Seeing colors, i propose, is a necessary step toward exposing the workings of coloniality in scriptures and theologies (see also Santiago Slabodsky, in this collection).

This essay brings color to the intersection of people and land, which i unfold over three parts.[7] First, i offer a color review of the Yahwist garden story (Gen. 2:4b–3:24), noting that color is not often considered in the intersection of people and land (see also Steed Vernyl Davidson, in this collection). I meander through this text with the question, what are the colors of the land? Second, with the same question, i turn back to the priestly creation narrative (Gen. 1:1–2:4a) and present the light, the waters, and the land as colored cocreators with God. I argue that the concern of the priestly narrative is broader than the interests of humans (people). It is even broader than the land, but my orientation in this essay is toward the land (for a broader orientation, see George Zachariah, in this collection). This reading challenges the traditional assumption that humans (people) are the pinnacle of the creation, and that we have been given authority to rule and to have dominion (which has been blamed for the ecological crisis;[8] see also Barbara Rossing, in this collection). Third, i turn my question into the affirmation in the title of this essay—the land has colors—and take a leap onto the shores of theological and biblical studies with a supplementing affirmation—readings and theologies have colors, and they also color. The resulting questions are critical: How might we be more sensitive to the colors in texts and theologies? How might we explain the colors that readers and theologians do or do not see? In other words, how do we avoid being color-blind in our readings and theologies? And, what are the privileges, burdens, and baggage of colors?

COLORS OF THE GROUND

In the biblical account, the connections between people and land go back to the Yahwist garden story (Gen. 2:4b–3:24; see also Garnett Roper, in this collection). *Ha'adam* (the human, for people) was made with dust from *ha'adamah* (the ground, for land) in Gen. 2:7, for the purpose of tending the ground (Gen. 2:5). *Ha'adam* is from and for *ha'adamah*. In this regard, *ha'adam* was of the same substance as *ha'adamah*. In other words, at the beginning, they were at one.

Ha'adam became a living being thanks to the "breath of life" that the LORD breathed into its nostrils, but its destiny was not to serve the spirit of the LORD. Rather, both its origin and destiny are grounded upon *ha'adamah* (Gen. 2:8, 15). The orientation of this story was not toward the LORD, but to the intersection of *ha'adam* and *ha'adamah* (see also Jude Lal Fernando, in this collection). According to the narrative, *ha'adamah* was moist for it had been wetted with a mist from "within *ha'arets*" (the earth; Gen. 2:6). In this connection, *ha'adamah* is like the "skin" of *ha'arets* (see next section).

So what color did *ha'adam* have? The answer is obvious: *ha'adam* would have shared the colors of dust and of *ha'adamah*. Seeing that the ground was fertile, for it responded almost immediately (in narrative time) to the LORD's first (narrative) attempt at gardening (Gen. 2:9), i imagine that *ha'adamah* had glistening rich black colors. *Ha'adamah* was already moist with its own lifegiving mists, flows, and streams (depending on how one translates Gen. 2:6), which welled up from *ha'arets* to water the garden, then branched out as four rivers (Gen. 2:10–14). Even though the color of pure water is blueish, and a shallow quantity of water appears to be clear, I do not see the water of *ha'arets* as pure or clear. Rather, I see it as earthly, so it would be closer to brown than to clear.[9] With respect to composition, compared to the breath/spirit that the LORD breathed into the nostrils of *ha'adam*, which would have been more airy and windy than watery, the water from *ha'arets* would have had body and shape (at least be firm, in a soluble way).

Ha'adamah had more than one color. "Every tree that is pleasant to the sight and good for food" as well as the "tree of life" and "tree of knowledge of good and bad" (Gen. 2:9) would also exhibit the colors of *ha'adamah*. The spectrum is wide when one takes into account the colors of their leaves, flowers, fruits, branches, trunks, and roots. Add to that spectrum the colors of "every animal of the field and every bird of the air" (also made from the same substance as *ha'adam* and the trees, in Gen. 2:20) and the colors of water (which depend on its surrounding)—such a spectrum would include most of the colors in the world. The land has more colors than a rainbow (an allusion to the sign of the covenant after the flood), and people alone, though colorful in our human ways, do not do justice to the wide spectrum of the colors of the land.

Ha'adam was to care for the garden of trees, some of which it could eat (Gen. 2:15–17), and the animals and birds were to be "helpers as partners" in the tending and caring duties (Gen. 2:18). *Ha'adam* did not find any of the animals or birds fitting, and the LORD knocked him out, took a rib out, and created "the woman" (*ha'ishah*). The woman was to be a helper as well, and her coming to life enabled "the man" (*ha'ish*) to also arise—both *ha'ishah* and *ha'ish* came from *ha'adam* (Gen. 2:23).[10] And *ha'ishah* (the woman) helped *ha'ish* (the man) into being. Appealing to a US military advertisement, the woman helped the man *be all that he could be* (at that time and in that context). This is an old reading around which readers tend to focus on gender differences, but i bring the two creatures—*ha'ishah* and *ha'ish*—into the question of colors around two textual moments: the privileging of becoming "one-flesh" (Gen. 2:24) and the curses meted out in response to what *ha'ishah* and *ha'ish* did as "one flesh" (Gen. 3:14–19).

First, the narrative looks beyond the two bodies that were separated in Gen. 2:21–22. The narrative sees similar bodies in the future, women and men (people), and inscribes that they become "one flesh" (Gen. 2:24). The prompt for this reading is the word "flesh," which appears at the point of separation (the rib was taken, and its place was covered with flesh; Gen. 2:21) and at the point of coming together (as "one flesh" in Gen. 2:24). They will continue to be separate bodies, but they can become "one flesh."

If the separation of bodies in Gen. 2:21 is seen to cause problems, to damage, or even to be a mistake, the LORD makes up for those with the call to get back together: "Therefore, a man shall betray his father and his mother but cleave to his woman, and they shall be one flesh" (Gen. 2:24). "Betray" and "cleave" are strong words, and "one flesh" is utopian. I do not take becoming "one flesh" literally, but as a desire loaded with meanings. In the separation of *ha'ishah* from *ha'ish*, the colors of *ha'adam* were also split; therefore, the direction to become "one flesh" aims to also restore the colors of *ha'adam*. This reading is not a comment on the patriarchal agenda behind heterosexual marriage, but on the at-one-ment of the colors of *ha'adam* that points to the at-one-ment of the colors of *ha'adamah*. The colors of *ha'adamah* and *ha'adam* are not worn on the bodies of men only, or on the bodies of women only, but on the bodies of both men and women who are "one flesh." Becoming "one flesh" is therefore corrective (with respect to the LORD) and restorative (with respect to the colors of the land).

Second, staying with the color query, the curse narrative shows that "one flesh" is too good to be true. The two bodies that stood side by side and ate from one of the forbidden trees (Gen. 3:6), then together realized that they were naked and tried to cover themselves up (Gen. 3:7), did not become "one flesh." Rather, they shifted the blame from one flesh to the other.[11] The man blamed the woman. The woman blamed the serpent. And even though the serpent could speak and reason, the LORD did not ask for an explanation or defense. Would the serpent have accepted the blame, or shifted the blame to another flesh? If given a chance, would the serpent have revealed something about (read: fleshed) the LORD?

The LORD was not happy and first cursed (which is a form of shifting the blame as well) the serpent (Gen. 3:14), then brought the woman into the domain of the serpent (Gen. 3:15), before cursing the woman on her own cause (Gen. 3:16). The LORD then cursed *ha'adamah* on account of the man (Gen. 3:17), then brought the man under the domain of *ha'adamah*: "In the sweat of your face you shall eat food until you return to *ha'adamah*, for from it you were taken; for dust you are and to dust you will return" (Gen. 3:19). In the curses, the LORD paired the woman with the serpent and the man with *ha'adamah*.

In light of my color-oriented reading, the curses have at-one-ment effects: the woman is "cursed" to be at one with the most wise (crafty, subtle) of the living creatures in the field that the LORD had made (Gen. 3:1). What wisdom the woman did not receive from the tree of knowing good and bad, she might get from the wise, sensible, and straight-talking serpent. In the case of the man, he is "cursed" to labor harder for his food until he returns to *ha'adamah*. It is not too bad for the man, for he here inherits the purpose for which *ha'adam* was created: to till and tend *ha'adamah* (Gen. 2:5, 15).[12] But why curse *ha'adamah* as well? I will return to this question in the next section, with the help of the priestly narrator, but first briefly explain the reason and impact of my affirming of the "curses."[13]

In Indigenous Australian communities, each person at birth receives what is called a "skin name" determined by the skin names of her or his parents, and there are different skin names for males and for females. Because of the intricate webs of indigenous relationships and blood ties, people from different communities and "countries" (or nations) could share the same skin name (in addition to their first and family names, and their so-called bush names). The skin name determines a person's roles, relationships, and responsibilities within her or his kinship network (or skin system). What one may do and where one can go, and with whom, are determined by the skin system. In this regard, the skin system is comparable to the way totems function among American first nations and the Māoris of Aotearoa New Zealand and the caste system of Hinduism. But whereas there are four castes plus the Dalits (or Untouchables) in Hinduism,[14] there are sixteen skin names in the Indigenous Australian cultures (eight for men and eight for women, and the names are spelled differently across the indigenous languages).[15]

The "skin" in "skin names" has nothing to do with the physical skin on bodies. Instead, for lack of an appropriate English term, it refers to the "covering" of a person.[16] One's skin name identifies as well as protects one from harm and wrongdoing. When someone breaks the protocols of her or his skin name, thus violating her or his skin (read: protection) system, she or he is said to be "wrong skin."

For nonindigenous people, on the other hand, "skin" is connected to a physical body, and with respect to Indigenous Australians, the body is expected to be rugged, scented, and black. As a nonindigenous (to Australia) person, i (1) see color in skin names and (2) respect that no one chooses her or his skin color. The darker the color of my skin is my lot or, to put it bluntly, my curse. I did not choose my skin. Rather, it was gifted to me. My skin, my curse, is a gift from my parents, from their lifeworlds, and from our ancestors. As such, i accept it. And in that light, i read the curses in Gen. 3 as *gifts* with at-one-ment opportunities.

With color and skin name lenses, i see and understand the curses placed upon the serpent, the woman, and the man as *gifts* (bearing in mind the linguistic twist, that "gift" means "poison" in German).[17] My native roots influence my reading (see also Nāsili Vaka'uta, in this collection), in solidarity with those who (like natives, indigenous, and black peoples) are rejected and cursed. My reading intersects the totemic skin system in Indigenous Australian circles with the color-prejudiced mind-sets (though often denied) in nonindigenous circles. As a native reader, however, i cannot figure out the curse upon *ha'adamah* since it did not do anything other than to channel the moisture of *ha'arets* and thus enabled life to spring in the garden and spread to other parts of earth. Was the LORD troubled by the life-giving gifts in and of *ha'adamah* and so cursed it for no apparent reason?

COLORS OF CREATION

Turning back to the priestly account, the horizon extends from a garden to "the heavens and the earth" (Gen. 1:1), "the deep" and "the waters" (Gen. 1:2). The world is presented in layers, with many colors (which are hidden in the darkness) and shades (depending on whether its day or night, under greater or lesser lights). In this regard, the "formless and empty" (*tohu wabohu*; Gen. 1:2) state prior to the separation of "light from darkness" (Gen. 1:4) had to do with colors—darkness suppresses the different colors and so the world appears to be without form or content (void). In this context, i stress two points: first, that light was extracted from darkness. Darkness was not a rival or an adversary against light, but the very source of light. In this connection, light corresponds to darkness. Second, that light brings out color. It is thus interesting that fisher(wo)men declare "we have color" when the fish they are pulling up reaches the point where it begins to reflect light. Light brings forth color, and both are possible because of darkness.

Light, darkness, and color are important in the priestly account, and it is not surprising that two of the six days of God's creation activities are spent on them (days one and four, Gen. 1:1–5 and 14–19). The paradox of separating light from darkness first (day one) then the sources of light later (day four) could easily be explained with a color-sensitive reading. The sun and moon (greater and lesser lights, on day four), and the seasons, were necessary for the sake of the plants that "the earth . . . brought forth" on day three (Gen. 1:11–12). Assuming that the sun and moon are primarily for giving light is an androcentric view; they are sources of clean energy as well, especially for plants. So i imagine God having an "oopsie" moment at the end of day three: the day started with the waters under the sky gathering to one place so that land may dry up—and the narrator witnessed that "God saw that it was good" (Gen. 1:9). Then God asks earth to "bring forth" all kinds of herbs, plants, and trees (Gen. 1:11), to which earth concedes—again the narrator witnessed, "God saw that it was [also] good" (Gen. 1:12). At this point, i imagine, God saying "oops": God realizes that plants need energy, hence the activities of day four! And God doubles up, with not one but multiple lights: for the day, and for the night.

The color-sensitive reading works because there is significant attention to light in this narrative. In that light, two details are worth repeating: first, in the priestly account the colors of creation are spread over a larger canvas—from the expanse of the sky/heavens to the dry land, the waters, the deep, the creatures that roam in and the plants that breathe into those domains. When total darkness falls upon those, their colors are not visible. They are still there, but formless and void of colors. It thus makes sense to have lesser lights, so that their colors are not lost. Light, darkness, and color play significant roles in "bringing out" the elements of creation.

Compared to the Yahwist garden story, the priestly account shifts the language from *ha'adamah* (ground) to *ha'arets* (earth). In this shift is the second detail to highlight: *ha'arets* is cocreator with God. God asks (Gen. 1:11) and *ha'arets* delivers (Gen. 1:12). God "made" the sets of lights (Gen. 1:16) and the animals (Gen. 1:25) and "created" the water creatures and winged fowls (Gen. 1:21), but not the greening of the dry land—that was the creation of *ha'arets*. *Ha'arets* was not just part of a canvas, but an active partner in giving form to and bringing to life the *tohu wabohu*.

In a similar way to the Yahwist garden narrative, the waters have *mana* (dignity, integrity, presence, energy) in the priestly account, and they were creative along with God and *ha'arets*. This reading is based on comparing the events on day five (Gen. 1:20–23) and day three (Gen. 1: 9–13). On day five, God asks the waters to swarm with water creatures and winged fowls (Gen. 1:20) but then, instead of waiting for the waters to bring forth the water creatures (as God allowed *ha'arets* to bring forth plant life), God "created" the creatures. On day three, on the other hand, God asks the waters to gather to one place so that dry land may appear, and the narrator reports that "it was so" (Gen. 1:9). I take this to mean that the waters gathered themselves to one place. On day three, therefore, the gathering of the waters enabled the dry-land to show its colors; in this regard, the waters were cocreators with God. This is similar to the lighting event on day one: God asks for light, and light obliges (Gen. 1:3). In this juxtaposition, the waters (*hamayim*) and the light (*'or*) were agents of creation alongside God and *ha'arets*. So when God jumps up to create the sea creatures and the birds on day five, God stops the waters from continuing to be cocreator.

On day six, when God calls out—"Let us make *[ha]'adam* in our image, according to our likeness" (Gen. 1:26)—to whom else was God calling but to the cocreators in the previous days: the light, the waters, and *ha'arets*? This reading affirms the *mana* of God's cocreators and pulls them up (as the fisher[wo]men pull up their catch) so that fishing-readers could see their colors. Critics who prefer the *imago Dei* option would object to my reading, but they would have a difficult time arguing that humans are *not* images of light, of waters, and of *ha'arets* as well. To see humans as image of *only* God is limiting. To deny that light, waters, and *ha'arets* are God's cocreators is to be hermeneutically and theologically color-blind.

Fear of the Land

I return to the question raised above: What was so threatening about the land (*ha'adamah, ha'arets*) that the LORD cursed it? The text, sadly, does not entertain (nor hint at how one might answer) my question. The LORD cursed the land, and critics concede that the LORD, understood to have sovereign authority over the whole universe, has the right to do so. I am nevertheless troubled because this way of thinking has functioned as unspoken endorsement for the occupation of lands (see also the essays in part I) and the displacement of peoples (see also the essays in part II) even in modern times. An example of the working of such unspoken endorsement is the Balfour Declaration (see also Mitri Raheb, in this collection).[18]

Arthur James Balfour (who had served as British prime minister from 1902 to 1905) was a former British foreign secretary who signed the declaration on November 2, 1917, on behalf of the cabinet. The setting for the declaration was the First World War, and it was addressed to Lord Rothschild, expressing the support of "His Majesty's Government" for "Jewish Zionist aspirations" toward the "establishment in Palestine of a national home for the Jewish People." While the Balfour Declaration asks for protection of non-Jewish communities in Palestine, these subjects are presented as *civil and religious* subjects rather than as citizens of the land and state of Palestine. This distinction is hurtful, seeing that the non-Jewish communities are named in comparison to "Jews in any other country," who are recognized to have "rights and political status." Jews outside of Palestine have *rights and political status*; Palestinians inside Palestine have *civil and religious rights*.

The unspoken assumptions of this brief declaration expose its imperial foundations and leanings. These may be seen, as Edward W. Said explained, in light of the facts that the declaration is,

> (a) by a European power, (b) about a non-European territory, (c) in flat disregard of both the presence and the wishes of the native majority resident in the territory, and (d) it took the form of a promise about this same territory to another foreign group, so that this foreign group might, quite literally, *make* this territory a national home for the Jewish people.[19]

Palestine was not empty when it was "promised" (see also Gemma Tulud Cruz, in this collection) to the Jewish people. Palestinians were not consulted, and no appropriate colonial or indigenous authority gave Balfour or the British government the right to take the land of Palestine and give it to, and for the interests of, Jewish Zionists. More than a century later, the Palestinians in Palestine and in diaspora continue to suffer under this declaration, and the British government has not owned it, nor has it done anything to correct its mistaken assumptions or to reverse its ongoing impacts.[20] In the light of the reflection offered above, the Balfour Declaration is a curse on the land and on the people of Palestine. If the British government would own and consequently reject the declaration, that double move would be a big step toward bringing justice for the Palestinians and exposing the injustice that the modern State of Israel rains daily against Palestinians.

The question raised against Balfour and the British government may also be raised against the LORD: Who or what gave the LORD any right to curse the land, which existed prior to the LORD deciding to plant a garden (in the Yahwist narrative) and even prior to the creation of the heavens and the earth (according to the priestly narrative)? This question sees the LORD cursing the land as the act of a colonialist. And with respect to the *mana* of the land (as cocreator in the priestly account, and source of water and of life in the Yahwist story), i wonder if the curse was because the LORD did not want the land to have so much power. Put more sharply, was the curse of the land an attempt to put a stop (as God did with the waters in Gen. 1:21, and with the earth—*ha'arets*—in Gen. 1:25) to the powers of the land?

My question comes out of (and with) native Pasifika respect for the land according to which, to borrow words from the Indigenous Australian group Yothu Yindi's song "Gone Is the Land," the land "is not forty thousand dollars or more, but forty thousand years of culture here."[21] The land has a special place in native Pasifika hearts, as it does in other indigenous communities: the land has *mana* to be respected, and even feared. In this frame of mind, when colonialists and settlers claim and take land, they give native hearts and minds the impression that they are acting out of *fear of the land*. Colonialists and settlers cannot be acting out of *respect* for the land, because they do not know how to relate to the land. They cannot be "bad skin" because they do not know what it means to be "true skin" in the first place. So the colonialists and settlers had to be acting out of fear.

This native view of the land is behind the reading offered above of the two stories in Gen. 1–3, and it subverts the usual denial—that indigenous people do not see the land simply as property to be taken and possessed, but as the combination of our mother, sustainer, healer, destiny, and everything.[22] Natives in Pasifika also take and use, buy and sell (with capital, goods, and favors), the land, and sometimes we burn the land,[23] all within the protocols of respect and fear. At a deeper level, therefore, this native reading resists the tendency to romanticize native and indigenous peoples and views.

Assuming that the curse over *ha'adamah* was God's attempt to put a stop to the powers of the land, i suggest that this was out of fear and/or respect for the land. This suggestion supplements the popular view that the land is vulnerable to being taken, whether by churches (see Kuzipa Nalwamba, in this collection) or by empires (see Garnett Roper, in this collection), with the native view that the land has *mana*.

THE COLORS OF RESPECT

To close this reflection, i bring my obsession (in this essay) with color to the subject of fear, thus bringing attention to "people," the pair for "land" in this collection of essays. I draw attention to people at the end not for the sake of privileging humans (see, e.g., Ps. 8), but in order to invite consideration of what it might mean for people to respect the *mana* of the land. I extend this invitation out of respect for the late queen of soul, Aretha Franklin.

Aretha Franklin borrowed what became her signature song "Respect" from Otis Redding (who wrote and recorded the song in 1965), and gave it her own twists (e.g., adding the line "you're runnin' out of fools" as a way of saying that she will not be fooled, and the powerful R-E-S-P-E-C-T chorus) two years later.[24] While Redding and Franklin duetted on several occasions, in the case of "Respect," it makes a difference if it is a man or a woman who demands respect. In the renditions by both Redding and Franklin, the singers announce that she or he is returning home soon, that she or he is willing to give "all of my money" to her or his "honey," and as a consequence demands "respect." But this demand means different things for the two artists. In Redding's rendition, the call for "respect" comes from a tired worker returning home and wanting his honey to give him a break; in Franklin's rendition, the demand for respect was toward empowering, both politically and sexually, African American women in particular. With Franklin, "Respect" became a women's liberation anthem, an emancipation song. I take from Franklin's use of the song a clue for the color of respect: that it paints empowerment and emancipation.

Reading for colors is an opportunity for readers to see and respect subjects who are condemned and cursed (burned) at the intersections of land and people in the ancient and modern worlds, in theologies, and in scriptures and their interpretations. The contributors to this collection meet this invitation in different terms, and for different causes: to assess and transform the businesses of theology and hermeneutics; to expose and challenge the logics and delusions of coloniality; to tally and demand restitution of stolen, commodified, and capitalized lands; to account for the free (touristy) and forced movements of people; and to scripturalize the undeniable ecological crises and our responsibilities to the watershed. May we see the colors of, and give proper respect to, these realities.

NOTES

1. My orientation in this reflection is toward *land* (see also Sifiso Mpofu, in this collection), and *people* provide my frame.

2. I use the lowercase with the first person in the same way that i use the lowercase with "you," "she," "he," "it," "they," and "others."

3. On art in Pasifika, see Caroline Blyth and Nāsili Vaka'uta (eds.), *Bible & Art, Perspectives from Oceania* (London: Bloomsbury, 2017).

4. See Benjamin Ellefson, *The Land Without Color* (Edina, MN: Beaver's Pond, 2016), which tells the story of Alvin finding himself in a world where everything was gray. Alvin teams up with several unexpected friends and goes searching for the color thieves (goblins), to stop them and thereby restore colors to the kingdom. And of course, to rescue the princess.

5. See Vine Deloria Jr., *God Is Red: A Native View of Religion* (New York: Putman, 2003).

6. See Anthony G. Reddie, *Is God Color-blind? Insights from Black Theology for Christian Ministry* (London: SPCK, 2011).

7. I imagine here the process of unfolding (or unraveling) a mat. The three parts of the essay are separable, but they belong to the same weaving.

8. See Lynn White Jr., "The Historical Roots of Our Ecological Crisis," *Science* 155.3767 (1967): 1203–7.

9. Billy Bragg uses "brown water" in his "King Tide and the Sunny Day Flood" in reference to the rising waters that will "sweep everything away" unless we all "act today" (https://www.azlyrics.com/lyrics/billybragg/kingtideandthesunnydayflood.html; accessed December 4, 2018).

10. I distinguish *ha'adam* from *ha'ish* (the man). *Ha'adam* is the subject in Gen. 2:5–22, and *ha'ish* is the subject from Gen. 2:23 onward.

11. See Danna Nolan Fewell and David M. Gunn, *Gender, Power and Promise: The Subject of the Bible's First Story* (Nashville, TN: Abingdon, 1992), 22–38.

12. The division created by the curse is an often-overlooked element in this narrative. The woman (*ha'ishah*) was not created as a lesser being, but cursed to be a lesser being. On the same note, the man (*ha'ish*) was not created to be a greater being but cursed to inherit the orientation of *ha'adam*.

13. The Hebrew word used in Gen. 3:14 (against the serpent) and Gen. 3:17 (against *ha'adamah*), "arur," does not have the ambiguity of "barak" (which could be translated as bless or curse).

14. For an introduction to Dalit theology, see Sathianathan Clarke, Deenabandhu Manchala, and Philip Peacock (eds.), *Dalit Theology in the Twenty-first Century: Discordant Voices, Discerning Pathways* (Oxford: Oxford University Press, 2010).

15. See Central Land Council, "Kinship and Skin Names," n.d., https://www.clc.org.au/index.php?/articles/info/aboriginal-kinship (accessed October 10, 2018).

16. In this regard, "skin" is the reverse of Frantz Fanon's "mask" (see *Black Skin, White Masks* [New York: Grove, 2008]). Black people put on "white masks" in order to fit in with the dominant culture; indigenous people give "skin names" to nonindigenous people in order that the "white fellas" could be engaged in the blackfella world. In other words, it is in order to serve indigenous interests. Ironically, nonindigenous people assume that their being gifted with a skin name is indication that they are accepted.

17. I quickly add a qualification: the word "curse" is not used with respect to the woman or the man (in Gen. 3:15–19), but since i see the woman being drawn into the domain (similar to the skin system) and domain of the serpent, and the man being drawn into the domain (or skin system) and curse of *ha'adamah*, the woman and man are (by transference) also cursed-gifted.

18. The declaration is available at https://en.wikipedia.org/wiki/Balfour_Declaration (accessed November 5, 2018).

19. Edward W. Said, *The Question of Palestine* (New York: Vintage, 1979), 15–16.

20. See Zena Tahhan, "More Than a Century Later: The Balfour Declaration Explained," *Al Jazeera* (November 2, 2018), https://www.aljazeera.com/indepth/features/2017/10/100-years-balfour-declaration-explained-171028055805843.html (accessed November 5, 2018).

21. Composed and performed by Mandawuy Yunupingu and Gurrumul Yunupingu on Yothu Yindi's *Garma* (Phantom 1091333, compact disc, 2007).

22. See Wali Fejo, "The Voice of the Earth: An Indigenous Reading of Genesis 9," in *The Earth Story in Genesis*, ed. Norman Habel (Sheffield, UK: Sheffield Academic Press, 2000), 140–46.

23. See Iutisone Salevao, "'Burning the Land': An Ecojustice Reading of Hebrews 6:7–8," in *Readings from the Perspectives of Earth*, ed. Norman C. Habel (Sheffield, UK: Sheffield Academic Press, 2000), 221–31.

24. Franklin's lyrics are available at https://genius.com/Aretha-franklin-respect-lyrics (accessed November 5, 2018).

Part I

Promises and Losses

Chapter Two

Lost Paradises

Tracing the Imperial Contours of Modern Tourism upon Land and Peoples

Steed Vernyl Davidson

In this essay I explore how Eden, as part of a biblical concept, and paradise, as an add-on to the biblical notion, circulate within tourism discourse. The connections between the biblical motif and the tourism brochure lie beyond the evocative images of blissful days in the sun. While holding similar intent, the search for the Garden of Eden and the modern quest to exploit the benefits of the tropics represent different expressions of European imperialism. These different elements are held together through the transmission of ideas, practices, and structures that stretch as far back as primeval times and enter into modern times through repetition but also through mutations. The ideas as they have come to exist in the present day represent a Eurocentric perspective that maps on to Genesis and its interpretations, as well as deployment of various forms of exoticization of what constitutes paradise. This essay describes different aspects of this exoticization and production in the tourism industry.

The word "contours" in the title of the essay points to a cartographical feature, as well as to the idea of flow and circulation across history and geography. "Contours" here disrupts the idea of evenness and highlights connections that are determined by economics and politics.[1] More than the one-directional movement from an imperial center to a periphery which, as Dennis Merrill indicates, makes the imperial West the sole actor and avoids paying attention to agency from the underside,[2] "contours" enables me to talk about the multidirectional histories around the ideas of the Garden of Eden and paradise as well as the current realities of the tourism industry. The realities that give shape to tourism as part of the continuation of modern-day empire, similar to contour lines on a map, flow not like water but, as Salazar describes it, like blood circulating in a living body.[3]

The essay begins by showing how the Garden of Eden grows into the idea of paradise as a potent aspect of the European colonial era, particularly in relation to the Americas. The next section looks at how paradise, as an important signifier of things tropical, supplies a crucial term for the tourism industry that connects it with imperial configurations. The following section analyzes the circulation of biblical ideas over time and space and the way these play out in formerly colonized regions like the Caribbean. The essay ends with an exploration of the challenges of reimagining the garden narrative.

Along overlapping biblical studies methodologies, I use postcolonial and tourism studies together with two works from Caribbean authors to illustrate specific reflections on the tourism industry. The imagined conversation by Jamaica Kincaid, *A Small Place*, that narrates the Antiguan sociocultural and political context for tourism, is complemented by Derek Walcott's epic poem *Omeros*, that deals with similar themes in relation to St. Lucia. Both of these works make strategic interventions throughout the essay, illustrating the assemblage of the different forces upon land and people.

THE FLOW FROM EDEN TO PARADISE

Genesis 2–3 performs several functions for the Christian imagination. The theological conceptions of a fall and original sin stand out as some of the more dominant dogmas to find a home in these chapters. One of the impacts of these theological precepts has been to draw a temporal division in the narrative marked by the humans' act of disobedience. Consequently, the belief in an Eden prior to sin characterized by innocence, perfection, and magnificence, and devoid of sinful humans, takes hold in the popular imagination. The belief that the original purity of Eden remains intact helps form the connection to the idea of paradise. Derek Walcott channels this belief as the expatriate characters to St. Lucia in *Omeros*, Maud and Major Plunkett, look out on Castries:

> After a while the happiness grew oppressive.
> Only the dead can endure it in paradise,
> and it felt selfish for so long.
> [. . .]
>
> "It's so still. It's like Adam and Eve all over,"
> Maud whispered. "Before the snake. Without all the sin."[4]

Genesis provides a surprisingly sparse description of the Garden of Eden that belies its reputation over the course of history. Eibert Tigchelaar notes that at best the text indicates that the garden consists of an orchard with rivers and two trees in the middle.[5] The text distinguishes between the garden itself and the region known as Eden. The notice that the waters of the river flow out of Eden to irrigate the garden (Gen. 2:10) points to this distinction. As indicated YHWH Elohim plants the garden in Eden (*gan be `ēden;* Gen. 2:8), not a garden called Eden. Although the other references in Genesis maintain a similar Hebrew construction (2:15; 3:23–24; 4:16), and arguably a similar geographical distinction, the absence of the preposition in these other references leads to the implication of a garden called Eden. Over time this conflation occurs, and Eden comes to be understood not as a region but specifically as the garden of God (Isa. 51:3; Ezek. 28:13; 31:9; 36:35).

The details Genesis offers become fairly specific over the course of the interpretive history. The eastern location as well as the names of the four tributaries of the river that flow from Eden serve as geographical orienting points for the location of Eden. Biblical scholars remain divided on whether Genesis intends to provide a specific geography or a symbolic geography of the area, especially given the names of the tributaries.[6] That the Tigris and Euphrates are easily identified but Pishon and Gihon appear to be contrived locations marks one of the splits in the scholarly consensus between a Mesopotamian location and an imagined Palestinian location. In my estimation, the river and its tributaries represent an imaginative geography.

Neither Genesis nor much of the Hebrew Bible anticipates or reflects the major role that these opening chapters would play in Christian theology. With minimal references to Eden and almost little to no acknowledgment that this primeval place and the events that occur there shape conceptions of sin or human anthropology in the Hebrew Bible, interpretations of these chapters have been driven by considerations outside of the biblical text. The bifurcation of the text into pre- and postlapsarian time creates with it a spatial demarcation that separates Eden as ontologically different from other geographical locations. This ontology has enabled Eden to acquire the status of heaven on earth. Details such as the presence of mineral wealth at Pishon—gold, bdellium, and onyx (Gen. 2:11)—suggest a site that would be the source of great abundance. Although only associated with Pishon and therefore a location outside of the garden, in time the idea of Eden as a place of magnificence and splendor would develop. Taken together with the expulsion of the "fallen" humans from the garden and the stringent measures to prevent their return, Eden appears as a place set aside for a select population.

The Old Greek translation of the Hebrew *gan* as *paradesios*—intentional[7] or otherwise—contributes to the development of Eden as a superlatively different place and the association of Eden with notions of paradise. This translation suggests a qualitatively different garden. The influence of other cultural streams, such as the Persian conception of a garden for the pleasure of the elites planted with trees in a well-watered location, changes the perception of Eden.[8] In several ancient Near Eastern myths, the primordial garden occupies a space of perfection that represents the unspoiled harmony of all aspects of the creation—humans, animals, vegetation, and divine beings.[9] Bremmer indicates that by Hellenistic times, the term *paradesios* would have implied a "royal park with many trees suitable for walking."[10] Ezekiel's reception of Eden shares some of these views, particularly the notion of Eden as the garden of god. Placing the garden on a mountain (Ezek. 28:12–19) that contains stones of fire rather than trees,[11] Ezekiel produces space that resembles a temple[12] and therefore one inhabited by deities,[13] but notably one characterized by splendor, magnificence, and luxury. Like Genesis, Ezekiel understands Eden as emptied of its original inhabitants as a result of a moral taint.

Even though Eden gains in prominence in Second Temple texts, it is viewed more as an idealized place rather than an actual earthly location, as would become dominant in later years. From Ezekiel (47:7–12 cf. 28:11–18; 31:1–18) to the Book of Watchers (25:3–5), Eden appears as an eschatological site that hosts the renewal of creation.[14] In addition to earlier ancient Near Eastern myths, these views exist alongside other Greco-Roman literary traditions of a golden era location of ultimate goodness, such as the islands of the blessed in Hesiod or the Elysian Fields in Homer and other concepts in Plato, Virgil, and Ovid.[15] While Christians initially resist these ideas, by the second century figures such as Justin Martyr and Tertullian insist that these texts unwittingly drew upon biblical material for their descriptions of these locations.[16] Over time Eden expands conceptually to include the notion of paradise as collected from various cultures that constructs it first as a staging location for the resurrection and then ahead of the age of exploration as an actual earthly location[17] not easily accessed by humans.[18] Despite the advances in mapmaking, several medieval period maps, like the Hereford Mappa Mundi, would feature paradise as an actual location, most often at the top of the map, an indication of its spatially superior position.[19] Pictures of the world in monasteries gather biblical insights from theologians such as Augustine, Ambrose, and Isidore of Seville.[20] In fact, most of these representations locate Eden outside of the known world in and beyond a mythical land such as the famed kingdom of Prester John.[21]

Spurred on by the actual geography in the text as well as the mention of the garden being in the east (Gen. 2:8), orientalist interpretations locate Eden in the Asian world both physically and metaphysically. John Calvin's map of Eden in his commentary on Genesis produces Iraq as a likely location for Eden.[22] The geographical distortions that marked early European westward sea travels led several of these explorers to search for Eden in what they mistakenly thought to be Asia. Christopher Columbus understood the location of Eden based upon the river and its tributaries in the four major rivers of the world as covering mostly southwest Asia, the Indian subcontinent, and North Africa.[23] This emphasis upon rivers and abundant waters convinced Columbus when he sailed past the mouth of the Orinoco River that he was at the actual location of paradise: "There are great indications of this being the terrestrial paradise, for its site coincides with the opinion of the holy and wise theologians whom I have mentioned."[24] Columbus's fascination with the confluence of fresh river water and the ocean thrills him in his belief that he is experiencing "the earthly paradise," and if not then something "still more marvelous."[25] He voices experiences of wonder that catapult the tropics beyond this world, as Kincaid notes with respect to exoticization in Caribbean tourism:

> Antigua is too beautiful. Sometimes the beauty of it seems unreal. Sometimes the beauty of it seems as if it were stage sets for a play, for no real sunset could look like that; no real seawater could strike that many shades of blue at once; no real sky could be that shade of blue—another shade of blue, completely different from the shades of blue seen in the sea—and no real cloud could be that white and float just that way in that blue sky; no real day could be that sort of sunny and bright, making everything seem transparent and shallow; and no real night could be that sort of black, making everything seem thick and deep and bottomless.[26]

Since the waters of the river appear as the most defining geographical feature for the location of Eden well into the seventeenth century, Europeans hoped that transatlantic journeys would be a gateway to Eden. This notion derived from cosmic maps that envisage a "world ocean" from which all rivers flow.[27] Explorers like Columbus reapplied the ideas of Eden/paradise located in the east to western territories. Accordingly, as Mimi Sheller, drawing on Édouard Glissant, points out, a "hybrid Orientalist and Africanist discourse" characterizes European edenic descriptions of their impressions of the tropics of the Americas. In this discourse she notes that the Caribbean is seen like Asia, a land of extravagance, requiring minimal work, where the senses can be indulged, but also like Africa, primeval, harsh, rough, and dangerously unknown.[28]

The conflation of Eden with paradise produces new conceptions both for how Genesis is interpreted and how these theological concerns surface in various human and geographical relationships. As Eden becomes synonymous with paradise, biblical referents, already undergoing expansion as seen in Ezekiel, are further expanded to construct Eden as the idealized site of beauty, luxury, and divine favor. Paradisal ideas over time flow from otherworldly thinking to earthly locations, as seen in the age of European exploration with the search for Eden. While in the modern period the search for Eden as an earthly location would not be completely eliminated,[29] the conception of paradise with particular application to tropical islands forms the basis of modern tourism.

FLOWS TO EARTHLY PARADISES: EMPIRE AND TOURISM

The quest to locate the biblical Eden in service of religious devotion soon gives way to the thirst for the riches associated with a space of luxury. The racial constructs imposed upon the world by Europeans devalued people of other races and would in turn be reflected in the territories and peoples subject to colonialism, slavery, and their attendant legacies.[30] The ideas of the biblical Eden provide one way through which Europeans could engage the contradiction that the world's less desirable people occupied the world's most desirable spaces. Applications of the biblical narrative of expulsion from the garden alongside the quest to regain the garden can be discerned in aspects of the discourse of modern European imperial history. Various aspects of European imperialism not only articulate civilizational advancement of indigenous peoples as a core mission but also argue that insufficient use of the land, such as immoral practices or even limited economic exploitation, justify the appropriation of the land to ensure its efficient use.[31]

Tropical regions of the Americas provide the basis upon which Europeans fill out their yearnings for Eden. Since these desires were not simply spiritual but manifestly carnal, conquest, occupation, exploitation, and genocide became crass expressions that could easily belie the seeming innocence around the Eden-paradise narrative. The uniquely evolved flora and fauna of the Americas that produced species unlike those of the other continents attached by land bridges confirmed for early European visitors the Edenic nature of these lands. For instance, due to their long life spans as well as their ability to talk, parrots earned the exotic name "birds of paradise." These birds served as evidence of a place that predates the fall since the formerly talking serpent loses speech as a result of human sin.[32] In addition, the "climate, abundant water; exceptional fruits; precious stones" and the presumption that the indigenous people possessed remarkable longevity filled out other exoticizing characteristics of the Garden of Eden.[33] Paradise becomes a way to express these exotic desires to acquire these territories and in fact to transport tropical landscapes to Europe in order to capture all of the benefits that come with such spaces of blessedness.[34] Within this yearning, the island holds a particular appeal given the European fascination with islands[35] as sites of restoration, whether it be for health,[36] moral,[37] or existential clarity.[38] The availability of abundant waters that surround islands make them perfect replicas of the distinctive geography of Eden and consequently as sites of paradise. Walcott writes of the island as a perfect getaway and gateway to paradise:

> . . . but somewhere on the other
> side of the world, somewhere, with its sunlit islands,
> where what they called history could not happen. Where?
>
> Where could this world renew the Mediterranean's
> Innocence? She deserved Eden after this war.[39]

The European nesomania—obsession with islands—responded to more than aesthetic and spiritual desires. In addition, islands facilitated various expressions of imperialism.[40] Caribbean islands formed the basis of a plantation economy designed to extract as much wealth from the land with as cheap a labor force as possible. Although the dreams of large gold deposits never fully materialized in the Caribbean, the sugar, tobacco industries, and other agricultural industries of the imperial age provided a measure of satiety for the European thirst for paradise. Building on the work of George Beckford, Ian Strachan describes the plantation economy as an extractive one designed for the sole interests of metropolitan capitalists. As a "monopolizing institution," the plantation captures the best lands and puts them into production through various types of coercive labor practices—whether slave, indentured, or low-cost labor that results from limited choices.[41] The assemblage of capitalism, race, empire, slavery, and plantation economy appears in Kincaid's interaction with the tourist interlocutor of *A Small Place*:

> Do you know why people like me are shy about being capitalists? Well it's because we, for as long as we have known you, *were* capital like bales of cotton and sacks of sugar, and you were the commanding, cruel capitalists, and the memory of this is so strong, the experience so recent, that we can't quite bring ourselves to embrace this idea that you think so much of.[42]

Although the plantation system fizzled out with the declining of territory-based imperialism in the modern period, the structural and economic ties of metropolitan centers and multinational companies keep in place features of the "asymmetrical economic flows"[43] of the plantation in the tourism industry. Strachan offers that the essential monopolization of land continues with tourism, except that seacoasts rather than farms become the captured territory.[44] Lacking the gloss and elegance that should characterize the pursuit of paradise, the plantation economy in the Caribbean has nonetheless set the stage for the emergence of tourism as the dominant industry, making the Caribbean among one of the most "tourism dependent region[s] of the world"[45] and entrenching paradise into various discourses about the Caribbean. Antigua and Barbuda's Redcliffe Quay, a former slave-trading yard that evolved into commercial use after emancipation, which now operates as a major retail center dependent upon tourism, stands as a striking symbol of the ironic turn between plantation and tourism. As Sheller puts it, "In economic terms, 'Foreign sun-seekers replace bananas. Hiltons replace sugar mills.'"[46]

THE FLOW FROM TEXT TO ISLAND TOURISM

The heavy reliance upon tourism ironically returns Caribbean islands to using notions of paradise as the draw to compel European visitors to enact centuries-old quests for Eden-paradise with its imperial legacies intact. The role that paradise plays in tourism illustrates how tourism "reinforces and is embedded in postcolonial relationships."[47] These relationships proceed along several tracks, among which are the moral calculations that shape how past and present imperializing tendencies relate to land and people. Given how paradise impacts the tourism discourse, aspects of the narrative of Genesis, particularly unstated and insufficiently examined ideas about sin, appear to influence these relationships. The notions of paradise produce what on the surface can appear as a contradictory set of relationships but are in fact rationalized by a seemingly coherent reading of Genesis.

The label paradise places a high value upon tourism-dependent areas that sets them apart as deserving of special attention. Richard Grove locates the origins of the modern ecological movement in one aspect of European relationships with tropical islands.[48] He identifies the European strain of thought of Eden as a tropical location as responsible for the heightened measures to protect these tropical islands.[49] The establishment of the first forest reserve in the Americas in Tobago in 1763 in response to the understanding of how forests affect rainfall, as well as the founding of the botanical gardens in St. Vincent in 1764, the second in the tropics, indicate some of these early efforts at protecting the environment in the Caribbean. The preference of some European tourists for ecotourism, sometimes called green tourism, with emphases upon sustainability and the preservation of fragile landscapes as a counterpoint to the excesses of mass tourism, provides continuities with these early efforts of maintaining tropical landscapes. To the extent that paradise as a spiritual concept supports ecological efforts and concerns in island tourism, this connection draws upon the belief that these islands are not part of the fallen world. As a replica of Eden that remains unspoiled by human sin, tropical paradises enable spiritual engagement and therefore confirm that travel to tropical islands exposes tourists to special wealth and riches that can only be experienced in the physical world,[50] thereby enabling a form of transcendence through reveling in the natural environment.

In the Bible deities appear on earth from time to time, but no single location serves as divine space. The description of God walking in the garden in the evening suggests a regular divine habit. Ezekiel's and Isaiah's equation of Eden with the garden of God (Ezek. 28:13; Isa. 51:3) explicitly enables thinking of divine space on earth. In Genesis the garden itself does not suffer any of the consequences of human sin or the curse placed on the rest of the earth (Gen. 3:17). The measures taken to hinder human access to the garden (Gen. 3:24) support this idea of Eden as maintaining its pristine value as a divine space. Therefore, paradise as a synonym for Eden confers similar values of divinity upon lands that make them worthy of protection if only to maintain them as earthly portals to divine space.

The other side of the quest for transcendence through the natural environment is the unbridled revelry in the landscape that poses threats to its sustainability. Tourism unleashes deleterious consequences upon the environment to complete a vicious circle.[51] Reminiscent of early European explorers and their response to the lure of gold in the Americas, Adam Stewart, CEO of Sandals Resorts, speaking in support of a projected resort in Tobago whose tourism potential the government wishes to maximize, remarked to the Trinidad and Tobago Chamber of Commerce: "Trinidad and Tobago is a gold mine just waiting to be discovered."[52] Tourist-dependent countries embrace the identity of paradise as the basis on which to market themselves as destinations with pristine natural environments and as a result invite the types of development on the land as well as impacts upon local culture that threaten that identity. Marketing paradise requires the continuation of the myth of the unspoiled and untouched land to sustain exotic narratives. Kincaid ridicules the idea of marketing the beach as unspoiled:

> How well I remember that all of Antigua turned out to see the Princess person, how every building that she would enter was repaired and painted so that it looked brand-new, how every beach she would sun herself on had to look as if no one had ever sunned there before (I wonder now what they did about the poor sea, I mean, can a sea be made to look brand-new?).[53]

Paradise as a concept that connects spirituality and landscape degenerates into a crass economic commodity[54] in the tourism industry, exploited by the players that make up the industry. Ironically, the land becomes the first victim in this struggle but the last to get attention, since no real connection occurs with the environment beyond the mystique created by tropical temperatures and the backdrop of the ecosystem that those temperatures generate. Imperceptible decays in the environments—bleaching of coral reefs, rise in sea levels that denude beaches, reduction in the biodiversity of wetlands flooded by sewerage or cleared to accommodate resorts, destruction of coastal vegetation that protect shorelines as a result of beach construction—pose little immediate threat to economic profitability, and concerns about the environment could be deferred or disregarded as impediments to greater economic development. To the extent that paradise is conceived as a garden emptied or independent of human presence, the beauty of the natural landscape can be seen as its inherent strength, capable of regenerating and sustaining itself without human intervention. Yet Genesis points to the necessity of a gardener to ensure its upkeep through the creation of the earth creature (*ha'ādām*; 2:7). Over the course of the history of interpretation attention to the gardener is reduced,[55] and under the influence of extrabiblical ideas the role of the gardener is essentially erased to privilege an elite perspective. This elite perspective both fails to feature the duty of the king to care for the garden[56] and renders the work and presence of lower status individuals invisible. Not surprisingly, the duty of care is lacking in the dominant narratives of paradise deployed in the tourism industry.

If the first humans are expelled as a result of their sin, then their moral failure justifies their expulsion and subsequent relocation out of the land. While the notion of a return to Eden does not exist in the Genesis account, the conflation of the story with paradise discourses opens the door to accommodate the idea of "paradise regained." Columbus's own sense was that access to Eden would be a divine gift, "by God's own permission."[57] Paradise discourses, as seen in contemporary tourism use, perform three major functions regarding humans and the land: erase all traces of humans to make the land appear untouched,[58] represent indigenous occupants as primitive, and imply access for a privileged elite. The third aspect of paradise as a benefit for a privileged elite combines theological thinking with the logic of imperial economics. As modern empires built wealth upon ideas of manifest destiny to claim resources and territory out of the hands of indigenous people, the belief in the tight relationship between moral purity and material wealth grew even further. That patterns of modern imperialism added race to this tight relationship means that indigenous people in the tropics or those who became the labor force for the empire—largely black and brown people—possess the opposite image to success and therefore are less deserving of paradise. Access to paradise as a concept in the tourism industry appeals largely to white Euro-Americans and plays to alchemic mixtures of moral purity, wealth, the desire for adventure, and race.

Desire for paradise operates both at the individual and corporate levels. In fact, the individual desire functions as an extension of the corporate (read here, in the case of tourism, as imperial). The multinational corporations as well as individual tourists serve as expressions of the continued linkages between imperial economic exploitation and tourism, as already noted. Their desires for paradise converge around the ideas of entitlement of access to divine space. This convergence enables a clear articulation of the economic interests of businesses and personal needs in the greater service of imperial designs. For instance, some expansionist platforms existed in the nineteenth century in the United States that advocated incorporating several territories into the country, using travel narratives that pointed to the beauty of the landscape and the economic potential of that land under the right leadership.[59] While these platforms eyed locations as diverse as California and Montana, there was also a push to acquire Cuba and Hawai'i. Interestingly, in these discussions Cuba is represented as an apple and Hawai'i as a pear.[60] While the Hawai'i discourse would go further to invoke biblical and theological tropes for its justification, the Cuba discussion relied mostly upon the signifier of the apple, reproducing aspects of the biblical Eden to heighten the attraction of the land as a national possession. The invocation of Eden around Cuba in a broad appeal to several constituencies—military, economic, political, recreational, and so on—demonstrates the interlocking nature of travel, tourism, and empire.[61] The implied superiority of the white Euro-American tourist to the entitlements of paradise becomes incarnate in the presence of that tourist, who bears the image of the cultural, economic, and military power of these former and present imperial powers. Merrill points to US tourists abroad as forms of "international soft power" that represent consumptive and cultural benefits that are supported and kept in place by military and economic power best labeled as empire.[62] The idealized Euro-American tourist serves not simply as an economic sign but chiefly as an indicator of ideal humanity deserving of paradise.

The idealization of wealth on its own that the tourism industry supports distracts from several other factors that constitute the tourist that walks through the constructed paradises of the tourism-dependent country. Subtly implying the moral purity of the visitor to paradise masks the economic, political, military, and other sins that produce the wealth that flows through the industry. The assumption of the ability and means to travel ignores global economic formations as well as historical realities. Kincaid pries apart the economic inequities that constitute the subject of the visitor and visited:

> For every native of every place is a potential tourist, and every tourist is a native of somewhere. Every native everywhere lives a life of overwhelming and crushing banality and boredom and desperation and depression. . . . But some natives—most natives in the world—cannot go anywhere. They are too poor. They are too poor to go anywhere.[63]

In the use of paradise in tourism discourse, economic ability stands in for the freedom from sin that enables the wealthy tourist to overcome the moral lapses that disqualify the natives from the garden. The ability to shake off the drudgery of the world and gain access to a portal to heaven needs to appear reserved for a select group rather than universal access, as the selectivity of tourism marketing confirms. The tourism industry sells this access not simply to those who can afford it the most but to those whom the imperial power structures of the world have determined to be the most deserving. The current motto of the Caribbean Tourism Development Company, "Life Needs the Caribbean," constructs the Caribbean as the threshold to a different life not marked by an awful commute, board meetings, workouts, and presumably uncomfortable boardroom chairs.[64] This politico-economic version of moral purity relies upon the readings of the Eden narrative that through various means envisage a way back into the garden for those who overcome the failures of the native inhabitants. That the idea of paradise, however, never flowed in the same direction as other universalist ideas of salvation means that paradise has always been deployed as a benefit for a select few. Paradise discourses tend to isolate aspects of the biblical texts as well as human history to serve a single perspective. Consequently, marketing the Caribbean as paradise papers over the historical realities of the Caribbean—genocide of indigenous people, slavery, indentureship—that reflect centuries of economic and military exploitation in order to repeat that exploitation in a different form. St. Lucia's current tourism marketing obscures this history with a historical account of the arrival of various groups at the island that seems like a series of peaceful intentional migrations, almost as proto-tourists:

> It began with the Amerindians who were drawn to Gros Piton and Petit Piton for their mystical protection. Generations of Africans made their home here bringing with them a variety of enchanting flavours. The British and French followed and along with them came customs and traditions that manifested themselves in the flavours of Saint Lucia.[65]

Greedy Spanish explorers responded to the staging of the territory as paradise and when gold failed to materialize turned to slaves—indigenous and imported—to yield their wealth.[66] Marketing it once again as paradise enables the land to serve up the exploitation of the people as sources of enrichment, entertainment, and adventure for those who engage in travel, exploration, and the transfer of cultural and other resources, a simulated world in which imperialist fantasies are played out again and again."[67] Kincaid points to exploitative travel as a source of difficult relationships generated by imperialism and tourism:

> You came. You took things that were not yours, and you did not even, for appearances' sake, ask first. You could have said, "May I have this, please?" and even though it would have been clear to everybody that a yes or no from us would have been of no consequence you might have looked so much better. Believe me, it would have gone a long way. I would have had to admit that at least you were polite. You murdered people. You imprisoned people. You robbed people. You opened your own banks and you put our money in them. The accounts were in your name. The banks were in your name. There must have been some good people among you, but they stayed home. And that is the point. That is why they are good. They stayed home.[68]

The dominant notion of blissful innocence as the life of the first humans in the Garden of Eden lost to the corrupting influences of sin, temptation, and carnality drives most interpretations of the Genesis text. From this perspective the humans are a curious mixture of primitivism and sensuality, not that different from early Greek thinking about indigenous people whom they encountered for the first time—savage, innocent, feminine.[69] Since the general interpretation of the narrative suggests that sinful humans cannot abide in the garden, when Eden or paradise is thought of as a place where humans live and not simply as a luxurious garden, human beings are perceived as either primordially innocent or sensually arousing. These ideas about indigenous populations are also true for the land seen as a paradise—virgin soils, stimuli that appeal to all the senses, generating immense desire. The consequent effect of representing the landscape in this way is that the inhabitants become icons of aboriginalism, abundant perversion, endless stimulation, that are all readily available.[70] Walcott adopts the European fantasy name for St. Lucia, the Helen of the West, liberally used in the tourism marketing of the island, and personifies it as Helen, a character in *Omeros*: "the island's beauty was in her looks."[71] Indistinguishable from the land, inhabitants of paradise therefore deliver the experiences associated with paradise. Helen not only becomes a source of attraction for Major Plunkett, the retired British military officer, but also subject to harassment from tourists, whom she is expected to tolerate as part of the performance of her job:

> . . . What the white manager mean
> To say was she was too rude, 'cause she dint take no shit
> from white people and some of them tourist—the men
>
> only out to touch local girls; every minute—
> was brushing their hand from her backside so one day
> she get fed up with all their nastiness so she tell
>
> the cashier that wasn't part of her focking pay[72]

Tourism when it operates under the notion of paradise requires certain performances of the perceived native culture. These perceptions, of course, settle fairly close to primitivism. As Salazar points out, tourism depends upon an "image-making-machinery" that draws upon already existing scripts about places and people.[73] While these scripts may originate from old tropes and ideas, they also serve modern needs expressed in various dimensions of neoliberalism—such as unbridled individual freedom and maximum efficiency as it relates to self-actualization—that make an experience in what is considered a slice of heaven a prerequisite for the good life. Salazar offers three myths that feed these modern drives in tourism: "the myth of the unchanged, the myth of the unrestrained and the myth of the uncivilized."[74] Interpretations of the Eden narrative circulate versions of these three myths about the garden. That is to say, the garden retains its pristine form as the apex of creation where humans lived or can live in the innocence of the uncivilized state. Despite anxieties around sexuality in Christian theology, popular Christian depictions of Eve—using visual erotic registers such as shorn pubic area,[75] flowing locks (at times blonde),[76] and the position of the body[77]—sufficiently feed prurient and other fantasies to support the myth of Eden as a place of sexual unrestraint.[78] Paradise, therefore, provides the avenue through which the tourism industry can exploit these myths to create an experience decidedly different from the quotidian. Tourism marketing consequently exaggerates differences—culture, race, gender, or sexuality; even if this means repeating some of the most grotesque conceptions Europeans have long harbored about indigenous people in the tropics, the payoff is worth it. The machinery produces the fantasy of being "in a paradisiacal environment, a vanished Eden, where the local landscape and population are to be consumed through observation, embodied sensation and imagination."[79]

Paradise as a selling point in tourism coerces the consent of the populations of tourism-dependent countries to enact exoticization discourses that circulate from Western sources and confirm an inferior status. Participation in staging the production of a version of primeval Eden means that workers in the tourism industry must appear native enough to produce an authentic local culture untouched by broader Western influences but at the same time knowledgeable of the needs of Euro-American tourists and the geopolitical realities that shape the interaction. Nostalgia for an imagined past, created in large measure by a broad variety of Western media[80] and circulated throughout the Caribbean, produces national identities that only exist and are performed within tourist enclaves. Walcott describes Helen's performance of the St. Lucian version:

> You can see Helen at the Halcyon. She is dressed
> in the national costume: white, low-cut bodice,
> with frilled lace at the collar, just a cleft of a breast
>
> for the customers when she places their orders
> on the shields of the table. They can guess the rest
> under the madras skirt with its golden borders[81]

These performances hardly feature anything heroic but instead retreat to servile concepts. In fact, as a service industry, tourism employs local labor in jobs that require limited specialist skills. And to the extent that training does occur in the growing field of tourism and hospitality as an education discipline, participants are socialized into the servant role. Kincaid's vivid but searing description of tourism education makes the point:

> the Hotel Training School, a school that teaches Antiguans how to be good servants, how to be a good nobody, which is what a servant is.[82]

The impact upon the self-worth of the local population also holds economic implications since tourism as the major income earner for a local economy depresses other forms of employment through the lure of workers to the tourism labor force. Tourism cannibalizes other forms of employment in the economy that could integrate strategically in the industry but are instead weakened, given the control of major corporate players. Walcott portrays the hapless Hector, an aspirant for the affections of Helen—land and woman—caught between his passion for fishing and the enticement of greater wealth in the tourism sector that compromises his true love:

> He'd paid the penalty of giving up the sea
> as graceless and as treacherous as it had seemed,
> for the taxi-business; he was making money,
>
> but all of that money was making him ashamed
> of the long afternoons of shouting by the wharf
> hustling passengers. He missed the uncertain sand[83]

As the servant class in the tourism industry, the local population takes on the role of the humans in Eden—resident workers rather than owners. However, since Genesis understands the garden as divinely owned, all humans, should they enter the garden, do not do so as owners. Nonetheless, the perception of the secondary status of the indigenous humans in the garden becomes all too real in a tourism industry that communicates to native populations their servile role in creating paradise for more deserving human beings.

THE FLOW FROM TOURISM TO REIMAGINING PARADISE

The contours that connect Eden to paradise to earthly locations to imperial desire to plantation slave economies and then to tourism reveal layered histories and complex postcolonial relationships. Biblical and theological conceptions facilitate and maintain these connections, suggesting important roles for oppositional readings of these texts and theologies. Reconceptualizing paradise can create more equitable geopolitical arrangements and meaningful relationships among people as travel continues to be a feature of human life. My concern in this essay to illustrate the material consequences of biblical interpretation serves as a platform to contribute to the unsettling of traditional theological interpretations of Genesis 2–3. As evidenced by the postcolonial focus of my work, attempting a neat containment of gender, sexuality, and human anthropology when dealing with native people and lands distorts the existing reality even further. The path to fairer global relations around travel requires more than simply decentering this passage in Christian theology; it also requires disrupting the flow of elitist ideas that (re)produce the privileging of certain lives and spaces.

Although "paradise" seems like a pseudo-theological term, it still retains links with biblical texts. To the extent that biblical interpretations circulate the idea of primeval innocence, words like paradise will continue to breathe that air and perpetuate unfortunate consequences of the exotic. Valorizing innocence to the point of fetishization and commodification, as occurs in tourism marketing, perpetuates the myth of civilizational progress and its attendant racist imperialisms. Primitivism functions as a basic building block that sustains persistent forms of racialized caste systems and ideologies. The teleology of progress builds upon Christian precepts that require a moment of human primal innocence. The tourism industry is therefore one aspect of a broader circulation of notions that either takes their origins from Gen. 2–3 or is projected onto the text and consequently maintained by the circulation of religious dogma.

The implications of this single narrative for people and land are enormous. Primordialism and its inherent linearity distort proper historical accounting of relationships with the land. The romanticization of a nonexistent past in the garden where humans commune peacefully with nature suggests that the ideal ecological balance is buried in the primeval abyss. Since the pristine moment of ecological balance where humans lived in "easy harmony with the rest of the natural world"[84] has long faded, participants in tourism are relieved of any responsibility to deal with the pressing environmental challenges. Further, since this warped environmental history indicts Western industrialization as the single guilty party in environmental decay, tourism-dependent countries can absolve themselves of any responsibility.

The language of "fall" reaffirms the unproven notion that an ideal humanity once existed. Consequently, the distinction between the idealized humans created in the garden and the fallen humans expelled from the garden makes space for racialized and other hierarchies as seen in imperialism and tourism: the expelled sinful humans over against the perfect humans who reenter paradise to rightly use its riches. The subject positions of indigenous people and colonizing travelers effortlessly fall into place. The imperialism of the age of exploration thrived as imperial powers told this story about themselves and indigenous people. Through tourism both the tourists and those who host them tell the same story about paradise, where native people internalize an identity as the outsider.

The intersections of Eden and tourism narratives reveal the need for reconceptualizing the narrative that disrupts their previous histories. Rethinking these narratives can provide different forms of relationships between peoples across the world and tourism destinations. Walcott offers, in my estimation, a starting point with his reimagination of a primeval narrative for St. Lucia that emerges from the conjuring of Ma Kilman and her African rituals, that ends not with the notes of satisfaction over the creation in Gen. 1 but with the starkness of the processes of birth; a confluence of several near histories that produce a stench and an unappealing picture that sets the stage from which the unknown potential of the future begins:

> That was why the sea stank from the frothing urine
> of surf, and fish-guts reeked from the government shed,
>
> and why God pissed on the village for months of rain.
> But now, quite clearly the tears trickled down his face
> like rainwater down a cracked carafe from Choiseul,
>
> as he stood like a boy in his bath with the first clay's
> innocent prick! So she threw Adam a towel.
> And the yard was Eden. And its light the first day's.[85]

NOTES

1. Noel B. Salazar, *Envisioning Eden: Mobilizing Imaginaries in Tourism and Beyond* (New York: Berghahn, 2010), 8.
2. Dennis Merrill, *Negotiating Paradise: U.S. Tourism and Empire in Twentieth-Century Latin America* (Chapel Hill, NC: University of North Carolina Press, 2009), 26.
3. Salazar, *Envisioning Eden*, 44.
4. Derek Walcott, *Omeros* (London: Faber and Faber, 1990), 63.
5. Eibert Tigchelaar, "Eden and Paradise: The Garden Motif in Some Early Jewish Texts (1 Enoch and Other Texts Found at Qumran)," in *Paradise Interpreted: Representations of Biblical Paradise in Judaism and Christianity*, ed. Gerard P. Luttikhuizen (Leiden: Brill, 1999), 37.
6. See Claus Westermann, *Genesis 1–11: A Continental Commentary* (Minneapolis, MN: Fortress, 1994), 210.
7. Jan Bremmer suggests that the Greek translators could have opted for *kêpos* instead of *paradesios*. See Jan N. Bremmer, "Paradise: From Persia, via Greece, into the Septuagint," in *Paradise Interpreted: Representations of Biblical Paradise in Judaism and Christianity*, ed. Gerard P. Luttikhuizen (Leiden: Brill, 1999), 1–20.
8. Bremmer, "Paradise," 10.
9. Jean Delumeau, *History of Paradise: The Garden of Eden in Myth and Tradition* (New York: Continuum, 1995), 6.
10. Bremmer, "Paradise," 18.
11. Tigchelaar, "Eden and Paradise," 37.
12. By the Second Temple period Eden would come to be regarded as the ideal temple location, as seen in Jubilees 3:12, 27; 4:26; 8:19. See Peter T. Lanfer, "Allusion to and Expansion of the Tree of Life and Garden of Eden in Biblical and Pseudepigraphical Literature," in *Christian Literature and Intertextuality*, ed. Craig A. Evans and H. Daniel Zacharias (London: T&T ClarkLanfer 2009), 98.
13. Ed Noort, "Gan-Eden in the Context of the Mythology of the Hebrew Bible," in *Paradise Interpreted: Representations of Biblical Paradise in Judaism and Christianity*, ed. Gerard P. Luttikhuizen (Leiden: Brill, 1999), 21.
14. Ben Sira, who views Eden as a more earthly reality, serves as the exception. See Martha Himmerlfarb, "The Temple and the Garden of Eden in Ezekiel, the Book of the Watchers, and the Wisdom of Ben Sira," in *Sacred Places and Profane Spaces: Essays in the Geographics of Judaism, Christianity, and Islam*, ed. Jamie Scott and Paul Simpson-Housley (New York: Greenwood, 1991), 65–69.
15. Delumeau, *History of Paradise*, 7.
16. Delumeau, *History of Paradise*, 11.

17. Christoph Auffarth, "Paradise Now—But for the Wall Between: Some Remarks on Paradise in the Middle Ages," in *Paradise Interpreted: Representations of Biblical Paradise in Judaism and Christianity*, ed. Gerard P. Luttikhuizen (Leiden: Brill, 1999), 171.

18. Christopher Columbus, *Select Letters of Christopher Columbus, with Other Original Documents, Relating to His Four Voyages to the New World* (London: Hakluyt Society, 1847), 137; Delumeau, *History of Paradise*, 171.

19. In the Mappa Mundi, housed in the Hereford Cathedral, Eden appears as "a circular island at eastern extreme of the world (the top) . . . inaccessible to humanity . . . surrounded by a ring of fire. Separated from the land masses by water, walled and battlemented, and its gates are firmly closed" (http://www.themappamundi.co.uk/mappa-mundi).

20. Delumeau, *History of Paradise*, 56.

21. Delumeau, *History of Paradise*, 90.

22. Brook Wilensky-Lanford, *Paradise Lust: Searching for the Garden of Eden* (New York: Grove, 2011), xvi.

23. Columbus, *Select Letters*, 135.

24. Columbus, *Select Letters*, 137. Walter Raleigh reflects similar ideas influenced by biblical and theological positions (Delumeau, *History of Paradise*, 15).

25. Columbus, *Select Letters*, 138.

26. Jamaica Kincaid, *A Small Place* (New York: Farrar, Straus and Giroux, 1988), 77.

27. Nicolas Wyatt, "A Royal Garden: The Ideology of Eden," *SJOT* 28 (2014): 14–15.

28. Mimi Sheller, *Consuming the Caribbean: From Arawaks to Zombies* (London: Routledge, 2003), 109.

29. See Wilensky-Lanford, *Paradise Lust*.

30. Robert J. C. Young, *Empire, Colony, Postcolony* (Malden, MA: Wiley Blackwell, 2015), 46.

31. Spanish colonization in the Americas relied for its legal basis upon thirteenth-century arguments in support of the Crusades that authorized the pope to enforce civilization upon non-Christian lands and conversion to Christianity. Richard Haklyut uses similar arguments—inefficient and underutilization of lands—to support British conquest of the West Indies and Ireland (Robert A. Williams Jr., *The American Indian in Western Legal Thought: The Discourses of Conquest* [New York: Oxford University Press, 1990], 14, 140).

32. Although Genesis never indicates loss of speech as a curse on the serpent, interpretations such as Jubilees 3:28 suggest that the serpent and all animals lost the ability to speak.

33. Delumeau, *History of Paradise*, 116.

34. The development of glass houses and "painterly scenes" representing tropical vegetation in British estates reflects the thirst for the new landscape (Sheller, *Consuming the Caribbean*, 46).

35. Richard H. Grove, *Green Imperialism: Colonial Expansions, Tropical Island Edens and the Origins of Environmentalism, 1600–1860* (Cambridge: Cambridge University Press, 1995), 34.

36. Greek writers like Hesiod describe the islands of the blessed as part of a golden age where uninterrupted peace reigns. Similarly, Pindar, as early as 476 BC, narrates the Happy Isles as the reward of the righteous as a result of their sufferings. These islands, with their restorative sea breezes, were believed to eliminate any form of suffering (Delumeau, *History of Paradise*, 6).

37. For instance, in Dante's *Purgatorio* an island serves as the site for purgatory and redemption (Grove, *Green Imperialism*, 34).

38. The popularity of *Robinson Crusoe* and the resulting robinsonade genre demonstrate the appeal of islands as sites of personal renewal for Europeans.

39. Walcott, *Omeros*, 28.

40. Elizabeth M. DeLoughrey, *Routes and Roots: Navigating Caribbean and Pacific Island Literatures* (Honolulu, HI: University of Hawai'i Press, 2007), 6.

41. Ian Gregory Strachan, *Paradise and Plantation: Tourism and Culture in the Anglophone Caribbean* (Charolttesville, VA: University of Virginia Press, 2002), 4.

42. Kincaid, *A Small Place*, 36.

43. Anthony Carrigan, *Postcolonial Tourism: Literature, Culture, and Environment* (New York: Routledge, 2013), 19.

44. Strachan, *Paradise and Plantation*, 9.

45. Carrigan, *Postcolonial Tourism*, 9.

46. Sheller, *Consuming the Caribbean*, 163.

47. C. Michael Hall and Hazel Tucker, "Tourism and Postcolonialism: An Introduction," in *Tourism and Postcolonialism: Contested Discourses, Identities and Representations*, ed. C. Michael Hall and Hazel Tucker (London: Routledge, 2004), 2.

48. Grove, *Green Imperialism*, 3.

49. Grove, *Green Imperialism*, 5.

50. Grove, *Green Imperialism*, 51.

51. Carrigan, *Postcolonial Tourism*, 33.

52. Kristina Rundquist, "Sandals Eyes Tobago for New Resort," *Travel Pulse*, November 24, 2016 (http://www.travelpulse.com/news/hotels-and-resorts/sandals-eyes-tobago-for-new-resort.html).

53. Kincaid, *A Small Place*, 33.

54. Melanie A. Murray, *Island Paradise: The Myth: An Examination of Contemporary Caribbean and Sri Lankan Writing* (Amsterdam: Rodopi, 2009), 21.

55. Luther, who helps shape the emphasis on sin and the fall in this text, has a single passing reference to this role in his commentary. See Jaroslav Pelikan (ed.), *Luther's Works: Lectures on Genesis Chapters 1–5* (St. Louis, MO: Concordia, 1958), 1:91.

56. Wyatt, "A Royal Garden," 24.

57. Columbus, *Select Letters*, 137.

58. Six of the eleven pictures in the 2017 photo stream on the website of the Caribbean Tourism Development Company (www.caribbeantravel.com) feature empty landscapes. The other five pictures depict potential tourists. Websites from individual countries overwhelmingly depict native people as performers.

59. Christine Skwiot, *The Purpose of Paradise: U.S. Tourism and Empire in Cuba and Hawai'i* (Philadelphia, PA: University of Pennsylvania Press, 2010), 3.

60. Skwiot, *The Purpose of Paradise*, 14.

61. Skwiot, *The Purpose of Paradise*, 3.

62. Merrill, *Negotiating Paradise*, xii.

63. Kincaid, *A Small Place*, 18.

64. See http://www.caribbeantravel.com. These and other phrases map onto series of pictures to describe the "life" that needs the Caribbean implicitly—life as led by highly paid but overly stressed Euro-Americans.

65. http://www.caribbeantravel.com/caribbean-islands/st-lucia.

66. Murray, *Island Paradise*, 22.

67. Sheller, *Consuming the Caribbean*, 122.

68. Kincaid, *A Small Place*, 35.

69. Strachan, *Paradise and Plantation*, 18.

70. Carrigan, *Postcolonial Tourism*, 35.

71. Walcott, *Omeros*, 96.

72. Walcott, *Omeros*, 33.

73. Salazar, *Envisioning Eden*, 21.

74. Salazar, *Envisioning Eden*, 43.

75. Ancient Greek statues of men displayed pubic hair, unlike those of women. These statues display the codified beauty of Aphrodite over and against the distaste for pubic hair among the Egyptians and their sex-worker cultures (Hastings Donnan and Fiona Magowan, *The Anthropology of Sex* [Oxford: Berg Donnan and Magowan, 2010], 33).

76. By the middle of the fourteenth century paintings of Eve featured long flowing blonde hair like that of Aphrodite. Blonde hair generally suggested beautiful but dangerous women; "a transgressive power that could be used to convey illicit sexuality" (Donnan and Magowan, *The Anthropology of Sex*, 30).

77. Polinska observes that artists tend to use various positions of Eve's body in relation to other characters as erotic suggestions. For example, Hans Baldung Grien's 1511 woodcut, *The*

Fall, depicts a fully nude Eve in front of the partially hidden Adam (Wioleta Polinska, "Dangerous Bodies: Women's Nakedness and Theology," *Journal of Feminist Studies in Religion* 16 [2010]: 50).

78. Milton's focused descriptions of Eve in the words of Satan depict a measure of sexual attraction (John Milton, *Paradise Lost* [New York: Norton, 2005], 5.420–430).

79. Salazar, *Envisioning Eden*, 21.

80. Salazar, *Envisioning Eden*, 44.

81. Walcott, *Omeros*, 322.

82. Kincaid, *A Small Place*, 55.

83. Walcott, *Omeros*, 231.

84. Martin W. Lewis, "Environmental History Challenges the Myth of a Primordial Eden," *Journal of Geological Education* 42 (1994): 474.

85. Walcott, *Omeros*, 248.

Chapter Three

When No Land on Earth Is "Promised Land"

Empire and Forced Migrants

Gemma Tulud Cruz

The twenty-first century has been called "the age of migration"[1] essentially because there are more migrants in the world today than ever before. Estimates by the International Organization for Migration indicate that the number of migrants worldwide could rise to as many as 405 million by 2050.[2] Today, there are an estimated 244 million migrants, who comprise more than 3% of the world's population.[3] While the percentage seems miniscule, it actually represents a lot of people. In fact, if all migrants in the world were to come together to constitute a country, theirs would be the world's fifth most populous. This immense movement of peoples is not only rearranging human geography but also transforming the economic, religious, and cultural landscapes of many countries and communities.

"Driven from home" is a description commonly associated with forced migrants[4] insofar as they are forced to leave their homes to flee from wars, violent conflicts, natural or environmental disasters, poverty, and persecution in various forms.[5] It could be argued that, with many migrants being forced to move due to loss of livelihood or literal loss of their land due to land-grabbing or development, forced migrants today could also be described as people driven from the land and victims of empire.[6] To be sure, the suffering of these migrants does not end when they leave their homeland or pass across international borders into another land. Forced migrants' lives are not all about suffering either. Indeed, contemporary human mobility is both a challenge and a gift; it offers both promise and peril. I now turn to sketch in broad strokes this double-edged character of the experience of contemporary forced migrants by exploring their experience of land and empire.

LAND AND EMPIRE IN THE EXPERIENCE OF FORCED MIGRANTS

Migration is both a cause and an effect of broader development processes entangled in empire. The analysis of international migration from 1990 to 2013, which shows the predominance of people from the Global South among people on the move, serves as evidence of this entanglement. Eighty-two million, or 86 percent, of the ninety-six million international migrants residing in the developing world in 2013 originated from the South, while fourteen million, or 14 percent, were born in the North. Although the annual growth rate in international migrant stock in the South has outpaced the growth rate in the North since 2000, of the fifty-three million international migrants added in the North between 1990 and 2013, forty-two million or 78 percent were born in the South.[7]

The people of the Global South, which includes 157 recognized states in the world, bear the brunt of some of the greatest challenges facing the international community: poverty, environmental degradation, human and civil rights abuses, ethnic and regional conflicts, hunger, and disease. Thus, for many people in the Global South, moving across borders is the best, if not the only, way to cope with life's risks and challenges. The recent case of about five hundred mostly African migrants simultaneously forcing their way into Spanish territory by breaking through the gates of the twenty-foot-high fence that separates Morocco from Spain's Ceuta enclave illustrates this "migration at any and all cost" mentality that has engulfed marginal(ized) countries and communities preyed upon by unscrupulous human traffickers.[8] Such cases starkly depict many migrants' desperation to leave their homeland in search of a new or different one. As Ousmane Kane puts it bluntly in the case of Senegalese immigrants, it is a matter of "immigration or death."[9] This is echoed by Syrian refugees who lament how the only choice is to flee, otherwise you have to "kill or be killed."

To be sure, forced migrants are victims of injustice before, during, and after migration. As mentioned previously the majority of the world's migrants and would-be-migrants come from developing countries that suffer not just from the uneven distribution of the world's wealth and resources but also from regional and global economic policies that burden or further disadvantage these developing countries. In most cases forced migrants have been driven from the land directly or indirectly. The droughts, famines, wars, ethnic and political conflicts, as well as natural or environmental disasters that have wracked developing countries, serve as examples of direct causes, while problematic trade agreements shed light on indirect causes. Take for example the North American Free Trade Agreement (NAFTA), which has disillusioned and displaced small Mexican farmers and forced them to either make their way into Mexico City, where they do bit jobs, or cross illegally into the United States to find work.[10] In a number of cases, migrants are victims of local or national economic crises that force them to sell and/or leave their land. A number of Guatemalans working in the meatpacking industry in Delaware, for example, were coffee farmers who were forced to move because of the coffee crisis.[11] As migrant workers, they are further victimized by regional and global economic crises. The Asian financial crisis that plagued much of labor-importing East Asian countries in 1997 is a case in point. As a result of the financial crisis Thailand deported thousands of Myanmarese laborers, while South Korea and Malaysia deported 300,000 and 10,000 workers respectively. In the case of Overseas Filipino Workers (hereafter OFWs), at least 3,000 Filipino engineers, draftsmen, architects, and others in the construction industry were laid off in Korea, and 2,000 were retrenched in Malaysia.[12]

Some migrant workers, meanwhile, end up in slave-like conditions and become part of the new slavery in the global economy that leads to what Kevin Bales calls "disposable people." According to Bales, three interrelated factors helped create the new slavery: (1) the enormous population explosion over the past three decades that has flooded the world's labor markets with millions of impoverished, desperate people; (2) the revolution of economic globalization and modernized agriculture, which has dispossessed poor farmers, making them and their families ready targets for enslavement; and (3) rapid economic change in developing countries, which has bred corruption and violence, destroying social rules that might once have protected the most vulnerable individuals.[13]

Forced migrants are victims not just of the injustice between and across countries but also within their own countries, particularly in the hands of governments that cannot provide jobs or protect peoples' livelihood. When they move across borders forced migrants also experience exploitation at the hands of their governments, which create a migration industry that turns them into primary exports or cash cows for their remittances, as well as at the hands of various local and transnational vultures, from exploitative recruiters, *coyotes*,[14] and abusive employers to multinational companies, banks, and agencies who prey on migrants' vulnerability. Worst, border crossing these days has become not only humiliating and difficult but downright dangerous. For asylum seekers and refugees, in particular, militarized borders combined with unforgiving elements and ruthless human traffickers have resulted in numerous tragic, horrific, and mass deaths, making deserts and seas the cemetery for countless people simply looking for bare life.

Even when forced migrants get inside another country legally, there are still a host of problems that they face disproportionately. They could suffer, for instance, from inequities in the educational or health care system. Health care providers unfamiliar with the migrants' language and culture and the pressures that migrants face may minimize or misunderstand their symptoms. For women there could be an added gender dimension to these inequities, especially for those who may be dependent on male family members for visas and/or access to health care and other benefits. Then there is the persistent issue of discrimination, particularly racism. As Nyarai, a Zimbabwean immigrant in Birmingham, laments, "You go to school to pick up your kids and the [white] mothers won't speak to you."[15] In some cases, they encounter resistance, especially if they do not share in the dominant religion of the country or local community. At the height of the European migrant crisis in 2015, for instance, Slovakia expressed that it wants to take Christian migrants only just as Australian politicians indicated they will prioritize Christian asylum seekers. The media highlighted these words of a Hungarian bishop: "They're not refugees. This is an invasion. . . . They come here with cries of Allahu Akbar. They want to take over."[16]

Aside from the problem that stems from differences *across* religious traditions there is also the problem rooted in differences *within* religious traditions. Within Christian communities, for instance, migrants experience difficulties because of various forms of differences. Take the case of the following Mexican immigrant church, which had to ask the bishop for their own church because they were rejected by the members of the local Catholic Church:

> It was really hard work and long days, still we were happy to have our Sundays free. Yet, even then we could not feel at home in the Catholic Church since we were denied pews at Our Lady of Perpetual Help (pseudonym). The Italians would tell us, "all seats are taken." No matter how early we arrived the pews were always reserved for Italians. That is why we asked the Bishop for our own church.[17]

It could be said that while it is true and good that migrants can use most local churches for their own services, Martin Luther King's statement that the most segregated hour of the week is 11:00 a.m. on Sunday morning still rings true in places of worship worldwide. Various forms of differences inhibit the formation of intercultural churches. Thus, for many forced migrants today the new land does not immediately nor necessarily become a home, and neither does it truly and fully become a substitute for the homeland that was "lost" or left behind.

For most forced migrants the old land, which is the original home, is not completely or utterly lost or forgotten. It lives on in their hearts.[18] It lives on in the language which continues to be spoken and passed on as much as possible to succeeding generations. It lives on in food and other cultural items sold in small ethnic stores or brought back from visits back home. It lives on in migrant associations and networks,[19] both formal and informal, local and global, real and virtual. It lives on, most of all, in religious and cultural practices that serve as reminders of, as well as keep ties with, the homeland, from hometown saints to festivals, ethnic church buildings, liturgies, etc. The establishment of migrant religious institutions and other social institutions such as schools that are attached to parishes and churches become the means to achieve cultural reproduction, pass on the heritage and religion to their children, negotiate and construct ethno-religious identities, and integrate newcomers.

DOWN BUT NOT OUT

It could be argued that forced migrants do not get completely swallowed up nor defeated by empire. Migration is fraught with problematic conditions that, in most cases, amount to oppression. Migrants, however, do not simply submit to or resign themselves to these death-dealing conditions. Under certain circumstances and using strategic means, they actively fight against oppression in their quest for well-being and liberation. These active attempts to resist oppression and transform their lives are not just on the level of the local but also that of the global; communal not just individual; formal and informal; public and private; and religious, cultural, political, and economic.

Creative Resistance

What is most instructive when it comes to migrant resistance against empire is the creative and imaginative strategies of migrants. The subtle resistance strategies are a combination of active and passive yet creative and potentially liberating strategies. They are akin to what Yale professor and anthropologist James Scott calls "hidden transcripts" or "weapons of the weak"[20] and to the unconventional ways such as folktales, jokes, songs, rituals, codes, euphemisms, etc. through which subjugated peoples refuse to give in to their oppression.

Take the case of migrant Filipina domestic workers in Hong Kong: on Sundays, fellow domestic workers serve as accomplices to their cash-strapped compatriots who sell the illegal *halo-halo* (a concoction of fruits, milk, sugar, and shaved ice), by providing the vendor with human camouflage every time the Urban Services Guard passes by.[21] When one of them is caught selling food by the patrol for illegal hawking, the cluster of customers suddenly sing "Happy Birthday" and instantly transform the activity into one of many birthday parties celebrated at the square.

Other migrants resort to dropping names that elicit suspicion or discrimination and/or change to names that will more easily blend with the general population. Chinese immigrant Te-Sheng Cheng became "Tommy" Cheng to more easily blend into the small town of Rothschild, Wisconsin,[22] while many German Lutherans who came to Adelaide to escape from religious persecution in Prussia and Silesia dropped German-sounding names to more easily blend in and/or be accepted by the local community.[23]

Creative resistance is also evidenced in the way forced migrants reconstitute or transform marginal(ized) public places that they are relegated to, spaces which help them in their struggle for well-being. Women migrant domestic workers in Singapore who work in the same building and are under strict surveillance by employers, for example, create "safe meeting places" out of the garbage area and the car park since these are places where employers do not "tail" them. The domestic workers then utilize garbage-throwing and car-washing time for S.O.S. and socialization. These migrants, like migrants in other parts of the world, have also transformed basements, car parks, warehouses, small shop lots, and auditoriums into ethnic centers or places of worship. In little, subtle, and often creative ways, and like water on stone, migrants slowly and painstakingly chip away at the empire. Today's migrants refuse to be completely marginal(ized) and are a bit more vocal and more organized such that they are increasingly becoming social capital for both the new[24] and the old homeland. The Vietnamese-Finnish community in Turku, Finland, for example, serves as a formidable source of assistance by offering various types of practical help such as interpreting assistance and help with paperwork (e.g., tax declarations, financial loans, remittances to relatives, temporary lodgings, etc.). As Kathleen Valtonen observes, this extended family role structure could be seen as one form of sociocultural capital.[25]

In many cases, migrants' activities transcend national borders. These transnational activities are worthy of consideration as they provide glimpses of how migrants navigate the possibilities for community formation and political engagement in a globalizing world. As Patricia Landolt shows in her study of Salvadoran migrants in Los Angeles, Washington, DC, and Toronto, exploring the spatial dimension of transnational politics is necessary to develop a more nuanced understanding of power relations, specifically of the ways in which migrants constitute meaningful forms of political membership (e.g., through civic engagement).[26] Jeremiah Opiniano's study of diaspora philanthropy sheds lights on this. In the case of Filipinos, Opiniano notes how diaspora philanthropy occurs through (1) overseas Filipinos and migrants' organizations; (2) hometown associations; (3) community or area-based groups of Filipinos in the host country; (4) professional organizations; (5) Filipino-run charities, nonprofit organizations, and foundations; (6) alumni associations; and (7) other types of organizations, e.g., sports clubs, groups run by citizens in the host country with Filipino members, church-based organizations, mutual-aid groups by Filipino migrants with programs in the Philippines, and sister-city organizations. Opiniano believes there is a development potential associated with transnational migration.[27] In fact, there is growing recognition of diaspora-driven development or diaspora groups as development actors in the sense that these groups have immense potential for human and social capital, as the skills they accumulate are invaluable in terms of the development of a variety of sectors such as health, education, and technology. In addition, the transnational networks that they maintain are crucial to facilitating a more open flow of trade, investment, skills, and knowledge and are based on relationships with families, friends, colleagues, or associations.[28] Last but not least, diaspora groups also provide cultural capital through the rich and diverse background that they bring to the societies in which they reside, as well as the new values and ideas they acquire, which may be helpful in addressing social issues in their old homeland, e.g., human rights and gender equality.

As faith communities made up of marginal(ized) people are often confined to marginal(ized) areas, migrant congregations are also increasingly filling the void for outreach to the areas and sections of the population that need serious and urgent attention. In fact, these congregations play a strategic role,[29] whether they like it or not, in serving constituencies (both immigrant and native) long abandoned by more established and affluent congregations, precisely because they are predominantly located in struggling urban neighborhoods and often forced to occupy the most unlikely places—cramped living rooms, hotel ballrooms, storefronts, rented halls or office buildings, crumbling buildings in industrial areas, and even ornate churches whose membership has declined.

African Christians in Europe, for instance, have set up evangelistic initiatives to reach out to groups of people that are rarely directly targeted by indigenous missionaries. These groups include drug addicts, alcoholics, prostitutes, victims of human trafficking, juvenile delinquents, and unauthorized migrants.[30] As the late Otto Maduro affirms, "in these dire circumstances it is often only religious congregations—especially those founded by migrants, with migrants, and for migrants—that are left to care for the 'collateral damages' wrought by national xenophobia, white supremacy and nativism."[31] This is what I call power among the powerless.[32]

BIRTHING A NEW HUMANITY

To do theology today means, in part, to face reality and raise it to a theological concept. Theology from this perspective needs to be honest with the real.[33] Anselm Min speaks of this theological perspective in the context of migration by drawing attention to the fact that theology is a reflection on the transcendent significance of all aspects of human experience, but especially of those aspects in which human dignity and solidarity are at stake.[34] It is within this understanding of doing theology that this essay now turns to theological reflections on forced human mobility as it intersects with land and empire.[35]

Borders and the Quest for the Promised Land

To migrate is to cross borders. For today's migrants, however, borders are no longer just the political membranes through which goods and people pass, in order to be deemed acceptable or unacceptable. Today, to cross the border is to live on the border. For the border, as Gloria Anzaldua posits, is an "open wound."[36] It is a gaping wound that serves as a testament to the ever-widening gap between the haves and the have-nots and the ever-expanding quest for homeland security as a result of global terrorism.

Borders serve as indicators of the limits of existence, identity, and belonging. When one crosses the border, one traverses the yawning gap between being a citizen to being an alien, an outsider.[37] Today, more than ever, to cross the border is to live on the margins and be a stranger. Xenophobia—fear of the stranger—is the curse of the migrant, "the image of hatred and of the other."[38] As people left at or pushed to the borders, literally and figuratively, migrants form part of today's marginal peoples. In the case of the USA "the central problems have to do, ultimately, not with ethnic groupings or the distinctness of [our] cultural heritages as such, but with racism and its manifestations in American economic policy, social rule and class relations."[39]

As strangers, migrants' experience challenges theology not only to utilize the biblical notion of the stranger, but also to reappropriate it by integrating the distinct experiences of today's migrants as the new strangers. Migrants' creative use of imposed marginal places like carparks and garbage areas, for example, is worth noting as it gives us a glimpse of how "bordered" or marginal(ized) places can be transformed into "spaces." The reconfigurations of borders into "spaces" by migrants bring a new frontier into theology. Their Sunday rituals, transnational families, and international links, for instance, challenge theology to articulate home not as a place "but a movement, a quality of relationship, a state where people seek to be 'their own,' and [be] increasingly responsible for the world."[40] This also means reassessing the adequacy of "land" as an analytical category for identity. More concretely, this means that "land" is no longer enough as a category to theologize about "home" and "identity" because home is no longer simply associated with the land or only one (home)land for that matter.

Today's forced migrants are like Israel in the wilderness that embarked on a journey believing that the promised land lies ahead. Unlike the Israelites, however, they do not necessarily experience their exodus as a "justice event," as some biblical scholars describe the said biblical narrative,[41] since forced migrants' quest for justice is an ongoing struggle. Moreover, unlike the Israelites, they do not always and necessarily find the promised land as the culmination of their exodus. If there is anything that can be gleaned from the very reasons that they leave their homeland and the difficult conditions they struggle with in the new land, it is the good news that no land on earth is a promised land.[42]

Being a stranger is the primary condition of the people of God (Exod. 23: 9; Deut. 24: 18). "The land . . . is mine" says the Lord and we "are but strangers and guests." (Lev. 25:23). King David eloquently acknowledges our fundamental and collective identity as strangers and the idea of God as the host in 1 Chronicles: "All comes from you; what we have received from your own hand, we have given to you. For we are strangers before you, settlers only, as all our ancestors were; our days on earth pass like a shadow." (1 Chr. 29:14–15).

The Call to Justice, Hospitality, and Solidarity

The migration of peoples, particularly those who are forced to move, is embedded in local and global inequities. Not surprisingly, Daniel Groody and Gioacchino Campese posit that migrants, particularly forced and undocumented migrants, are today's "crucified people."[43] This is a perspective that Peruvian theologian Gustavo Gutierrez echoes by referring to the contemporary immigrant as iconic of the face of the poor in the modern globalized world.[44] Thus, in the context of human dislocation, there can be no meaningful mission without costly incarnation. Justice, in other words, becomes an imperative for Christian witness. As Jonathan Bonk writes,

> To be a Christian entails recognizing and resisting the terrible reductionisms of all self-serving nationalisms, tribalisms, and racisms—and their ever attendant legalisms—that undervalue or even dismiss the stranger, the refugee, or the immigrant, or the enemy. When we cooperate in such systemic reductionism we subvert our own identities as men and women created in the image of God, since we yield to Caesar something to which Caesar has no ultimate claim—human beings, including ourselves. *Legality*, for Christians, can never be an acceptable substitute for *justice*.[45]

This witness to justice entails, first and foremost, the recognition of the centrality of the human person, who tends to get lost in the sometimes abstract, objectified, and politically exploited discourse on migrants, e.g., the use of "boats" or "boat people" to refer to refugees and asylum seekers. As the document *Welcoming Christ in Refugees and Forcibly Displaced Persons: Pastoral Guidelines* indicates, the first point of reference should not be the interests of the state or national security, but the human person.[46] Groody locates the basis for this argument in the incarnation and contends that "arguments about the economic, political, and social implications of migration must first find a reference to the human face of the migrant or else the core issues at stake become lost and easily distorted. If we do not get the human face of the migrant right, a just society is not possible."[47]

The call to hospitality,[48] meanwhile, draws inspiration from the notion that the God we believe in is a God of the stranger (Deut. 10:17–18; Ps. 146:9). Thus, from a Christian perspective, all of us are strangers and, just as God exhorted the Israelites to love the strangers for they were once strangers in Egypt, our witness to hospitality as Christians is tantamount to a practice of anamnestic solidarity. This means that God is, ultimately, the host in hospitable encounters. What happens in these encounters, therefore, is a form of hospitality and solidarity among strangers, albeit there is a need for strategic solidarity because certain groups of migrants, particularly forced migrants, are more vulnerable than others.

The image of God as a host augurs well since it presents the migrant and the citizen as guests and, consequently, as strangers.[49] It is a more egalitarian way of looking at the experience of hospitality and it is very much Christian, as exemplified in our experience of creation, grace, healing, and forgiveness as God's gifts. This means that whenever Christians receive or practice hospitality they are actually sharing in God's hospitality. This challenges Christians to move from the notion of hospitality *to* strangers to hospitality *of* strangers, and from the understanding of solidarity *with* strangers to solidarity *among* strangers.

Dying to Live

While many forced migrants are pushed to live in ghettoes or on the fringes of their destination countries, they refuse to be marginal(ized) completely and often create spaces for themselves to survive. The subversions of oppressive conditions constitute a frontier for theology today in the way it simultaneously symbolizes the human drama of exclusion and inclusion, of death and life. People move in order to survive and, in some cases, thrive despite obstacles and unjust policies that they encounter in the migration process. In the annals of human history, borders have been redrawn, people's stories have been rewritten, and communities have been transformed because groups or masses of people crossed either by land, sea, or air. Indeed, time and time again people's liberation, or the need for it, is caused by human movements. Even Christianity's central narratives are embedded in migration stories.

The glimpses of human liberation in the midst of profound oppression make migration a lens for a contemporary understanding of salvation. As could be seen in the preceding section, migration provides windows into human suffering and, at the same time, human well-being; it is rich with situations where death meets life and hope overcomes fear and despair. This dialectic underscores the notion that redemption's "already" aspect is as real as its "not yet" aspect. It drives home the point that the divine is both present and absent and life is both horror and love. As Silvano Tomasi stresses, "migration is graced even in difficult circumstances. . . . [It can be seen as] part of the ongoing mystery of redemption, contributing to solving the great problems of the human family. [Migrants] are, thus, also part of God's plan for the growth of the human family in greater cultural unity and universal fraternity."[50] P. Giacomo Danesi more explicitly articulates the link between migration and redemption:

> Against the Gospel ideal of brotherhood, migrations, whatever form they may take, are always revealed as ways of gradually forming a new social fabric, a new body, which the Gospel message is called to animate; by virtue of the tragic aspect they often entail, they are transformed into appeals to brotherhood on a world scale; by virtue of the conflicts that accompany them, they are an aspect of the painful birth of the pilgrim Church; by virtue of the discords and disparities they disclose, they become an appeal for a juster universal order; and by virtue of the rapprochement they effect between the most diverse components of the human family, migrations are ways to—and the foundation of—a pentecostal, universalistic, catholic, and ecumenical experience of Christian brotherhood.[51]

This ensemble of conditions and experiences embedded in contemporary migration is a reminder that salvation never takes place in isolation but in communion; salvation is not achieved in a static state but in dynamic, purposeful, life-changing movements. Migrants move in order to live. In the process they encounter death but, like Jesus, dying is not the last word. Rather, the last word is that life comes after death. Migration is thus a microcosm of the Christian belief in dying to live. It is, in other words, a witness to hope.

CONCLUSION

The search for a better life binds all people on the move. Thus, forced migrants move despite the array of obstacles and even in the midst of real dangers. This hopeful and courageous quest for well-being is the enduring theme of wave after wave, generation after generation, of migrants worldwide. The experience of land and empire among forced migrants today, therefore, calls all of us to imbibe and embrace an ethic of risk. A person who risks, Sharon Welch says, cares for and loves life in all its forms. This is made possible by grounding the struggle in a redefined, responsible action. This means that the struggle for justice should be informed with the recognition that we cannot guarantee changes and the achievement of desired ends; we can only create a matrix or conditions in which further actions are possible and in which desired changes are possible. Drawing from African American literature, Welch goes on to say that an ethic of risk as responsible action can be seen when the resistors name, find, and create other resources that evoke persistent defiance in the face of repeated defeats. For Welch, this "sheer holy boldness" is about deciding to care and act, although there are no guarantees of success. It is not easy, she says, as such action requires immense, deep daring. At the same time, however, it also enables deep joy.[52]

This, I reckon, is the heart of Christian mission. It is about persistently believing and witnessing to the reality that in the midst of pain and sin it is possible to work for and discover God's abundant grace in unexpected and amazing ways. It is about insisting that life is bigger than death; that love is greater than hatred; that goodness is far deeper than evil. Thus, like the migrant way of life, we are called to embrace Christian mission as about moving . . . and moving on without giving up on the vision for a better life, and never giving up on oneself, others, the world, and one's faith even in the midst of hardship. It is, in other words, about being midwives and night-watchers of hope.

NOTES

1. See Stephen Castles and Mark Miller, *The Age of Migration: International Population Movements in the Modern World* (Basingstoke, UK: Palgrave MacMillan, 2009). Whereas other previous great migrations have been largely based on and described according to ethnic or regional groups, migration today, or migration in the age of globalization, literally has "the world on the move" (John Haywood, *The Great Migrations: From the Earliest Humans to the Age of Globalization* [London: Quercus, 2009], 244–49).

2. International Organization for Migration, *World Migration Report 2010: The Future of Migration: Building Capacities for Change* (Geneva: IOM, 2010), 3.

3. International Organization for Migration, *World Migration Report 2018* (Geneva: IOM, 2017) https://publications.iom.int/system/files/pdf/wmr_2018_en_chapter2.pdf (accessed May 20, 2018).

4. "Forced migrants" is used in this essay to refer to asylum seekers and refugees as well as economic migrants, particularly migrant workers.

5. See, e.g., David Hollenbach (ed.), *Driven from Home: Protecting the Rights of Forced Migrants* (Washington, DC: Georgetown University Press, 2010).

6. "Empire" is used in this essay to refer to the massive concentration of power that permeates all aspects of life and that cannot be controlled by any one actor alone. Empire seeks to extend its control as far as possible; not only geographically, politically, and economically but also intellectually, emotionally, psychologically, spiritually, culturally, and religiously (Joerg Rieger, *Christ and Empire: From Paul to Postcolonial Times* [Minneapolis, MN: Fortress 2007], 2–3). Rieger argues that theology needs to address the issue of empire as it shapes the way we do theology—how we think about God, humanity, and how we are related to God

and creation. Empire's connections with the history of colonialism and the ever-expanding process of globalization also make theological attention to it important.

7. United Nations Department of Economic and Social Affairs, *International Migration Report 2013* (New York: United Nations, 2013), 17.

8. See Aritz Parra, "Almost 500 Migrants Smash into Border Fence with Spain," https://www.yahoo.com/news/red-cross-assists-hundreds-migrants-entered-spain-084555096.html (accessed February 19, 2017).

9. Ousmane Oumar Kane, *The Homeland Is the Arena: Religion, Transnationalism and the Integration of Senegalese Immigrants in America* (New York: Oxford University Press, 2011), 209–26.

10. David Bacon, *Illegal People: How Globalization Creates Migration and Criminalizes Immigrants* (Boston: Beacon Press, 2008), 23–26.

11. Jerry Gill, *Borderland Theology* (Washington, DC: EPICA, 2003), 111.

12. Peter Tran, "Migrant Workers in Asia: The Call by the Synod for Asia to Assist Migrants," *Migration World Magazine* 26.5 (1998): 32–34.

13. Kevin Bales, *Disposable People: New Slavery in the Global Economy* (Berkeley, CA: University of California Press, 2012).

14. A "coyote" is a guide who takes migrants across international borders in exchange for money.

15. Dominic Pasura, "Religious Transnationalism: The Case of Zimbabwean Catholics in Britain," *Journal of Religion in Africa* 42 (2012): 36.

16. Griff Witte, "Hungarian Bishop Says Pope is Wrong about Refugees," *Washington Post*. https://www.washingtonpost.com/world/hungarian-bishop-says-pope-is-wrong-about-refugees/2015/09/07/fcba72e6-558a-11e5-9f54-1ea23f6e02f3_story.html (accessed March 20, 2017) .

17. Kathleen Sullivan, "St. Mary's Catholic Church: Celebrating Domestic Religion," in *Religion and the New Immigrants: Continuities and Adaptations in Immigrant Congregations*, ed. Helen Rose Ebaugh and Janet Saltman Chafetz (Walnut Creek, CA: Altamira Press, 2000), 126.

18. See Mojubaolu Olufunke Okome, "African Immigrant Relationships with Homeland Countries" in *Africans in Global Migration: Searching for Promised Lands*, ed. John Arthur et al. (Lanham, MD: Lexington Books, 2012), 199–224.

19. See, e.g., Thomas Owusu, "The Role of Ghanian Immigrant Associations in Canada" in *Africans in Global Migration: Searching for Promised Lands*, ed. John Arthur et al. (Lanham, MD: Lexington Books, 2012), 19–44.

20. See James Scott, *Domination and the Arts of Resistance* (New Haven, CT: Yale University, 1990); James Scott, *Weapons of the Weak: Everyday Forms of Peasant Resistance* (New Haven, CT: Yale University Press, 1995).

21. Federation of Asian Bishops' Conferences-Office of Human Development, *Pilgrims of Progress??? A Primer of Filipino Migrant Workers in Asia* (Manila: FABC-OHD, 1994), 13.

22. John Allen, *The Future Church: Ten Trends Revolutionizing the Catholic Church* (New York: Doubleday, 2009), 338.

23. Peter Mares, *Borderline* (Sydney, NSW: University of New South Wales Press, 2002), 1.

24. See Patricia Madigan, "Graced by Migration: An Australian Perspective," in *Christianities in Migration: The Global Perspective*, ed. Elaine Padilla and Peter Phan (New York: Palgrave, 2016), 135–152; Michael Foley and Dean Hoge, *Religion and the New Immigrants: How Faith Communities Form Our Newest Citizens* (New York: Oxford University Press, 2007), 91–114.

25. Kathleen Valtonen, "East Meets North: The Finnish-Vietnamese Community," *Asian and Pacific Migration Journal* 5.4 (1996): 476–77.

26. Patricia Landolt's study looks at grassroots community organizing among immigrants ("The Transnational Geographies of Immigrant Politics: Insights from a Comparative Study of Migrant Grassroots Organizing," *The Sociological Quarterly* 49 [2008]: 53–77)

27. Jeremiah Opiniano defines diaspora philanthropy as both individual and organized giving to causes or organizations in an original homeland by a population outside of its homeland

("Filipinos Doing Diaspora Philanthropy: The Development Potential of Transnational Migration," *Asian and Pacific Migration Journal* 14.1–2 [2005]: 225–41).

28. See the various publications by the International Organization for Migration, such as *Developing a Road Map for Engaging Diasporas in Development: A Handbook for Policymakers and Practitioners in Home and Host Countries* and *Migration for Development in Africa*, https://publications.iom.int/books/developing-road-map-engaging-diasporas-development-handbook-policymakers-and-practitioners and https://www.iom.int/mida (accessed March 11, 2017).

29. See also Gemma Tulud Cruz, "Light of the World?: Christianity and Immigrants from the Global South," in *World Christianity and Global Theologizing: Perspectives and Insights*, ed. Jonathan Tan and Anh Tran (New York: Orbis Books, 2016), 85–107.

30. See J. Kwabena Asamoah-Gyadu, "To The Ends of the Earth: Mission, Migration and the Impact of African-Led Pentecostal Churches in the European Diaspora," *Mission Studies* 29.1 (2012): 30–31.

31. Otto Maduro, "2012 Presidential Address: Migrants' Religions under Imperial Duress: Reflections on Epistemology, Ethics and Politics in the Study of the Religious 'Stranger,'" *Journal of the American Academy of Religion* 82 (2014): 45.

32. See Gemma Tulud Cruz, "The Power of Resistance: An Inquiry into the Power of the Power-less." *CTC Bulletin* (December 2004): 131–37.

33. Jon Sobrino, *Witnesses of the Kingdom: The Martyrs of El Salvador and the Crucified Peoples* (Maryknoll, NY: Orbis, 2003), 13.

34. Anselm Min, "Migration and Christian Hope," in *Faith on the Move: Towards a Theology of Migration in Asia*, ed. Fabio Baggio and Agnes Brazal (Quezon City, Philippines: Ateneo de Manila University Press, 2008), 187.

35. See also Gemma Tulud Cruz, "The Moral Economy of Labor Mobility: Migration and the Global Workforce," in *Religious and Ethical Perspectives on Global Migration*, ed. Charles R. Strain and Elizabeth W. Collier (Lanham, MD: Lexington Books, 2014), 35–51.

36. Gloria Anzaldua, *Borderlands/La Frontera: The New Mestiza* (San Francisco, CA: Spinsters/Aunt Lute, 1987).

37. Virgilio Elizondo, "'Transformation of Borders': Border Separation or New Identity," in *Theology: Expanding the Borders*, ed. Maria Pilar Aquino and Roberto S. Goizueta (Mystic, CT: Twenty-Third Publications, 1998), 29.

38. Julia Kristeva, *Strangers to Ourselves* (New York: Columbia University Press, 1991), 1.

39. Andrea Smith, "Walking in Balance: The Spirituality/Liberation Praxis of Native Women," in *Lift Every Voice: Constructing Christian Theologies from the Underside*, ed. Susan Brooks Thislethwaite and Mary Potter Engel, 53–68 (New York: Orbis, 1998), 61.

40. Nelle Morton, *The Journey Is Home* (Boston: Beacon Press,1985), xix.

41. For Carlos Abesamis, for example, the exodus is the most primitive article of faith about justice and about a God of justice (*Exploring Biblical Faith* [Quezon City, Philippines: Claretian Publications, 1991], 30, 32).

42. Graziano Battistela, *For a More Abundant Life: Migrant Workers in Asia* (Hong Kong: FABC, 1995), 9.

43. See Daniel D. Groody, "Jesus and the Undocumented Immigrant: A Spiritual Geography of a Crucified People," *Theological Studies* 70 (2009): 307–16; Gioacchino Campese, "Cuantos Más?: The Crucified People at the U.S.-Mexico Border," in *A Promised Land, A Perilous Journey: Theological Perspectives On Migration*, ed. Daniel Groody and Gioacchino Campese (Notre Dame, IN: University of Notre Dame Press, 2008), 271–298.

44. Gustavo Gutierrez, "Poverty, Migration, and the Option for the Poor," in *A Promised Land, A Perilous Journey: Theological Perspectives On Migration*, ed. Daniel Groody and Gioacchino Campese (Notre Dame, IN: University of Notre Dame Press, 2008), 76–86.

45. Jonathan Bonk, "Whose Head Is This and Whose Title?" Presidential address delivered at the International Association for Mission Studies 13th Quadrennial Conference, Toronto, August 15, 2012. https://sites.google.com/a/iams2012.org/toronto-2012/ (accessed March 11, 2017).

46. See no. 58 of Pontifical Council Cor Unum and Pontifical Council for the Pastoral Care of Migrants and Itinerant People, *Welcoming Christ in Refugees and Forcibly Displaced Per-*

sons: Pastoral Guidelines, http://www.pcmigrants.org/documento%20rifugiati%202013/927-INGL.pdf (accessed March 20, 2017).

47. Daniel D. Groody, "The Church on the Move: Mission in an Age of Migration," *Mission Studies* 30 (2013): 36.

48. See also Gemma Tulud Cruz, "I Was a Stranger and You Welcomed Me: Hospitality in the Context of Migration," *CTC Bulletin* 28.1 (2012): 96–118.

49. See also Ross Langmead, "Refugees as Guests and Hosts: Towards a Theology of Mission Among Refugees and Asylum Seekers," *Exchange* 43 (2014): 29–47.

50. Silvano Tomasi, "The Prophetic Mission of the Churches: Theological Perspectives," in *The Prophetic Mission of the Churches in Response to Forced Displacement of Peoples* (Geneva: World Council of Churches, 1996), 41.

51. P. Giacomo Danesi, "Towards a Theology of Migration," in World Council of Churches, *Church and Migration: WCC Fifth Assembly Dossier No. 13* (Geneva: WCC Migration Secretariat, 1981), 35.

52. Sharon Welch, *A Feminist Ethic of Risk* (Minneapolis, MN: Fortress Press, 2000), 68; cf. Toni Cade Bambara, *The Salt-Eaters* (New York: Vintage Books, 1981), 265.

Chapter Four

Empty Land

Righteous Theology, Sneaky Coloniality

Santiago Slabodsky

In June 2017 over seventy scholars of religion and church leaders from thirty-five countries met in Bangkok, Thailand. This gathering was part of the DARE program run by the Council for World Mission (CWM). If one reads closely the final communiqué presented and discussed during the conference, it becomes clear that many organizers and attendees share one underlying presupposition. While they acknowledge theology's collaboration in oppressive constructions of empire, they still express a clear belief that religion can be at the heart of hope and resistance against these global designs. In their message there is a genuine trust that theology can become the preferential option to confront both the roots and manifestations of twenty-first-century versions of empire.

On the one hand, this presupposition has its merits. The gathering was attended by theologians who have been engaged in the struggle against different manifestations of empire for decades. Some of the participants fought against the apartheid system in South Africa and others resisted the military dictatorships in South America. Some others have been an integral part of the Black Lives Matter movement in the USA, a few have struggled against occupation in Israel/Palestine and a number of others are struggling against the Islamophobia that runs rampant in present-day Europe. Yet this discourse may alarm some of the purists among the secular anti-imperialist militants. They would surely point out that we need to be alert and argue that religion is the "opium of the people" and that it ultimately reproduces the same structure we intend to combat. But theology cannot be dismissed so quickly. Karl Marx, the famous author of this phrase and one of the most influential critical voices in the critiques of imperialism, was thinking dialectically in his critique. Only a few lines before his famous proclamation, he expressed that religion can also be the "expression of popular suffering." Marx, who early in his life worked under the guidance of a theologian, went as far as to express that religion can even be a "protest" against popular suffering.[1] In this way, the struggle represented by global activists and scholars who understand theology as a legitimate mode of resistance can be supported even from the most classical definitions of "empire" and "imperialism."

THEOLOGY AND THE USURPATION OF PEOPLE'S LANDS

But we should not celebrate the role of theology too quickly either. In this essay I argue that to be effective in this revolutionary path, theology needs to accept not only its complicity with empire but also its pioneering role in the construction of this problem. I will explore how, from the very beginning of modernity, theology helped to construct patterns of domination that eventually became the keystone in the reproduction of coloniality in the twenty-first century. In particular, I will show how the theological formulation of the relation between "land" and "people" may be at the very root of colonial enterprises for the last five hundred years. And I will highlight why those scholars, activists, and church leaders who intend to use this theology need to evaluate the way that even some of its more liberal proposals collaborated with the usurpation of lands in particular and with coloniality in general. The intention of this essay, then, can be reduced to one suggestion or, if I may, provocation. I would like to ask our partners in this conversation (from church as well as academic institutions) to ponder whether or not the same theology that they believe is the hope for liberation may very well be at the root of the problem.

A quick look at a map that follows geopolitical reconfigurations of the last five hundred years will highlight a striking fact. Over 80 percent of the lands of the world have been at one point or another colonized by European powers (and their heirs). Given this overwhelming history of usurpation, one can only wonder if there is any clear connection between the dispossessions in the Americas, Asia, Africa, and Oceania, beyond taking into account that the same empires (Spanish, Portuguese, Dutch, French, British . . .) seem to be largely responsible for modern colonialism and imperialism. And if there is a common thread, it is necessary to explore how theology, a mode of thinking that was hegemonic at the beginning of this process, may not have planted the pernicious roots for that which we are experiencing today. I will soon suggest that theology may be the very ground for the different manifestations of empire, imperialism, colonialism, and what is even more important for this essay, coloniality (or the patterns of domination that emerged during colonial times but transcend that time and space to operate globally).[2]

I will argue that coloniality can help us explain the link among the different enterprises, and that the theological collaboration with land usurpation is a prism through which to understand the lasting strength of colonial patterns. For over five centuries, the multiple usurpation of lands was generally legitimized by a conception held by Europeans that the land they were colonizing was empty. This trope of "empty land" does not mean, as Edward Said very well points out, that they are necessarily ignoring that there were actual people living in the land. The colonizers often recognized that these lands were inhabited by indigenous populations. But these populations, according to this narrative, were incapable of offering transcendence to the land because they lacked the right formulation of religion, economics, politics, or civilization.[3] According to this narrative, these populations were "Christian-less," "capitalist-less," "civilization-less," or "democracy-less" and, as such, they lacked the ethos to make the lands meaningful, and Europeans therefore had the responsibility of bringing these lands back into productive history for the common good of humanity at large (including, perversely, the same populations that had been the victims of the usurpation). This program would be implemented even if a "Just War" was needed to redeem the land. This trope of the "empty land destined for development" can be seen across time periods and imperial enterprises up to the twenty-first century itself.

From the very early stages of this process, theology, even some of the best well-intentioned versions, collaborated as an active participant of this enterprise. The problem here is not located in the distinct answers that conservative and liberal theologies can provide. The problem is that Europe presumed it had the right to ask that question. It is true that some theologies supported the genocide of the natives whereas others demanded a less violent treatment of the colonized. The normative theological arch nevertheless arrogated to itself the right to determine, according to very provincial sources of Western Christianity, the conditions according to which a land could be defined as empty and put in practice an irredentist project of ethnic supremacy that would seal the fate of native populations. Conservative projects, based on biological racism, turned native populations into victims of genocide. Liberal proposals, based on social racism, prescribed their cultural annihilation. The influence of theology in laying the base of land dispossession was so prevalent that even modern secular projects beyond the West end up reproducing the same structure of land usurpation in our day.

Here I call into question the role that theology has had in the construction of what I define as narratives of "redemptive violence." I am asking that we evaluate how the zealous crusade for redeeming lands has led to genocides and usurpation and has ultimately self-condemned theology to a very difficult position for those who want to use the discipline to help in the liberation of the people who have suffered centuries of racialization instead of simply . . . well . . . disciplining them.

REDEMPTIVE VIOLENCE

In modernity we live under the perverse shadows of the reification of inequality in the treatment of violence. One only needs to turn to any news outlet (both "fake" and "not-fake" news) to realize that an act of violence is not judged according to the action itself but to the social space that the alleged perpetrator occupies. If an act of violence is conducted by a Muslim, 1.3 billion people are quickly blamed and narratives of an Islamic plot to destroy the Western World reemerge. If the perpetrator is someone of African descent (and is not Muslim), the act is generally understood as an uncivilized act, often viewed as a product of gang-related violence. Now, if the person who perpetrates the act is white, they are typically described neither as the product of an attempt to conquer the world nor of uncivil gang violence. He (as this is generally a masculine character) is described as a lone wolf with emotional issues (or parking problems). Finally, when the person (typically but not exclusively white) wears a Western uniform, they are described as a national hero.

While the latter model corresponds to a long-standing rhetoric of redemptive violence, the first two models describe these acts as regressive violence. This is not new. The present-day portrayal of the Muslim overlaps with the past portrayal of the Jewish Bolshevik. This collective is often described as "Oriental" and as one whose only aim was to dominate the world through their pervasive ways. The person of African descent was yesterday the "Indian" who was launching nonconducive attacks against the advance of civilization due to the inability to understand the progress of history. This stereotypical connection between the tropes of the Oriental plot to conquer the world and the Indigenous/enslaved's childish attempts to stop the forward march of history unveils a long-standing construction of otherness that uses the unequal discursive treatment of violence to reify it.

This is indeed a stereotypical construction that has been popularized since the seventeenth century. This is the moment in which in colonial theological circles, violence was interpreted according to a tripartite division in function of the role of the interpreted "faith." The first group was composed of people who held the "true religion" of Western Christianity, and their violence was justified by their role in spreading or in developing civilization. In the seventeenth and eighteenth centuries, this "true religion" was defined as Christianity; in the eighteenth and nineteenth centuries, as civilization; in the nineteenth and twentieth centuries, as development/capitalism; and in the twenty-first century, as democracy. The second group, and the first to be condemned, was comprised of people who had the "wrong religion" and were usually described as attempting, through their alternative plots, to destroy what Western Christianity was building. In other words, they were "enemies of God." A third group was comprised of people who were described as "lacking religion" (and lacking any ethos of civilization) and were trying to stop the inescapable development of the nascent West, due to their inability to understand what development meant.[4]

Eventually the description of the two groups that were condemned to "regressive violence" merged, especially during the second half of the nineteenth century. Since the seventeenth century the first group, generally integrated by Jews and Muslims, was characterized as having the wrong religion, as being stuck on religion, history, or an old regressive civilization. The second group, generally integrated by Africans and natives, was described as lacking characteristics of civilization and modernity. But beginning in the nineteenth century (given the discussion of Jewish integration in the nation-states and the colonization of Muslims in North Africa and the Middle East) all of them were accused of lacking the central characteristic that made someone human: civilization in the nineteenth century, capitalistic development in the nineteenth and twentieth centuries, and democracy in the twentieth and twenty-first centuries. This is why, as an example, the Caribbean intellectual Aimé Césaire claimed that the Holocaust cannot be explained only through the lens of European history.[5]

This construction had clear consequences for the narratives that justified land usurpation. The land was empty because it needed to recover its past splendor (Egypt, Israel/Palestine, Iraq) or develop its transcendence under Christian/European designs (America, Africa, Oceania). The inhabitants of either place did not have the right to the land because their "lack" (of civilization, development, technique, democracy, etc.) stripped them of their power. To legitimize this situation a "Just War" was sometimes declared against the native inhabitants. But sometimes, and even more perversely, this was carried out as an altruistic project to help advance these populations who were viewed as "lacking" or "stuck."

This is why we need to consider that theology may not be the solution but, rather, the problem for land usurpation. The colonizer usually presented "his" project as an altruistic mission to advance society for the good of the world as a whole. The problem, then, is not hatred. The problem is love. Theology becomes the first legitimizer. Europe was able to conquer over three-quarters of the world supported by the strength of its ideological dictums. In the seventeenth and eighteen centuries this was "Convert (for your own good!) or I will kill you." In the eighteenth and nineteenth centuries, it was "Civilize or I will kill you." In the twentieth century the commandment was "Develop or I will kill you." And finally, in our days, it is "Democratize (for your own good) or I will kill you." Each time, each commandment is preceded with a rhetoric that presumes that this is the best path not only for the colonized populations but also for humanity as a whole.[6]

The reproduction of this usurpation of land (and its resources) challenges us to evaluate the kind of project that we have in front of us. This is not simply colonialism. This is interpreted as the political imposition of one political system over another. While this may have started as a colonial project, it outlived its temporal dimensions. It is not neocolonialism either, since the structures I am discussing here were not developed after the political independence of the colonies. When we analyze the problem of land in the context of modernity, it becomes clear we are in the presence of coloniality. Coloniality refers to the patterns of hierarchical domination that were developed during colonialism and that subsist in their capacity to order global relations of race, sexuality, labor, and landownership well after nominal political colonialism is over. Theology, in this context, was not only a collaborator but a pioneer in justifying these patterns of domination that usurp people of their lands (including their resources and even humanity). This construction and reproduction of coloniality was not conducted exclusively via theories of "Just War" but also through narratives of "Just Love." Theological missiology is not the solution for twenty-first-century empire. It may well be the root of the problem.

EXEMPLIFYING THE USURPATION

In order to exemplify the pioneering role of theology's collaboration with this process I bring together two a priori distinct cases that extended coloniality through land usurpation. The first one is that of fifteenth-century theological discourses of colonization in the Americas and the second, the biblically infused discourses of land usurpation in Israel/Palestine. While these two cases could not look more distinct, they share a very important feature: both cases intertwine presumably competitive trends (conservative/exclusivist and liberal/inclusivist) to perpetuate the conception of "empty land" that aims to "redeem" the territory in search of "transcendental irredentism." They do this by employing one of the most pernicious structures of modernity: the interplay between evolutionism (or the assertion that there is only one path toward redemption under the leadership of European civilization) and dualism (the inability of some populations to achieve this monolithic European design).[7] I examine these cases not because they are obscure but for the opposite reason. That these are two highly debated cases shows that even the most normative of modern theological discourses—independent of the content of this discourse—delimit clearly the discussion and, in doing so, implicitly reify Europe's right to conquer ("redeem") the land.

In 1492 a new world emerged. The colonization of the South of Spain first and then of the Americas added to the intensification of the transatlantic human trafficking and started a long-standing process that forced Jews, Muslims, and populations that would soon be conceived as Native and African into a hierarchical construction that would ultimately be the seed for a racialized conception of the world. Since this very moment, theology and its heritage has been constructing a world in which Europeanness (Western-ness, Whiteness) would arrogate itself the superiority of defining the ownership of land. It is in these very early years, in 1521 to be more precise, that a very renowned debate took place in the courts of Valladolid. Two intellectuals, Juan Ginés de Sepúlveda and Bartolomé de las Casas, debated the "nature" of the natives, the just war/just love against them, and ultimately the right to land usurpation. The debate is traditionally presented as a confrontation between two perspectives, one conservative (reactionary, exclusivist) and the other liberal (liberationist, inclusivist). Here I follow commentators who point out that both trends function more as partners than as competitors in the destitution of the colonized.[8]

Sepúlveda considered natives to be "barbarians" who hardly had "any trace of humanity." He deemed them to have completely "meaningless lives," guided by their "lack" of religion, political organization, and economic development. The Spaniards, on the other hand, were the leading force chosen by God to liberate the land by asserting their "innate superiority." The natives, "animal-like" creatures, were unlikely to understand their divine designation as "natural servants or slaves." Problematically, their inability to understand their "nature" leaves them in a condemnable state of heathenism. So, it is the responsibility of Christian Europe to represent truth by declaring an altruistic just war against the natives for their own sake. The ownership of land, in this context, is lost due to the natives' inability to develop it without the salvific intervention of Christian Europe that will perpetuate itself as the only redeeming force. In Sepúlveda's narrative, then, we see the strength of the interplay between evolutionism and dualism. The evolutionism entailed in his project will insist that there is only one path toward redemption (Christendom), and the (soon-to-be) European has the responsibility of bringing the empty land and its creatures to this path as an altruistic project of redemption. While the conquistador would keep the land, the strength of the dualism will still define the native as hardly human, with natural limitations beyond servitude/slavery and with no claim to the territory. The lack of the native was sealed. Resistance would lead to death in the war. Acceptance of the condition (or inability to rebel) would lead to murderous labor or sexual slavery. In either case Europe arrogates to itself the altruistic right to the empty land while proposing the physical annihilation of native populations.[9]

Bartolomé de las Casas, his rival, seemed a priori to be standing for the opposite. He was defined by multiple interpreters as the "Defender of the Indian Tears" and identified as the precursor of Latin American liberation theology. He disputes Sepúlveda's conception of the natives as natural slaves, critiques the ferocity of the conquest, and puts in question the true aim of the conquistadors. But de las Casas's proposal is more problematic than it seems prima facie. Anticipating discourses on "noble savages" he defined the "Indians" as "peaceful creatures" who could be "easily subjugated." So he was proposing to redeem them by "peacefully" converting them to Christianity, which amounted to erasing any previous cultural background as the condition for their salvation. This insistence on the irredentist project of salvation is at the very core of the project of modernity. The native cannot develop or know what to do with his/her land without accepting "Just Love" from Christian Europe that reifies itself as the only path for salvation.

If Sepulveda's project supported the physical annihilation of the natives, de las Casas supported their cultural annihilation. The latter needed to accept their underdeveloped condition and the permanent suspicion of the Spaniards, who will be the judges of the native's adaptability. A number of scholars have pointed out that the problem of de las Casas was that he defended "Indian Tears" with a proposal to alleviate the pressure on the native by intensifying transatlantic trafficking of Africans. Here I add my voice to a minority of scholars who believe that his support for black slavery is just the beginning of the problem. De las Casas insists, first of all, on the evolutionism shared by his contemporaries. There is only one path toward redemption, Europe holds a transcendental truth, and the responsibility of the natives is to abandon their culture and accept Europeans' superior designs. This discourse deepened its interrelation with the dualism of his proposal by presenting, perhaps in ways even more pronounced than Sepúlveda, this as a discourse of "Just Love" negating the rights of the natives to live and possess their land according to their own system. Yes, he protested against the violence of the conquest. But his protest left intact the salvific project that would intensify the cultural alienation necessary for the legitimation of the European claim of superiority first and, then, that of the "empty land" soon after.[10]

From the very beginnings of modernity conservative and liberal theologies seem different in their formulation, virulence, and justification. One represents a rhetoric of "Just War" and the other of "Just Love." One forces the natives into servitude/slavery; the other offers an inclusion of natives as future Christians. Where one represents an apology for physical elimination, the other leads to cultural alienation. What both projects agree on is their combination of evolutionism and dualism in order to reify Christian superiority. Both insist that there is no salvation, redemption, or development outside Christianity. And the acceptation of Christianity, by force or love, due to the natives' perceived inability to give transcendence to their own land, is the stepping-stone for their destitution. The conception of empty land is presented in both cases as there is a pernicious combination between a self-appointed superiority of Christian Europe that grants rights and redeems lands, and there is an emphasis on native inability (either proto-biological or cultural) to possess the land without the developmentalist leadership of the redeeming European Christianity. Theology, independently of its conservative or liberal tendency, ends up supporting the usurpation of land because of its inability to question its own presuppositions. The problem is therefore not which theology to choose but rather, theology itself is the problem. Conservatives and liberals are not competitors, but partners in this project.

Our second case would seem a priori very distinct. But it is a natural extension of the coloniality built from this first debate. We will take a few paragraphs to see how this combination between evolutionism and dualism that culminates in the irredentist conception of empty land was employed to justify usurpation in Israel/Palestine. It is important to clarify, as I am a Jew writing to a largely Christian audience perhaps concerned with potential anti-Semitism in times when all critiques of Zionism are branded as anti-Semitic, that this is not a condemnation of Jewish discourses. Nor am I questioning the right to self-determination of any people including my own (Jewish). This is a critique of a particular Jewish discourse that even before Jews were welcomed as white and/or Western took over long-standing Western designs in a nationalistic framework. But political Zionism, the discourse I will engage now, was until the Second World War only a minority within Jewish projects and only one among a number of varieties of Zionism (a landscape that included versions of cultural, revisionist, materialist-dialectic Zionisms). Yet by the end of the 1940s, this discourse became hegemonic within Zionist discourses and, by the end of the 1960s, it had become the normative Jewish response in a post-Holocaust world.[11] In recent years, it has become difficult to separate political Zionism from modern Jewish aspirations. This relation (or reduction) and partnership has been normative for just over a century, whereas the Jewish network of communities has survived for over four thousand years.

In the previous paragraphs we explored the founding fathers of the ideology behind Spanish colonization in the Americas. Now I explore the thought of a figure that is unarguably the founding father of political Zionism, Theodor Herzl, who was made an icon in the pantheon. Perhaps even more than Sepúlveda and de las Casas, Herzl became "one of the most powerful elements of the Zionist creed," his life "acquired legendary proportions," and "his portrait" under which the State of Israel was declared became "one of the trademarks of Zionism."[12] His contribution to our discussion will be key because, in contrast with the previous debate, we do not need to demonstrate the conceptual partnership between conservative and liberal trends à la Sepúlveda and de las Casas. Herzl himself intertwines both trends. While in his most well-known programmatic manifesto (*Der Judenstaat* or *The Jewish State*) he presents a conservative perspective that includes Euro-Jewish superiority and the reduction to servitude of a "lower" population, in his little-read novel (*Altneuland* or *The Old New Land*) he presents a very liberal trend including Jewish superiority and inclusiveness of the natives who needed to leave behind their culture to accept European developmentalist enlightenment. Both cases, then, become nationalistic adaptations of the discourses created by theology in the fifteenth century. They become irredentist projects of "empty land" or, as the popular Zionist slogan goes, "a land with no people for a people with no land."

Herzl's political program, developed in *The Jewish State*, is without any doubt the most popular text emanating from political Zionism. At the start of the twentieth century, Herzl writes to Cecil Rhodes, by then one of the key imperialist players, that he should take interest in Jewish resettlement because "it is something colonial."[13] After flirting with two other colonial locations (Africa and South America), he decides to throw all his support behind the colonization of Palestine. It is in his 1896 manifesto that he will explain in detail not only the project itself but the reasons for the project. Specifically, he pits the Jewish state, an "Outpost of Western civilization," against the "barbarism" of the Middle East. Jews suffered anti-Semitism in Europe because they were abnormal among Europeans. While early in his life Herzl supported individual assimilation to solve anti-Semitism (each Jew should become like any other European), now he would support the collective or national assimilation (the Jewish people as a whole becoming a nation-state like any other European).[14] In this way Herzl fully accepts the European designs of his own people. Jews were abnormal, to an extent responsible for anti-Semitism, and the only possible solution was to recover their "transcendence" as a people through the colonization of an "empty land."

It is precisely in this search for transcendence that we can start to elucidate Herzl's adaptation of the conservative combination of evolutionism and dualism. In the first place he directly defines the place as an "empty land" that can only recover its transcendence by being conquered and developed by European (Jews). He offers a detailed technical project that presumes that only a Westerner has the knowledge necessary to liberate the land or "make the desert bloom." (It is important to point out that Herzl was by profession a journalist and had very little education in any of the necessary areas—especially engineering and agriculture, but also regional history or politics.) The project becomes even more interesting when we examine the dualism in Herzl's approach to the division of labor. The leadership of the process would lie in the hands of Western Jews. While in the text he largely ignores that there are other populations, in his diaries he recognizes the existence of Arabs who should forcefully be "transferred" out.[15] If he decides to ignore that there was a native population, who would do the hard labor to open the path for Western Jews? Pauper Oriental Jews (in his mind the "Eastern European Jews" who, after the Holocaust, were replaced by the "Arab Jews") who would be forced to recognize Western European superiority, trained in their ways, and follow the illumination of their direction.

Herzl divides Sepúlveda's treatment of the natives in an extension of fifteenth-century colonialism into twentieth-century settler colonialism. On the one hand, the "Just War" is declared to the native populations in order to empty the territory. On the other hand, a new population is brought in and declared a "natural servant" of Western leadership. European Jews will not only be responsible for redeeming the land by displacing Palestinians, but also for making the Oriental Jew work to exhaustion and, in the process, become Jewish (acquiring an identity defined by "civilized" Western Jewry). Just as in the last decades the fate of Palestinians has broadly gained recognition for the luck of Palestinians, the use of the Oriental Jews did not go unnoticed by Herzl's contemporaries. Even some former Zionists broke with the movement due to Herzl's proposal to bring non-Western Jews "by their noses" as servants (or even worse "forced labor") in the service of Western European middle classes that would only settle after the hard work had been accomplished. Herzl, then, extends Sepulveda's evolutionism and dualism by describing an "empty land" that could only recover its transcendence thanks to the leadership of the superior Western Europe and the forced labor of those who were natural servants among non-Westerners.[16]

The second version of his proposal, the liberal inclusive project of colonization, will be described a few years later in his novel *Old Land/New Land*. The novel, to be succinct in this explanation, narrates the voyage of two Westerners (an Austrian aristocrat and a young Central European Jew) who were traveling to the Pacific and bumped into Palestine on two occasions over a period spanning a decade. The first time, they see a desolated unproductive land, an empty "land with no people" awaiting "a people with no land." The second time, however, they are surprised when they see Palestine is a miraculously flourishing land. What took place within the two visits was the Jewish colonization that had created a cooperative and made the desert bloom. This time Herzl does not ignore the existence of "Arabs" (nor recommend their "transfer out"). In the novel, Herzl is much more nuanced. In the second trip he gives voice to a "local Arab" who speaks about colonization in a way that de las Casas could only have dreamt that his native would speak.

The local "Arab," Rashid Bey, is used ventrilocuously to explain that he is nothing but thankful to European Jews for having resolved the problems of Palestine by bringing "economic and cultural development" to a place that before was voided from (Western) progress. Herzl, who had already acknowledged that this was a colonial project, makes the European travelers object to the Euro-Jewish plan because it implies the dispossession of natives from their land and the annihilation of their culture. Bey stands strong, stoic in his orientalism one may say, explaining that the Europeans altruistically created a society of full inclusion. The "transcendence" of the land was recovered under Western leadership. The "native" acknowledges European superiority, places "himself" under this project, and does not question the stripping of "his" economical or political ethos. The land belongs to the developers. As we can see the liberal discourse of Herzl adapts de las Casas's inclusivist project. First, the project insists on the evolutionist conception of development by portraying the European version as the only right path for development. In this discourse, the native acknowledges that the land could only recover its transcendental development with the leadership of the Jewish project and renounces the "possession" (of land, ethos, etc.) in favor of a Western project.[17]

The two cases bring to light a clear conception of empty land. This is the discovery of a land that is unproductive and can only recover true transcendence through the direction of those divinely chosen to carry the truth. The local population's ownership over the land is negated due to their inability to carry out the Western design by themselves. In some versions, the more liberal ones, they would be invited into the new society as long as they recognize the superiority of the European power and submit to its leadership. In some other, more conservative versions, they will be subjected to forced labor or eliminated in order to fulfill the divine mission. From cultural to physical annihilation, theology, both liberal and conservative, has collaborated with this process for five hundred years.

DELINKING FROM "JUST WAR/LOVE" THEOLOGIES

For a long time, liberal theologies supporting conceptions of "Just Love" have reified their moral superiority by showing how distinct they were from those narratives that justify "Just War." In this essay, however, we have shown that they are partners in this crime. They collaborated to reify European superiority, forced others into a foreign system that would always be suspicious of them, and ultimately ended up reproducing the same irredentist project that justified the annihilation of native populations and the usurpation of their land (and, with it, their economical/political ethos and ultimately their humanity). It is time to recognize that theology, presented as the preferential option to combat "empire," may be the very root of the problem.

If we were to coin a theology capable of confronting its pioneer role in the collaboration with coloniality, we need to develop a theology that could permanently question itself. In other words, we may need to de-link theology not only from hateful theologies of war but also from supposedly naive theologies of love. What we need is a way of formulating the relation with the divine and between humans that does not require the monopoly on truth but rather recognizes the multiplicity of avenues to achieve the desired goals. In this way, we need to confront not only the reactionary narratives of just war but also those allegedly altruistic discourses of just love. The impetus to share the "Good News" has been used to physically or culturally annihilate destitute populations from their lands and humanity in the process of evangelization through religion, politics, or economics. In a few words, I am saying that Christians should stop talking only to one another. It is time to surrender the privilege in their discourse and to realize that the solution cannot be found just by themselves, as the problem started when they thought only by themselves.

Interreligiosity and interculturality are first steps toward understanding this multiplicity of avenues, as it escapes from the monopoly of Western Christianity. But those are not enough. We have seen how other traditions eventually adopt the pernicious projects of Christianity and how others were also negated in their religiosity. What we need is to acknowledge that cultures and knowledges emerge in disparate ways and to start a conversation among the internal critics of these traditions to confront the twenty-first-century empire. If we continue to talk only to each other (either within the academia, activism, or the Christian Church) we again run the risk of reproducing the same discourses that have destituted millions and millions for five centuries. We have an imperious need to confront the current manifestations and roots of empire. But to do this, we need to start being more and more uncomfortable with our own traditions and to question the true legacy of coloniality in our times.

NOTES

1. Karl Marx, "Zur kritik der hegelschen rechtsphilosophie," in *Ökonomische-philosophische Manuskripte* in *Marx/Engels Gesamtausgabe* (Berlin: Dietz Verlag, 1982), 36–37; "Toward a Critique of Hegel's Philosophy of Law," in *Writings of the Young Marx on Philosophy and Society* (New York: Anchor Books, 1967), 249–50.
2. Walter Mignolo, *Local Histories/Global Designs: Coloniality, Subaltern Knowledges and Border Thinking* (Princeton, NJ: Princeton University Press, 2000), 87–91.
3. Edward Said, *The Question of Palestine* (New York: Vintage, 1979, 9.
4. See also Santiago Slabodsky, *Decolonial Judaism* (New York: Palgrave Macmillian), 39–66.
5. Aimé Césaire, *Discours sur le colonialism* (Paris: Présence Africaine, 1955), 31; Aimé Césaire, *Discourse on Colonialism* (New York: Monthly Review Press, 2001), 36.
6. Ramon Grosfoguel, "The Structure of Knowledge in Westernized Universities: Epistemic Racism/Sexism and the Four Genocides/Epistemecides on the Long 16th Century," *Human Architecture: Journal of Sociology of Self-Knowledge* 11.1 (2013): 8.
7. Anibal Quijano, "Coloniality of Power, Eurocentrism, and Latin America," *Nepantla: Views from the South* 1.3 (2000): 533–80.
8. Enrique Dussel, *1492: El encubrimiento del otro: Hacia el origen del "mito de la modernidad"; conferencias de Frankfurt, octubre de 1992* (La Paz: Plural Editores, 1994); Enrique Dussel, *The Invention of the Americas: Eclipse of "the Other" and the Myth of Modernity* (New York: Continuum, 1995); see also Immanuel Wallerstein, *European Universalism: The Rhetoric of Power* (New York: The New Press, 2006).
9. Juan Ginés de Sepúlveda, *Democrates Segundo; O De Las Justas causas de la Guerra contra los indios* (Madrid: CSIC, 1951), 35–47; see also Luis Rivera-Pagan, *A Violent Evangelism* (Louisville, KY: Westminster/John Knox Press, 1992), 134–36.
10. Bartolomé de las Casas, *Brevísima relación de la destrucción de las Indias* (Madrid: Alianza Editorial, 2005); cp. Walter Mignolo, *The Darker Side of the Renaissance* (Ann Arbor, MI: Michigan University Press, 1995), 441–43.

11. Zeev Sternhell, *The Founding Myths of Israel: Nationalism, Socialism and the Making of the Jewish State* (Princeton: Princeton University Press, 1988), 6, 43.

12. Shlomo Avineri, *The Making of Modern Zionism* (New York: Basic Books, 1991), 98–99.

13. See Hatem Bazian, *Palestine, It Is Something Colonial* (The Hague: Amrit Publishers, 2016).

14. Joseph Massad, "The "Post-Colonial: Time, Space, and Bodies in Israel/Palestine," in *The Pre-occupation of Postcolonial Studies* (Durham, NC: Duke University Press, 2000), 313–14.

15. Theodor Herzl, "Letter 6/12/1985," in *The Complete Diaries of Theodor Herzl* (New York: Herzl Press, 1960), 88–89.

16. Theodor Herzl, *Der Judenstaat* (Berlin: Jüdischer Verlag, 1920), 24; Herzl, *The Jewish State* (New York: Dover Publications, 1988), 96.

17. Theodor Herzl, *Altneuland: Roman* (Berlin: H. Seeman, 1900); Lotta Levenshon, *The Old-New-Land* (New York: Bloch Pub., 1941).

Chapter Five

Religious Diversity, Political Conflict, and the Spirituality of Liberation

Mitri Raheb

There is no other region in the world where religion and politics interact, collide, and conjoin—around land (territory, inheritance, property) and land matters (theme, subject, struggle)—like the region from where I come, the Middle East. On the one hand, the Middle East is the cradle of three monotheistic religions (Judaism, Christianity, and Islam), and on the other hand, the Middle East is a region of diverse ethnicities, religious minorities, and multiple identities. The interactions, collisions, and battles around land are therefore about people and their religions as well. Add to those the fact that this region has been marked for over a century by colonization, conflicting imperial interests, the Israeli-Palestinian conflict, and regional instability.

CONFLICTS OVER LAND

In this chapter I present and reflect on three contemporary case studies that show the use and misuse of religion in contexts of political conflicts, around struggles over land. In the first case study I look at the latest debate at the United Nations Security Council regarding Israeli settlement in the West Bank and East Jerusalem (this is a Jewish-Israeli case). In the second case study I look at the interaction between religion and state in the Arab world in relation to power (this is an Arab-Islamic case), and in the third case I look at the role Christian Zionists play within the current context (this is an intra-Christian Western case). After analyzing these case studies, I draw three important conclusions from a liberation theology point of view.

Israel-Palestine Context: Occupation of Land and Rights

The Israeli-Palestinian conflict is one of the longest ongoing conflicts in modern history. The roots of this conflict, however, are not in the Middle East, but in nineteenth-century Europe. On November 2, 1917, the British lord Arthur James Balfour promised the land of Palestine to the British-Jewish lord Rothschild. It was not the Lord God who promised the land to the Jews of Europe, but Lord Balfour of Britain. This was not done out of religious convictions, but as part of British imperial expansion policy on the one hand and of interior political necessity on the other. On the one hand the European Jews were to colonize Palestine and to settle there serving British imperial expansion and interests. On the other hand, the sending of the European Jewish community to Palestine was supposed to solve an interior European issue, the integration or nonassimilation of Jews in Europe. Religion indirectly played a role behind this declaration. For many Zionist Christians in Great Britain, the restoration of the Jewish people was a precondition for the second coming of Christ. A subtle anti-Arab and anti-Muslim theology was the other side of this coin. The Balfour Declaration was issued at a time when the British army, stationed in Egypt, was ready to storm southern Palestine. The plan for a national home for the Jewish people was thus one of the deals and outcomes of World War I.

This plan was made possible in the aftermath of World War II. It was in this context that in 1947 the United Nations adopted the partition plan to divide Palestine into two states. A year later the State of Israel was established. The new state chose the biblical name "Israel" for itself. The branding of the Israeli state as "biblical Israel" accelerated after 1967, when Israel occupied the West Bank, including East Jerusalem, the Gaza Strip, and the Golan Heights. The name chosen for the war, "Six Days," had a biblical connotation: as God finished the creation in six days, so Israel finished its job by occupying the rest of Palestine before it can rest.

The war didn't bring rest to the Israelis nor to the Palestinians. When the international community and the political leadership of both peoples failed in achieving a just peace, people started turning more and more to religion for answers. The longer the conflict remained unsolved with human intervention, the more religious connotations it accumulated. The outcome of the 1967 war gave a boost to Jewish religious nationalism and to "messianic" extremist Jewish groups within Israel, who started settling in the West Bank, claiming it as ancient "Judea and Samaria." Judea and Samaria was not so much a geographical description as a religious claim with a clear political agenda. The Iranian revolution and the petrodollars that flooded the Gulf region gave a boost to certain forms of political Islam. Christian Zionism experienced a revival, and its followers started celebrating Israeli victory as direct divine intervention.

After the 1993 Oslo Accords and when political leaders were ready for a political compromise, the opposition utilized religion to empty that peace agreement. Rabin was killed by a religious Jewish Israeli person, and Hamas started a series of suicide attacks on Israeli targets. Expanding Israeli settlements in the Palestinian land became a tactic of the Israeli government, which has been subsidizing the building of settlements through soft loans, tax exemptions, and a modern infrastructure. This is the background for the first case study.

On December 23, 2016, the UN Security Council met to discuss the expansion of Israeli settlement in the West Bank and East Jerusalem. A resolution 2334 (2016) was adopted by fourteen countries in favor and with a US abstention. The resolution reaffirmed the Security Council stand that Israeli settlements have no legal validity and constitute a flagrant violation of the Internal Law. The full text of Resolution 2334 is readily accessible.[1]

I was watching the debate live and listened to the fourteen council members talk about the fourth Geneva Convention and international law and how important it is to abide by them. The US representative explained the decision to abstain rather than veto the resolution by saying that settlements are undermining Israel's security and eroding the prospect for a two states solution, thus peace and stability. Once all fifteen Security Council members were given the floor, Danny Dannon, the Israeli representative to the UN, addressed the council:

> Mr. President today is a bad day for this council. . . . This council wasted valuable time and efforts condemning the democratic state of Israel for building homes in the historic homeland for the Jewish people. We have presented the truth time and again for this council and implode you not to believe the lies presented in this resolution. I ask each and every member of this council who voted for this resolution: Who gave you the right to issue such a decree denying our eternal rights in Jerusalem? . . . We overcame those decrees during the time of the Maccabees and we will overcome this evil decree today. We have full confidence in the justice of our cause and in the righteousness of our path. We will continue to be a democratic state based on the rule of law and full civil and human rights for all our citizens and we will continue to be a Jewish state. Proud live and reclaiming the land of our forefathers, where the Maccabees fought their oppressors and King David ruled from Jerusalem.[2]

And before ending his speech, something interesting captured my attention. Mr. Dannon pulled out a Hebrew Bible, lifted it up in his hand, and said, "This holy-book the Bible contained 3,000 years of history of the Jewish people in the Land of Israel. No one, no one can change this history."

It wasn't a surprise for me to hear such rhetoric from an Israel politician, but what struck me was the act of raising the Hebrew Bible at a UN Security Council meeting with the aim of undermining international law and the Geneva Convention articles. It is interesting to see the words and language Mr. Dannon used in his speech. Mr. Dannon was convinced that he owns the truth: "We have presented the truth time and again." And he was convinced of the justice of his cause and the "righteousness of his path." He used words like "historic homeland" and "eternal rights." He kept shifting between biblical Israel and the State of Israel of today as if they were one and the same: "Proud live and reclaiming the land of our forefathers, where the Maccabees fought their oppressors and King David ruled from Jerusalem." And "This holy-book the Bible contained 3,000 years of history of the Jewish people in the Land of Israel. No one, no one can change this history."

The Israeli-Palestinian conflict is a political conflict over land and rights. The UN Resolution clearly refers to international laws applicable in contexts of occupation. Mr. Dannon doesn't address this issue. He avoids it on purpose because there is no human excuse for it and there is no way that one can excuse Israel's colonial expansionist policy. The last resort to defend the Israeli settlement policy is God.

I heard Mr. Dannon basically state that Israel does not adhere to international law, does not abide by the Geneva Convention, does not care about the bill of human rights, because Israel possesses divine and eternal rights. In this regard, Israel uses religion and the bible to avoid a political solution and to legalize what is politically an aggression. I asked myself: How come we arrived at a situation today where scripture and divine rights trump human rights? Is it appropriate to violate human rights in the name of the Bible and divine rights? Is it just to use the biblical text to whitewash military occupation and the oppression of whole nations? Can religious convictions lead to a severe violation of international law? The matter here is not about religious convictions, but rather how the Bible and religious convictions are instrumentalized for political ends. And how divine rights are utilized to allow for the violation of human rights and to avoid solving a political conflict. And while Jewish Israelis are given land to occupy in the West Bank and the Gaza Strip, Palestinian towns and villages are stripped of any possibilities for expansion or natural growth. This situation is a clear case of discrimination, segregation, and apartheid and can't be defended by modern international standards—thus the resort to the Bible as the last resort and legitimizing tool.

Arab-Islamic Context: Religion, State, and Power

The second case is from the Arab-Islamic context. Following the 1967 war, the defeat of the pan-Arab ideology of Nasser and the loss of Palestinian land to the State of Israel, the situation in the Middle East changed drastically. The outcome of the war was a political earthquake. Regime changes took place in Iraq in 1968, bringing Saddam Hussein to power. In 1969 military coups saw Qaddafi take power in Libya, and Numayri in Sudan, followed by

Assad in Syria (in 1970). The death of Nasser in 1970 brought Sadat to power. In all of these countries, there was only one political party—that of the president, and no other parties were allowed. Political diversity was not tolerated. Elections took place with only one candidate. While political parties were forbidden, religious groups could not be outlawed. The rulers however used religious groups against each other: Saddam with the Sunnis, Assad with the Alawites, and Sadat with the Muslim brotherhood.

The other place where people could gather without becoming suspicious to the state was in the mosque. The mosque thus became the alternative to the political castle. Where political disagreement was not possible, religious space became the outlet for a kind of subtle opposition. A critique of the leader was not possible, but criticizing the government was tolerated. The mosque and the political leader were able to exist side by side.

However, whenever the legitimacy of the political leader was in question, he would resort to religious legitimacy to stay in power. The weaker the political leader, the more daring religious groups were in their attempts to seize power.

A good case here is Iraq. Under Saddam Hussein Iraq was ruled by the one and only party of Baath. The Arab Socialist Baath ideology was a secular ideology developed by an Arab Christian by the name of Michel Aflaq. Although Saddam ruled based on the Sunni community in Iraq, all religious groups were more or less free to perform their religious duties. In 1991 Saddam invaded Kuwait, a neighboring Arab and Islamic country, which isolated him in the whole Gulf region. As long as he was fighting Iran, he had legitimacy in the neighboring Arab countries. The moment he invaded Kuwait, he lost that legitimacy and needed it badly. This is when he resorted to religion, adding the *takbir* slogan "Allahu Akbar" (God is Greater) to the flag. It was clear that Saddam was losing many of his allies and wanted to gain legitimacy and support by adding an important Muslim slogan to the flag. In a post-Saddam era, ISIS adopted the Islamic Shehada "La illah ila allah" (There is no God but God and Muhammad is his Prophet) on their one color black flag as a means to get Islamic legitimacy and support. Religion, in this case Islam, was utilized as a tool by Arab political leaders to remain in power, while the same religion was utilized by religious movements to seize power. The current unhealthy relationship between religion and state in the Middle East has to do with the way the ruling regimes on the one hand, and opposition movements on the other, manipulate religion as a tool to exert control and unilateral authority, or, conversely, to overthrow them. This means that religion is being exploited for the political ends of control and access to power, and power is exercised over land.

There is a correlation between the terror of the state and that of religious groups. The more aggressive the state acts against religious groups, the more extreme they become. In the clash between the state and the religious terror groups, marginalized groups pay a high toll and diversity is weakened. Often religious and ethnic minorities are not a target per se, but Christians, Yazidis, and other groups become a kind of a collateral damage in the power battle between the state and the opposing religious movements.

Christian Zionism Context: Tool of the Israel Lobby

The third case study is an intra-Christian debate. At an international conference on August 20, 2015, meant to commemorate the thirtieth anniversary of Kairos South Africa, a delegation from Palestine was present. One of the members of the delegation was Robert O. Smith,[3] at that time serving as the program director of the Middle East and North Africa at the ELCA and co-moderator of the Palestine-Israel Ecumenical Forum of the World Council of Churches.

During the conference, Smith and two other Palestinians were invited to speak at an evening panel organized by one of the South African Palestinian Solidarity groups. In his short input, and after describing himself as a citizen of the United States and a citizen of the displaced Chickasaw Nation, and as a current resident in Jerusalem, Smith talked about the responsibility of international Christians to the Christians of Palestine and raised questions about why the Christian communities in the world react to the suffering of the Palestinian community the way they do and why they allow Israel to behave the way it does. He proposed three reasons:

> [First,] I would say that the Christians in the United States and I assume also in South Africa often do not know that Christians are present in the West Bank and East Jerusalem and within the State of Israel. They have a false imagination of what Israel is and what Palestine is. They falsely assume that Israel is made up solely of Jews and that the West Bank is made of solely of Palestinian Muslims but this is not true [. . .]. Secondly, Christians in the United States and in many other places have negative conceptions of Islam and Muslims. They operate out of a fundamental fear of Islam and Muslims along with the false understanding that the conflict is at its foundation religiously formed; that it is a conflict between Islam and Judaism. This is so far from the truth; it is a conflict over land; it is a political conflict over resources; it is a political conflict over self-determination and decolonizing principles. [. . .] And finally Christians in the United States and in many other places [. . .] are influenced by the Imperial theology known as Christian Zionism. Christian Zionism is first and foremost political activity. It is not really a theology; it is not a commitment to doctrines and principles of faith; it is a political ideology that supports Jewish control over the land that now contains Israel and Palestine.[4]

Soon after, on April 4, 2017, Smith became a target for a social media smear campaign orchestrated by an American Christian who describes himself as a media analyst, Dexter van Zile. The smear campaign uses a quote from

Smith's presentation in South Africa: "The biblical narrative of Israel has almost nothing to do with contemporary Israel other than the intentional manipulation of sacred texts to justify a political project."

In any debate about any Christian doctrine, theologians can speak their mind and criticize almost everything. One can question the existence or non-existence of God, the divinity of Christ, the historicity of any biblical story, but dare anyone question anything regarding the State of Israel? There are watchdogs who watch every word, watch every YouTube, follow every tweet and every post. It seems that when it comes to the State of Israel, neither are religious disagreements allowed nor are diverse political opinions tolerated. Even worse, every credible Christian theologian or researcher who dares to question the religious Hora of the State of Israel becomes a plausible target for all kinds of Israeli watchdog groups.

The Israel lobby is very clever. They don't want to be at the front of such attacks, so they hire Christian Zionists to do the dirty work for them. Dexter van Zile is one of those hired in 2005 by Charles Jacobs to be the director of Christian Outreach and to oversee an initiative called the Judeo-Christian Alliance at the David project. A year later, van Zile moved to another watch-dog group called CAMERA, "The Committee for Accuracy in Middle East Reporting in America." He does the dirty work of targeting Christians. If one follows the smear campaign over two days, one notices the following: the campaign is intended to scare Smith so that he starts censoring himself. By mentioning Notre Dame University, Smith's employer, in the campaign, the university is dragged into the conflict and will either exert pressure on Robert or even fire him. One religious or political view on Palestine can therefore cost people their jobs or their reputations, and comes close to being a form of character assassination. And last but not least, there is no room for dialogue or diverse opinions or academic or political disagreement. The message is not debated, but the messenger is targeted. The tactic of the State of Israel and that of Christian Zionists is close to the tactic of radical Islamic groups that can't tolerate modern Muslim critical thinkers by declaring them as Kafer, that is apostate, and thus deserving the death penalty. Killing as well as character assassination in the name of God becomes a religious duty.

LIBERATION CONCLUSIONS

From these three case studies I draw theological conclusions around three concerns that are critical for the situation in Palestine-Israel, especially with regard to the intersection of land and people.

Divine Rights and Human Rights

In contexts of conflict, as in the Middle East, groups often utilize divine rights to deny others having equal human rights. We find these groups within all three monotheistic religions. These are not only Islamist groups in Iraq and Syria, but also Jewish groups in Israel as well as Israeli politicians. These are also Christian Zionists, who keep attacking fellow Christians who dare to challenge the Israeli occupation.

Two forces are currently violating human rights in our Middle East region: so-called security states that don't allow people to move, to have an opinion, to publish controversial books, to question policies, or simply to think critically; and religious movements who leave no room for people to choose their beliefs and to breathe freely. Both forces create systems based on fear. The fear of the state and the fear of God become two sides of the same coin. A society that is based on fear rather than on freedom kills the soul and spirit of its people, their innovation and their creativity. There will be no future for the Middle East until we break out from the bondage of the security state as well as of oppressive religious laws to a wide open space where human lives and security are protected, where freedom is free to blossom, and where human rights become sacred.

For us as Christians, in Palestine and everywhere, a spirituality of liberation is a spirituality of creation and incarnation. All people are created equally in God's image. In fact, all three monotheistic religions could agree on this. As Christians we believe also that in Christ and in Bethlehem God became human so that all human lives are sanctified. Such a theology of liberation is essential in our region today. But in today's world we adhere to the universal declaration of human rights that clearly states "All human beings are born free and equal in dignity and rights." It should not be acceptable by religious or political terms to violate human rights in the name of divine rights, or to play God against humans. Groups who do that misuse God and their scriptures for their own political ideologies. The scriptures and the Human Rights charter are there for one and the same reason: to defend the meek, protect the rights of the weak, put limits to those in power, and make sure that the state adheres to the laws. Both religion and state have to ensure that the power of law and not the law of power prevails. No religion or human legislation is entitled to give the Israelis more rights than Palestinians, Muslims more privileges than Christians, or men higher wages than women. Equality is something we cannot compromise when it comes to people and land.

The Cross as Critique of State and Religious Terror

For too long we have spiritualized the notion of liberation in the Bible. We replaced liberation with salvation, and the cross became nothing but atonement. I propose that we have to put the cross in its original context of political and religious violence. Jesus was one of the many who experienced on his own body the violence of state as well as religious terror.[5] The cross is a permanent reminder of the millions of people who are persecuted by the state or by the religious establishment because they raise their prophetic critique to an unjust ruler or to corrupt forms of religion and government. The cross is a reminder of all those innocent killed in the name of God. There is an urgent need today to discover this dimension of the cross. The fact that Jesus died on the cross by a combination of state and religious terror is of utmost importance as a critique to both powers. The cross becomes the ultimate critique of state as well as of religious violence. The cross becomes a mirror that shows God's vulnerability and the cruelty of political and religious behavior. For the peoples of the Middle East who live in contexts of Israeli occupation, or in the context of political despotism, or are affected on a daily basis by religious extremism, this dimension of the cross is of utmost importance.

Both religion and the state must be under the rule of law as a means of protection from, on the one hand, political despotism, and on the other hand, from tyrannical and repressive religious extremism that bans what it dislikes and legitimizes what suits its ambitions. The role of the state is to safeguard the rights of all its citizens. On the other hand, religion has an important role to inspire its followers to be compassionate. Securing human dignity and the well-being of the people is at the core of religion and the ultimate raison d'être for statehood. There is a dire need for a prophetic and dynamic faith that does not run away or hide from the challenges of the society but instead engages the society for the good of all citizens. The alternative to state and religious terror is a society based on civil laws, freedom, compassion, and equal citizenship irrespective of one's religious convictions, cultural identity, socioeconomic status, or race.

A World Marked by Diversity

The story of Pentecost in the Book of Acts (2:1–13) is imperative to understanding the spirituality that is needed in the Middle East because it provides a counternarrative to the logic of the oppressive regimes. The narrative of oppressive regimes is found in Genesis in the story of the Tower of Babel (Gen. 11:1–9), where a mighty empire with a strong economy reaches to heaven and with one language holds the empire together. This is exactly what Alexander the Great and the Greeks tried to do by imposing Greek and

Hellenistic cultures on their conquered peoples. Alexander and company had the ambitious plan to pour all tribes and groups into one gigantic melting pot. The outcome of this forceful unification was utter confusion. The empire fell apart and dissolved. The Romans tried the same experiment and were no more successful. The Byzantine emperor, Constantine, thought that by forcing one creed at Chalcedon he could unite his empire behind one emperor and one faith. The Oriental identities and expressions of faith were thus declared heretical and were persecuted. The Arabs tried to push their language onto the Berbers of North Africa and central Asian countries, which led to the opposite effect—of less identification with their empire by those tribes.

This issue is central for a Middle East which is pluralistic in nature. No single empire has been able to force the region into uniformity. And there was never a single Catholic Church that monopolized the Christian faith in the Middle East; instead, there are national churches: Copts, Syriac, Marinates, Greeks, etc., each worshipping in their own native language and possessing, as they do today, a distinct cultural identity. The same is true for Islam. It too has different expressions according to different regions: Shiite, Sunni, Alawite, Druze, etc. All efforts to forcefully unify them have come to naught.

The Middle East continues to be one of the most diverse regions in the world, with multiple ethnicities, religious affiliations, and plural identities.[6] For any empire, this was and is both a challenge and an opportunity. A challenge because the region resisted all attempts of forceful inclusion. But also an opportunity because the empire was forever keen to play one group against the other and ensure that the region remained preoccupied with internecine fighting so that the empire's job of control was easier. This is part and parcel of colonial history in the Middle East.

In this context, the story of Pentecost shows an alternative vision of the region by reversing the story of the Tower of Babylon. Jerusalem becomes the counternarrative of Babel. Here various nations and cultures meet. They don't speak the language of the empire, but rather their own native languages. Their identities are respected and embraced. The Spirit provides the software for communication so that they understand each other. In this story the rich diversity of the region is embraced and celebrated. It is regarded as a strength rather than a deficiency. The multiple identities of the region are viewed not as contradictions, but as a treasure to save. In Jerusalem the people from the whole *oikumene* "stood" on equal footing: "Parthians, Medes and Elamites; residents of Mesopotamia, Judea and Cappadocia, Pontus and Asia, Phrygia and Pamphylia, Egypt and the parts of Libya near Cyrene; visitors from Rome (both Jews and converts to Judaism); Cretans and Arabs." The moment Pentecost was taken out of its original context it became a nice story without any particular significance. It became a tale about speaking in tongues, and thus lost its contextual relevance. The church born in Jerusalem was meant to counter the empire, not by creating another empire, but by providing a new, ecumenical vision. The spirituality so urgently needed today, more than at any previous time, is one that embraces diversity and celebrates it as strength.

A Christian spirituality of liberation is a crucial contribution not only to the survival of the Christian community as such, but also for the future of the Middle East at large, ensuring that human rights are protected, prophetic critique is raised, and diversity is celebrated over and throughout the land and among all of the people.

NOTES

1. See http://www.un.org/webcast/pdfs/SRES2334-2016.pdf.
2. The full speech is available at https://www.youtube.com/watch?v=hPxSx8qdpWA.
3. Smith is the author of *More Desired Than Our Owne Salvation: The Roots of Christian Zionism* (New York: Oxford University Press, 2013), which was his doctoral thesis at Baylor.
4. Smith's presentation was taped along with other presentations. See Robert Smith, Jerusalem World Council of Churches, https://www.youtube.com/watch?v=etTBIHHYq6M
5. Cf. Mitri Raheb, and Suzanne Watts Henderson, *The Cross in Contexts: Suffering and Redemption in Palestine* (Maryknoll, NY: Orbis, 2017).
6. See Mitri Raheb, *Faith in the Face of Empire: The Bible through Palestinian Eyes* (Maryknoll, NY: Orbis, 2014), 110–12.

Chapter Six

A Theology of Land and Its Covenant Responsibility

Sifiso Mpofu

Land is the most important resource in the history of humanity. Interestingly, the entire Bible, from the Genesis creation stories to the final vision in the book of Revelation, contain many stories around land and land issues. The Bible goes further to reflect on the setting of God's people amid the various empires of the biblical world—from Egypt and Babylon down to Rome. There is constant reference to conflicts around the land and God giving land to certain people; all of these accounts are clear testimonies to the significance of land in the Bible and among people who appeal to and are influenced by the Bible.

Surprisingly, a theology of land has not featured prominently in the theological discourses of the reformed tradition. Protestant theologies in Africa in particular (so in the rest of the world) have never supported a radically rudimentary perspective as regards the subject of land and empire. One may infer that protestant theologies in Africa in general and Zimbabwe in particular are informed by the historical links of evangelicalism with colonialism. The two institutions were both after land for different but related reasons (the church needed land for its mission institutions while colonial settlers needed land for economic reasons). Both parties were from Europe and shared the same religious interests, cultural values, and civilization thrusts.

In the processes of Christianization and colonialization, the rights and hopes of the indigenous peoples whose land was acquired by these two institutions were trampled and the values of love, justice, and peace enshrined in the Bible were violated, even by those who called on the name of God. The fatal inconsistency of the message of the Bible and the conduct of European missionaries when they grabbed land for their missionary activities would, later on, cause many to question the motives of the missionaries in the newly created colonies. It is thus no excuse that African nationalism manifested itself from within the African educated Christians, and the driving spirit of African nationalism was the ideals of justice, freedom, and return of the land to the indigenous peoples.

To the African nationalist and Christian alike, the issue of the land could not be compromised because land has always been viewed as a divine provision for the good of the people. This sacred value associated with the land influenced the need to fight for what the people believed was their rightful entitlement instead of merely denouncing colonialism. From the 1950s, many members of the clergy responded to the call for "land return" by having recourse to a model of liberation theology according to which hope is fused with political and pastoral concerns to form a critique that is highly political and even confrontational. In this context, the call for the equitable redistribution of the land vibrated across the social order. This is not a mere political call but a critical theological statement that affirms the rights to justice, property ownership, and food production. Theologically, no human being must be deprived of land since the land is a gift from God (Gen. 15); the value of land is irreplaceable, and land is the core resource for people's political, economic, and social development in any society.

PEOPLE, LAND, JUSTICE, AND HUMAN RIGHTS

The subject of religion and land dominates the book of Genesis. The biblical text pictures God as taking pleasure in creating human beings and giving them a piece of land as their home and source of sustenance (Gen. 2:7–8). In the order of God's creative work, it was crucial that human beings have land. Clearly, the biblical creation account pictures God as the great giver of land and life, from the dawn of time.

The significance of land for the common good of humanity and all creation runs across the formation and history of empires so loud and clear to the extent that any talk of the land evokes emotional sentiments. In emphasizing the significance of land to humanity, Sebastian Bakare argues that "land has played a vital role in the history of human beings . . . it has been a source of life and sustenance, hope, freedom and redemption."[1]

In the Biblical account it is clear that God desires all people to have fair access to land for their sustenance. This is summed up in Genesis: "And I will establish my covenant between me and you and your offspring after you throughout their generations for an everlasting covenant, to be God to you and to your offspring after you. And I will give to you and to your offspring after you the land of your sojournings, all the land of Canaan, for an everlasting possession, and I will be their God" (Gen. 17:7–8 ESV). This covenant promise becomes the pedestal for a theology of land. The earth (land) is given to human beings and was created for them, but it is not a final personal possession. Rather, it is held in trust since land belongs to God, and those who occupy the land must always remain accountable for its management.

Having been given land by God, the people of Israel entered into a covenant relationship based on "love, justice, and equitable distribution of land amongst the twelve tribes."[2] Under this theocracy, the people of Israel enjoyed fair and just access to land by all citizens since land was a critical commodity for their sustenance. Under this model of land access, whenever powerful citizens attempted to usurp the land of the poor the prophets cried out and condemned their actions: "The Lord has taken his place to contend; he stands to judge peoples . . . the elders and princes of his people: 'It is you who have devoured the vineyard, the spoil of the poor'" (Isa. 3:13–15).

The gifts of land and environment come with responsibilities and opportunities—human beings are stewards over the land. Bakare points out that when human beings become irresponsible and selfish and hoard the land, then the land can easily become a source of "exploitation, dispossession, disillusionment, captivity and even death."[3] The problem originates out of a desire to manipulate, possess, and hold title to the land by a few powerful and privileged in the society. As regards the hoarding and exploitation of land, this came with the birth of monarchy (empire) when the people of Israel cried out to Samuel that they wanted to be like other nations (1 Sam. 8:20).

With the emergence of agrarian societies, land became more and more critical as a source of sustenance and wealth. In the precolonial history of Zimbabwe, land was held by peasants. The usurpation of land from the peasants is nothing but a political tool of neutralizing and controlling the masses by empire. It is noteworthy that when land was extensively grabbed from the peasants, those who now own land used their control of the land to enslave the peasants, who now have to "sell their labour to the landlords as a daily wage earner."[4] In the Zimbabwean context, when one wants to fairly and justly address the issues of empire, land, and religion one has to ask whether "there exists a gap of time and place (between the) Bible and African religio-cultural worldview and life."[5] This critical analysis helps toward locating and dealing with critical issues and not mere cosmetic issues. The need to dialogue with both religion and culture is very important because culture and religion are key aspects of people's identities.

The tragedy of a flawed land tenure system is that you can have a few people that own land at the expense of the peasant majority who actually need land for their sustenance. What has become the norm in many cases is that such landlords are actually absentee landowners who happen to live "in urban centres far away from their properties."[6] and most of the time their land lies barren and idle. Such "abuse" and neglect of this fundamental commodity becomes a threat to societal economic interests in terms of food production. The sad reality is that the churches that own mission farms tend to be the main culprits that underutilize the vast tracts of land they own.

THE CASE OF ZIMBABWE

The land issue in the African continent in general and in the Zimbabwean context in particular is not merely about a commodity but an essential element for sustenance and the realization of economic prosperity and human rights. Land is a cross-cutting issue that impacts directly on the enjoyment of quality life and basic human rights. For the people of Africa in general and Zimbabwe in particular land is a source of livelihood, central to their economic rights; hence the growing call for fair land redistribution. Land is also often linked to people's identities, as it is also tied to social and cultural rights. Disputes over land frequently lead to violent conflicts and place many obstacles to sustainable peace. In short, the human rights aspects of land affect a range of issues, including poverty reduction and development, peacebuilding, humanitarian assistance, disaster prevention and recovery, urban and rural planning, to name a few. From such a context, the land issue is a fundamental matter for any country that wishes to build permanent and strong structures of peace, development, and prosperity.

An increasing number of people in the developing countries have been forcibly evicted or displaced from their land to make way for large-scale development or business projects such as dams and mines, among others. However, such developments have been carried out without any compensation to the affected families or individuals. In many countries the shift to large-scale farming has led to forced evictions, displacements, and local food insecurity, which in turn has contributed to an increase in rural to urban migration and consequently further pressure on access to urban land and housing. A considerable portion of this displacement violates the human rights of the affected communities, thus further aggravating their already precarious situation. Such trends are common in the African continent, and Zimbabwe is no exception.

Another sad development is the costs associated with landownership in developing economies. In many developing cities of Africa, the development projects have led to socioeconomic polarization owing to escalating costs of land and housing on the one hand and the depletion of low-income housing on the other hand. Such trends have a huge impact on the lower income classes's ability to access land (housing stands), as the land is basically priced beyond their reach. In order to understand the contextual challenges as regards the land question in Zimbabwe, one must appreciate that the colonial policies of land tenure remain in force; hence the glaring inequalities, which are summed up by Katerere:

> The history of land in Zimbabwe is the history of alienation and marginalization of the peasantry. The land alienation process favoured the white settlers who occupied the more fertile parts of the country while the peasantries were forced into more marginal lands.[7]

The alienation of indigenous people from their land as noted by Katerere has created a perpetual social evil that must be washed away if justice, genuine peace, and economic empowerment are to be achieved. For Banana, the church must speak out toward addressing the mistakes of the past and it must do so with humility and understanding. In speaking out against the mistakes of the past, the church may have to repent for its failure to forgive and seek to reconcile. In doing so, the church may need to work with the government for the good of all "even at the cost of sacrifice. This way, we not only serve our people, we also fulfill the Mission of Christ."[8]

In Zimbabwe, the indigenous people based the liberation struggle on the need for land. The land question remained at the core of political tensions in Zimbabwe as well as Zimbabwe's political, social, and economic transformation; hence the need for the church to develop a clear theology of the land. A theology of land is necessary to help people deal with the utter discontent prevalent in our communities and societies.

The talk about land has also become an environmental issue in our modern world. In the case of Zimbabwe, measures taken by the Environmental Management Agency (EMA) to protect the environment are at times in conflict with the interests and human rights of poor populations that depend on land for subsistence and survival. This is in direct reference to urban farming along river banks, wetlands, and open recreational places. On the same platform, failure to effectively prevent and mitigate environmental degradation and the negative impact of climate change could drastically reduce access to land, especially for marginalized groups. The results of such a paradox when it comes to proper management of the land versus traditional and cultural usage of the land results in tension, which often leads to conflict. In post-colonial conflicts, the subject of land has resulted in serious tension between the landowners and the peasants. Many ordinary citizens were deprived of their land through the colonial land tenure systems (which parceled out lots of land to a few white farmers while grouping many African families in poor reserves); hence these ordinary citizens who were deprived of the land have called for land appropriation policies to redress the colonial land imbalances. Sadly, the Western governments in particular have often criticized the post-colonial land appropriation policies in Africa and Zimbabwe as land grabs. What this basically means is that any logical attempt to resolve the land questions results in more tension and at times, open conflicts.

The roots of the land dispute in the Zimbabwean society are located at the beginning of colonial settlement in September 1890. Prior to the European colonial settlements, the indigenous peoples of Zimbabwe had a communal attitude toward landownership—land was the collective property of all the residents in a given chiefdom, with the chief mediating disagreements and issues pertaining to its use.[9] The European concept of individual landownership was unheard of and its implementation caused tension.

In terms of landownership dynamics, it is noted that between 1890 and 1896, the colonial settlers owned up to 16 million acres of land (about one-sixth the area of Southern Rhodesia).[10] By 1913, Europeans had extended their land ownership to 21.5 million acres. To demonstrate the roots of the problems that came with the settlers, who reduced chances for land apportionment and economic competition, note the following:

> In 1900, Southern Rhodesia's black population owned an estimated 55,000 head of cattle, while European residents owned fewer than 12,000. Most of the pastureland was being grazed by African-owned cattle, accordingly. However, in less than two decades the Ndebele and Shona came to own over a million head of cattle, with white farmers owning another million as well. As the amount of available pasture for the livestock quickly dwindled, accompanied by massive amounts of overgrazing and erosion, land competition between the three groups became intense. A number of successive land commissions were thus appointed to study the problem and apportion the land.[11]

The problems related to the land question spring from the creation of Tribal Trust Lands and the Land Apportionment Act of 1930 and the Land Husbandry Act of 1951. These policy measures divided the country into fixed racial compartments of "whites" and "blacks." White people were allocated quality productive farmland, while black people were grouped in poor arid and less productive land called reserves with no infrastructure for production.[12] The Land Apportionment Act of 1930 reserved productive and fertile rainfall regions for white settlements while indigenous people (who constituted over 95 percent of the population) were moved to arid and poor rainfall regions. This resulted in the pushing of blacks to the labor market.

The Land Apportionment Act development created two new problems: first, in the areas reserved for whites, the ratio of land to population was so high that many farms could not be exploited to their fullest potential, and some prime white-owned farmland was lying idle when local black people needed it (land). The overcrowded conditions in the Tribal Trust Lands compelled large numbers of the indigenous people to abandon their livelihoods in the so-called reserves and seek wage employment in the cities or on white commercial farms. This was a clear sign of enslavement and economic disempowerment of the indigenous peoples.[13] Second, the legislation resulted in enforced overuse of the land in the Tribal Trust Lands due to overpopulation and as a result the discontentment around the land issue was a solid foundation for the birth of African nationalism that ultimately led to war in Zimbabwe's liberation struggle. [14]

Geographically, Zimbabwe covers 96,600,000 acres of land. The 1930 Land Apportionment Act allocated 49,060,000 acres of land to 50,000 white settlers; 22,060,000 acres of land to black indigenous people, whose population numbered 1,100,000 people; 560,000 acres were classified as forest areas; 90,000 acres were termed undetermined land; and 17,600,000 acres were categorized as unassigned land. The segregation of all land was meant to be permanent "until the Native has advanced very much further on the path of civilization."[15] The Land Tenure Act of 1969, which was an attempt to make more land available to the fast-expanding population of indigenous people, reserved 45 million acres of land for white ownership (450,000 white people) and allocated 45 million acres of land for black ownership (5 million black people). However, this act did not change anything since the most fertile farmland continued to be under the white enclaves.

The 1979 Lancaster House settlement allowed the Zimbabwean authorities to initiate the necessary land reform measures "as long as land was bought and sold on a willing basis and the British government was mandated to finance half the costs of such agreements."[16] However, in the 1990s the British government of Tony Blair terminated this arrangement, claiming that funds available for this program were exhausted, thereby repudiating all commitments to land reform programs in Zimbabwe. The government of Zimbabwe responded by embarking on a "fast track" land redistribution program, which resulted in forced confiscating of farmland owned by white farmers without compensation.[17] The fast track project was followed by events of intimidation and violence that, in some cases, resulted in the loss of life by some farmers and loss of formal employment by many workers. Unfortunately, the fast track land reform coincided with the collapse of Zimbabwe's economy.

The tragedy of landownership by a few in Zimbabwe is glaring when one looks at the statistics since independence in 1980:

> Almost 6,000 white commercial farmers owned 15.5m hectares (45 percent of the most productive land in the high rainfall regions where the potential for agriculture output is greatest). Small scale commercial farmers (8,500 mainly black farmers) controlled 5 percent of the land, in mostly drier regions; and 700,000 black farming families occupied the remaining 50 percent of the land (75 percent of which was in the low rainfall areas with very poor soil fertility).[18]

These statistics help one to appreciate why during the Lancaster House Conference negotiations (the dialogue that led to Zimbabwe's independence) both Joshua Nkomo and Robert Mugabe (leaders of Zimbabwe's liberation movements) threatened to walk out over the land issue unless Britain agreed to fund the land reform program which sought to correct the colonial imbalances. "The Conference resumed only when Britain and America made certain commitments to assist the Zimbabwean government to acquire land from white farmers for distribution to blacks."[19] Interestingly, the new government that was ushered into power through the 1980 elections declared a policy of reconciliation which was aimed at appeasing the white community, especially the farming community and industrialists:

> The statement was made to avoid scaring the settlers, particularly large-scale farmers, most of whom were aware of the unjust land tenure they had created in the country. They feared retaliation and were therefore reassured that no revenge would be taken against them. The past was to be forgotten and buried, and a new era ushered in where all persons, regardless of colour or creed, would live together equally and in harmony.[20]

Zimbabwe's 1980 reconciliation statement was basically a political statement whose thrust was for political mileage and not focused toward what it purported to achieve. What the statement missed was the fact that true reconciliation entails changed attitudes and relationships for the better between two concerned parties that were previously hostile toward each other. The reconciliation statement should have promulgated a road map toward addressing and/or removing the political and economic structures that were responsible for creating and promoting a poor landless peasantry on one hand, and a small, powerful, rich group of landowners on the other hand. The flawed nature of such a reconciliation policy is that it attempted to "cover up the past as if it never was—(thereby) deepening the roots of hostility."[21]

With politicians playing politics, the Christian church could have taken upon itself to push for a just solution to the land question. But did the church, then, understand the necessity of a theology of land? For me, it is implicitly clear that the church did not realize the need to put in place mechanisms that would promote a moral and just process toward addressing Zimbabwe's land question, which was at the center of the country's liberation struggle, and the war which was a result of that struggle. If the church had, by then, realized the need for a land theology then it would have concluded that Zimbabwe's independence could only be meaningful to the majority of the poor people after the land question was solved by empowering people, through giving them adequate land in order to create a just society which enables all citizens toward self-sustenance with practical and sustainable development.

A REFORMED THEOLOGICAL REFLECTION ON LAND AND COVENANT

Recent trends in modern theology have developed interest in the holistic approach to issues of justice and human rights over and above mere "anthropologies which present the essence of human personhood in terms of spirit, consciousness or mind essentially distinct from the body. The human being, it is argued, is essentially embodied, finite, social and rooted in space and time."[22]

Theologically, one cannot justly define the rights and privileges of all people without appreciating the fact that a complete person requires territory in which one can "reside and flourish in communities. Requiring daily sustenance, housing and a settled existence for cultural flourishing, human persons are thus bound to the land in ways that are non-accidental."[23] With this type of anthropology, we can better understand the pervasiveness of land throughout the history of humanity. Interestingly, the Bible declares that human beings are created from the soil (land) and are to live and feed from the land: "Then the Lord God formed the man of the dust from the ground and breathed into his nostrils the breath of life, and the man became a living creature" (Gen. 2:7). This implies that human beings can never be separated from the land since they are a product of the land and their sustenance is in the land. Therefore, any attempt to strip peasants of their land by way of manipulative political instruments and financial power is ungodly. Period!

The delay by the church to seriously promote a land theology has presented empire with ample freedom to perpetuate land tenure systems that are disempowering to the peasants, whose right to land has been relegated to the backyard while promoting powerful personalities and institutions to grab land on account of their financial muscles.

When Jesus proclaimed the Kingdom of God, he explicitly declared that the reign of God brings about a holistic environment that promotes quality life. And when the same Jesus condemned the evils that attend to human beings, Jesus "implicitly questioned the Pax Romana (the dominance of Rome). He juxtaposed the true peace of God's kingdom with the 'imperial good tidings of a pacified world and human happiness in it'. To say God's kingdom is at hand implies that Caesar's kingdom is not ultimate."[24] Such reading of the biblical text demands grace of wisdom, complete faith, and divine courage that thrusts us into new frontiers of biblical exegesis.

That the land is a central theme in the Bible finds support in recent exegesis of the image of God in Gen. 1 and in the Hebrew anthropology where the person is a psychosomatic unity belonging to communities of family, tribe, and nation (land/location).[25] In the context of covenant theology, we need to deliberately have a clear and bold theology that entails a faith response that is articulated in terms of our engagement with the sociopolitical challenges of our time. Such a theology must clearly attest the rule of God throughout the cosmos and be able to protect the interests of the peasants who have been scandalized by empire. An authentic and relevant Christian theology must help to deal with discontentment among the peasantry communities and the emptiness prevalent in the industrialized societies, because human beings deserve justice, peace, and the enjoyment of human rights. The overbearing power of empire must be checked by any serious religion for the good of God's people in society.

NOTES

1. S. Bakare, *My Right to Land—in The Bible and in Zimbabwe* (Mutare: Delsink Publishers 1993), 1.
2. Bakare, *My Right to Land—in The Bible and in Zimbabwe*, 1.
3. Bakare, *My Right to Land—in The Bible and in Zimbabwe*, 1.
4. Bakare, *My Right to Land—in The Bible and in Zimbabwe*, 26.
5. F. J. Verstraelen, *Zimbabwean Realities and Christian Responses: Contemporary Aspects of Christianity in Zimbabwe* (Gweru, Zimbabwe: Mambo Press, 1998), 79.
6. Bakare, *My Right to Land*, 29.
7. Y. Katerere et al., "Zimbabwe: An Environmental Profile," ZERO Working Paper, no. 27 (1991): 33
8. C. S. Banana, *Turmoil and Tenacity: Zimbabwe 1890–1990* (Harare, Zimbabwe: College Press, 1989), 288.
9. Shoko T. Karanga, *Indigenous Religion in Zimbabwe: Health and Well-Being* (Oxford: Routledge, 2007), 9–12.
10. P. Mosley, "The Settler Economies: Studies," in *Economic History of Kenya and Southern Rhodesia 1900–1963* (Cambridge, UK: Cambridge University Press, 2009), 13–24.
11. H. Nelson, "Zimbabwe: A Country Study," in *Zimbabwean Realities and Christian Responses*, ed. F. J. Verstraelen (Gweru, Zimbabwe: Mambo Press, 1998), 137–53.
12. Verstraelen, *Zimbabwean Realities and Christian Responses*, 79–87.
13. G. G. Makura-Paradza, "Single Women, Land and Livelihood Vulnerability in a Communal area in Zimbabwe" (Wageningen: Wageningen University and Research Centre, 2010).
14. Nelson, "Zimbabwe," 137.
15. https://www.colonialrelic.com/appendixes/appendix-vi-the-land-tenure-act-1969-and-the-land-apportionment-act-1930/ (accessed October 25, 2019).
16. https://sas-space.sas.ac.uk/5847/5/1979_Lancaster_House_Agreement.pdf (accessed October 25, 2019).
17. https://en.wikipedia.org/wiki/Land_reform_in_Zimbabwe#cite_note-Security-4 (accessed October 25, 2019).
18. http://www.raceandhistory.com/historicalviews/2000/june.html (accessed October 25, 2019).
19. http://www.raceandhistory.com/historicalviews/2000/june.html (accessed October 25, 2019).
20. Bakare, *My Right to Land*, 58.
21. Bakare, *My Right to Land*, 63.
22. http://www.churchofscotland.org.uk/__data/assets/pdf_file/0009/13230/Theology_of_Land_and_Covenant.pdf (accessed October 25, 2019).
23. http://www.churchofscotland.org.uk/__data/assets/pdf_file/0009/13230/Theology_of_Land_and_Covenant.pdf (accessed October 25, 2019).
24. http://pauldouglaswalker.blogspot.com/2013/06/loving-your-enemy-part-4-what-did-jesus.html (October 25, 2019).

25. http://www.churchofscotland.org.uk/__data/assets/pdf_file/0009/13230/Theology_of_Land_and_Covenant.pdf (accessed October 25, 2019).

Part II

Dispossessions and Responsibilities

Chapter Seven

Landed Churches, Landless People

Kuzipa Nalwamba

"The Earth is the Lord's—But the land and water belong to financial capital" was the apt title of a workshop conducted by the World Council of Churches at the 2017 Lutheran World Federation Assembly held in Namibia. It is a play on the words of Psalm 24:1—"The earth is the Lord's, and everything in it, the world and all who live in it." The title captures the contradiction that commodification of land poses to the foundational Christian belief in a Creator-God to whom everything belongs. It distressingly heightens the scandal of church landownership which, in the case of African churches, proceeds from Africa's colonial and contemporary expressions of empire.

Fair and equitable access to land and other natural resources like water, forests, and biodiversity ensure sustainable development of people. Exclusion from those places and resources makes people vulnerable. Access to land and the lack thereof define prevailing power relations between the landless and landowners, and African churches are among the major bodies that hold (received from overseas mission societies) African lands. For this reason, we must problematize church landownership.

This essay offers a threefold reflection. First, it presents a historical overview of the church landownership issue as a legacy of colonial and postcolonial expressions of empire, casting landlessness in Southern Africa as a tool of oppression and exclusion of poor, powerless, landless people. Thus, the church as landowner does not share the powerlessness of the landless. The church is located on the side of oppressive, dispossessing powers. Second, this essay proposes that a relational ontology founded on African cultural and intellectual infrastructure that ensues from a holistic, life-affirming worldview offers a hermeneutical lens that could shape a theological alternative that confronts the internal life-denying logic of empire. Third, the essay concludes with an outline of recommendations for the church to nurture a life-affirming land-justice ethos.

The value of this contribution does not lie in its novelty. Rather, its location within the continuum of the broader debate on land reform in the individual countries and the Southern Africa region accentuates the role the church could play in contributing to development and alleviation of poverty by practicing and calling for land justice. The church's credible contribution is premised on understanding its missional identity as being counter-imperial. The church's ethical responsibility toward the land-dispossessed is a non-negotiable prophetic obligation.[1]

A HISTORICAL OVERVIEW

Historically the people of Southern Africa were nomadic hunters, gatherers, and pastoralists who wandered in their quest for water, grazing land, and game. Their rhythm of life followed the seasons that allowed for these basic survival activities. By the Iron Age, semipermanent settlements had emerged and agricultural land became important. Agricultural activities transformed the environment. Land, which supported agricultural, hunting, livestock, and gathering activities, was the basis for wealth.[2] Political and social organization around land as a key resource consolidated a community's power.

The arrival of Europeans in the mid-seventeenth century changed the land tenure system to individual ownership, which conflicted with the African communal land tenure. The political subjugation that followed during the colonial period reduced the landholdings of African communities. Rural land increasingly became "white owned." State intervention sanctioned control and domination of rural economies by commercial farmers. At this time, the land question was a source of insecurity for African people. Black African people were subject to forced removals and unequal competition with white farmers, who had access to capital, markets, and political influence. With respect to landownership, black African people were disadvantaged.

Church mission stations tended to be located in rural areas, and the church became a major landowner. The church was cash poor, but land rich. A favorite quote of Africans on the land question that the white man took African land in exchange for the Bible sums up that narrative, albeit crudely. Maluleke, commenting on the well-rehearsed anecdote, innovates when he interprets it in the light of empire. He aptly notes:

> This anecdote has been interpreted variously and divergently. Most commentators agree that the "bible" and "land" in the anecdote carry more than a literal meaning—without excluding their literal meanings. Here the bible stands, amongst other things, for Christendom and its allies and consequences in . . .

> Africa while the land stand, amongst other things, for Black dignity, livelihood and culture (in the most comprehensive sense).[3]

Some of the "land" (literal and metaphorical) taken by whites went to the church. Consequently, being "land" rich, the church took over the function of defining and managing "Black dignity, livelihood and culture."

The extent to which Christian mission colluded with the colonial imperial project is well recognized and documented. The postcolonial scenario is a carryover of that historical baggage as the political elite use their power to acquire land and to preside over its annexation by global financial capital. For instance, market-driven agrarian reforms benefit big business by expropriating land from poor small-scale farmers.[4] Church-owned land, when commercialized, is complicit in these practices.

The subject of church landownership in Southern Africa is well documented and has been a subject of theological reflection for some time, particularly in South Africa. The *Economic Project* (University of Stellenbosch) has collections of documents on church land—theological reflections, case studies, and church statements on the issue of church landownership. The *Bulletin for Contextual Theology* (University of Kwazulu Natal) dedicated its September 1998 issue to the question of church and land. The documents of the two projects demonstrate the extent to which the church has historically been complicit in the dispossession of the landless. Many mainline churches in the region own vast amounts of land, but their members remain landless. How will the church emerge from such a compromised state to make room for life-affirming theologies to inspire practical initiatives to redress land injustice?

This reflection is set against such a background. I, however, acknowledge that certain nuances and complexities of the land question may be lost in such a broad brushstroke. This is a theological reflection on an ongoing issue which does not purport to have mastered the actuality of complex and constantly changing sociopolitical nuances around this issue. The aim is to appropriate the mood, movement, and features which dominate the issue of church landownership in order to provide a backdrop for the subsequent theological analysis in this discussion.

Land injustice is a reality that people experience at different levels in Southern Africa. The wide divide between extreme wealth and extreme poverty can be explained in terms of historical land dispossession and power relations in the present. In a country like South Africa, the divide starkly runs across racial lines, which is a legacy of the apartheid policies of the past. The apartheid system economically advantaged white people. Black people were moved into small, impoverished, poorer areas in the outskirts and in separate areas in the cities. The scandal of church land ownership is its participation in historical disinheritance and exploitation. However, when the church remains silent, that exploitation becomes both spiritual and economic. A lack of commitment to address historical and contemporary land dispossession implicates the church more deeply.

Reading of biblical texts as tools of resistance that nurture life is largely absent. The land issue, which is such a deeply troubling contextual issue with felt sociopolitical consequences, is not prominent in church deliberations. In this light, I suggest that the church needs to confront and unmask its violent missiologies.[5] When the church upholds the status quo of holding onto land and/or not using it to benefit the dispossessed, it perpetuates a colonial and violent legacy.

The communal ethic embedded in African legal, philosophical, and cultural perspective pertaining to land offers a life-affirming lens. Such a critical interpretive lens is accessible as a cultural resource that potentially underpins theological reflection on the subject.

LAND IN AFRICAN THOUGHT: A LIFE-AFFIRMING HERMENEUTICAL LENS

Land possession in traditional African societies is grounded in a communal ethic.[6] It is the basis for identity, community consciousness, and well-being. For that reason, land was held in trust on behalf of the community. From that perspective, commodification of land is against cultural norms because it excludes weaker and poorer members of the community. A land tenure system that espouses such life-affirming values as care for the weak and poor promotes equitable use of land. Such a cultural hermeneutical lens interrogates the church's approach to the land question.

Land is an indicator of the extent to which justice and equity exist in our societies. As such, the church as landowner remains at the center of the theological critique that surrounds the land question. As Philpott and Zondi aptly observe, in this matter the church is "an embarrassed party."[7] In this regard, they wonder if shame should be the starting point for a more radical theological engagement.

Community consciousness that is grounded in land encounters the divine, as Creator, through the natural world. In that conception, the concrete world and the spiritual realm exist as a unitary whole. Land has particular significance as the concrete place and space in which communal life finds expression. Land also enshrines the community's memories for generations as the realm of the divine in which the community is invited to participate. African theologians underline the need to harness *participation* as an insight for theology. The Ghanaian thinker Emmanuel Asante has coined the term *pan-vitalism* in the African conception of community participation:

> Reality is inseparable. The African is kin to all creatures—gods, spirits and nature. . . . The whole of nature must be understood as sacred because it derives its being from the Supreme Being who is the Creator-Animator of the Universe.[8]

The Malawian theologian Harvery Sindima characterizes the same line of thinking as "bondedness, sacredness and fecundity" of what he terms the "community of life." Sindima explains further:

> African idea of community (which) refers to bondedness; the act of sharing and living in the one common symbol—life—which enables people to live in communion and communication with each other and nature . . . (which) allows the stories or life experiences of others to become one's own.[9]

The Congolese thinker Vincent Mulago's ideas of *union vitale* and *participation vitale* similarly enunciate God-centered communal life, in which the Supreme Being imbues everything and (inter)connects everything within a web of dynamic, elaborate relationships.[10] The union-of-life-in-participation (at the level of humans) echoes the Trinitarian relationship of Christian tradition.

The above insights enunciate the life-affirming principle inherent within a relational ontology, which explicates the African notion that the natural world is in kinship relationship. The implication is that before anything in nature (including land) is an economic commodity, it is bound up with divinity, people's identities and consciousness in a deeply spiritual sense. Ethical responsibility toward the natural world and other human beings shaped by such relational inclusivity excludes exploitation and commodification—in principle at least. Nel argues that the practical implication of such a worldview is that:

> this cosmology is the integration of three distinguishable aspects, namely environment, society, and the spiritual. All activities are informed by this holistic understanding so that they singularly or collectively maintain or transform the socio-cultural and spiritual landscape. An act is never separated from its environmental, societal, or spiritual impact. The cosmology becomes visible in that indigenous knowledge informs acts of technology, agriculture, animal keeping, music, song, dance, ritual, family . . . etc. It is a system of thought embedded in action. One may even go so far as to state that this thought structure is embodied.[11]

The integrative sensibility toward nature implies that the world lives within and in connection with the divine as its milieu of existence. This integrative and incarnational way of thinking echoes the words of Acts 17: 28: "In (God) we live and move and have our being. . . . We are (God's) offspring." In incarnational terms, we may speak of being *with* and *in* God because as John

1:3 states, "Through him all things were made; without him nothing was made that has been made."

The Christian scriptures that depict the interpenetrating and permeating realm of the Spirit using metaphors of water, breath, and air emphasize nature's dependence on God for its growth and flourishing. "This understanding says that we live within the body of God; that the world *is*, and *is not* the body of God; and that all things exist within the one reality that is and that reality is on the side of life and fulfilment."[12]

Land is a primary theological category in the Bible, too. It is spoken of in concrete as well as in symbolic terms. Biblical reference to land is a vast subject that cannot be systematized into one heading or view. However, a theme that runs through from the Old to the New Testament is that land is a gift of God's promise. It is a place and space of historical significance for its occupants because it is enshrined with memories that provide continuity and give identity across generations to its occupants.[13]

Protest, resistance, and the pursuit of justice also take place in that place and space. Land therefore anchors the dignity of its dwellers. The absence of land is a denial of that which dignifies humans. In the Bible, when the land was managed outside the relationship with God, defined by covenant, and when kings who were divinely tasked with the responsibility to hold the land in trust became instruments of land loss, the sad consequence was landlessness for the people (cf. Deut. 28:63–68; Hos. 2).

The inclusive participatory ethos points to the permeating power of the divine as the theological grounding for land justice. The convergences between African thought and Christian tradition, albeit with conceptual and cosmological discontinuities, make them feasible resources for a life-affirming grounding land theology that takes the well-being of all people, and indeed all of life, into consideration.

From an African perspective, coexistence and healthy relationships signal the goodness of nature as a divine gift and milieu for encounter with the divine. Maintaining harmony in relationship is therefore the standard for the humanness of an individual and community. The well-being of one assumes the well-being and flourishing of the entire community (*Ubuntu*). Conversely, the deprivation of one is the deprivation of the entire community, and equally the deprivation of the community is the deprivation of each of its members.

The strife and insecurity caused by historical land dispossession in some countries in Southern Africa is self-evident. A neocolonial practice is emerging in Africa that will lead to further land dispossession. Foreign companies and governments are purchasing land to grow food for export.[14] The volatility and disruption that this development could cause locally and globally illustrate the absence of a life-affirming ethos in the global economic system.

A hospitable approach to the land issue that emphasizes the well-being of the entire community resists materialistic views of land that underlie the logic of commodification of land. On the other hand, when the well-being of the land itself and that of the landless people is kept in view, land is understood to be inspirited by the divine. It has inherent value, and so do the poor and powerless people. In this perspective, life tends toward rapprochement within an enchanted[15] world in which life has value for its own sake.

A life-affirming land theology developed through such a holistic interpretive lens inspires an ethic that takes embodiment, participation, and intersubjectivity in the community seriously. Isaiah 32:15–20 resonates with such connections and interrelationships that are a symphony of well-being of the whole:

> till the Spirit is poured on us from on high,
> and the desert becomes a fertile field,
> and the fertile field seems like a forest.
> The Lord's justice will dwell in the desert,
> his [sic] righteousness live in the fertile field.
> The fruit of that righteousness will be peace;
> its effect will be quietness and confidence forever.
> My people will live in peaceful dwelling places,
> in secure homes,
> in undisturbed places of rest.
> Though hail flattens the forest
> and the city is levelled completely,
> how blessed you will be,
> sowing your seed by every stream,
> and letting your cattle and donkeys range free. (NIV)

A life-affirming theology of land that places emphasis on the well-being of the community is not a mere private transformational process. Rather, it is embodied. As a result, the judicious appropriation of land that calls for just living and actions in the concrete world matters. Every action is interwoven within an eschatological[16] frame, to glorify God.

The juxtaposition of African life-affirming ethos and the biblical one provides a compelling theological undergirding that interrogates utilitarian attitudes toward land and landownership.

TOWARD LIFE-AFFIRMING LAND JUSTICE

The church in Southern Africa can play a prophetic role in pursuing radical land justice. However, its problematic legacy of participating in centuries of land dispossession remains its albatross. The church, as beneficiary of past injustices, must confront its past (and present) regarding land dispossession. How will the church engage in restorative action, and where possible use its land as a strategic resource for poverty eradication? Could the church work with communities to transform land tenure systems through advocacy? Without paying attention to its own accountability, the church has a credibility gap that stifles its prophetic impulse.

In addition, major changes in African economies and societies, such as demographic growth, urbanization, monetarization of the economy, livelihood diversification, greater integration in the global economy, and cultural change, have had profound implications for land tenure systems. Decades of government interventions that have continually adapted and reinterpreted land tenure systems because of social, economic, political, and cultural change have transformed communities in relation to land. For that reason, it is not possible to recommend uniform practical interventions. A multi-layered approach to reorient theological perspectives and to provoke self-interrogation will lead to concrete action. I recommend intentional, systematic education and nurturing of attitudes over time in some of the following ways.

Through *proclamation*, we can show how Word and Spirit hold together, thereby nurturing a holistic worldview that nurtures a communal ethic. Insights from the Africa traditional worldview offer a critical hermeneutical lens for engaging with the biblical text in ways that bring polemical and doxological aspects of the text to bear on the land question. We, therefore, should not underestimate the power of sermons. The cumulative impact of churches preaching land-justice-sensitive sermons for a span of years could make a difference and shape an ethic. Listening to such sermons will shape personal and communal prophetic actions such as advocacy, protest, and restorative justice, as the case may be. Bad sermons devoid of a justice imperative will have the reverse effect.

The role of *prophetic ministries* requires the church to ask what prophetic mode is meaningful for the particular land issues in a given context. The broader question from this perspective is whether the land question is at the heart of church practice. If so, is the prophetic stance theologically consistent with the inalienable interconnectedness that promotes the well-being and flourishing of all. Such a prophetic stance can only arise from Christian content that takes seriously the position that land is a gift of God and that it is profoundly connected to people's identity, consciousness, and well-being.

The power of *studying biblical texts* should not be underestimated either. Even familiar biblical texts read through critical life-affirming hermeneutical lenses can inspire a consistent portrayal of the character of the God of mercy and justice that could incrementally shape a sense of justice.

There is power in *teaching, learning, research, and publications*. These activities analyze and debate the complex issues that surround the land question. The nature of the activities themselves lends them to taking advantage of influential transformative platforms and formations. The impact of many years of teaching, learning, research, and publishing could therefore confront and deconstruct the church's legacy of participating in violent land dispossession, shape church practices, and inform public policy vis-à-vis the land question in the region.

CONCLUSION

Christianity is widespread, and it has a public role in Southern Africa. The missionary-founded (mainline) Protestant and Catholic churches that inherited land have a dual identity. They bear the imperial baggage of being landowners, but they are also viable contributors to a constructive process that upholds the dignity of people. For the churches in Southern Africa that own land, repentance and just action are in a continuum. In his critique of the American empire, Amjad-Ali warns about "sleight-of-hand application of covenant theology" that justifies land possession and "places the victims on the losing side of this unethical theology."[17] Churches in Southern Africa as beneficiaries of the colonial legacy of empire would do well to heed that warning, not only in historical terms, but as a way of nurturing life-giving theologies that do not negate land issues and historical context as sites for theological reflection.

NOTES

1. Philpott and Zondi have coauthored an extended discussion of this question, outlining the church's responsibility to use its land as a strategic resource in the fight against poverty. See Graham Philpott and Phumani Zondi, "Church Land: A Strategic Resource in the War against Poverty," *Bulleting for Contextual Theology on Church and Land* 5.3 (1998): 17–39.
2. The Anglican Church in Southern Africa's report on this matter offers an assessment that, though focused on South Africa, is representative of the region in regard to Church land ownership. See Southern African Anglican Theological Commission, "The Land and Its Use in Southern Africa: Report of the Southern African Anglican Theological Commission, 26th January 1995," *The Bulletin for Contextual Theology on Church and Land* 5.3 (1998): 6–16.
3. Tinyiko Maluleke, "The Land of the Church of the Land: A Response to the Whole Issue," *The Bulletin for Contextual Theology on Church and Land* 5.3 (1998): 61.
4. Reuters Africa, "Zambia's Poorest Farmers Risk Becoming Squatters on Their Own Land," http://af.reuters.com/article/topNews/idAFKBN18905S-OZATP.
5. Maluleke, "The Land of the Church of the Land," 61–64.
6. An appreciative retrieval here does not valorize the communal and relational aspects of African culture in absolute terms. Life-denying practices such as the normalization of the subjugation of women and children for communal objectives are not absent. Whereas it is not my intention to valorize such elements, the inadvertent by-product of pursuing a single train of thought is a tendency toward apparent absolutism.
7. Philpott and Zondi, "Church Land," 4–5.
8. Emmanuel Asante, "Ecology: Untapped Resource of Pan-Vitalism in Africa," *AFER: African Ecclesial Review* 27 (1985): 290, 292.
9. Harvey Sindima, "Community of Life," *The Ecumenical Review* 41.4 (1989): 537. See also Harvey Sindima, "Community of Life: Ecological Theology in African Perspective," in

Liberating Life: Contemporary Approaches in Ecological theology, ed. Charles Birch, William Eaken, and Jay B McDaniel (Maryknoll, NY: Orbis Books, 1990), 137–147.

10. John Kapya Kaoma, *God's Family, God's Earth: Christian Ecological Ethics of Ubuntu* (Zomba, Malawi: Kachere Series, 2013).

11. Philip J. Nel, "Morality and Religion in African Thought." *Acta Theologica* 2 (2008): 37–38.

12. Sally McFague, *A New Climate for Theology: God, the World, and Global Warming* (Minneapolis, MN: Fortress Press, 2008), 116.

13. See Walter Brueggemann, *The Land: Place as Gift, Promise, and Challenge in Biblical Faith* (Minneapolis, MI: Fortress Press, 2002).

14. See Roy Laishley, "Is Africa's Land Up for Grabs," *Africa Renewal: Special Edition on Agriculture* 2014, http://www.un.org/africarenewal/magazine/special-edition-agriculture-2014/africa%E2%80%99s-land-grabs (accessed September 21, 2017).

15. Enchantment, not in an ethereal sense of seeing spirits in everything, but rather, the emphasis is on the interconnectedness of all of life (compared to being "distinct from").

16. Eschatology here is understood as a theology of the future, i.e., the beginning of the life of God. It is not the end of life or even the end of time, but as life bursting forth.

17. Charles Amjad-Ali, "Christian Ethics in the Context of Globalism, the Clash of Civilisations and the American Empire," in *Globalisation, vol. 1: The Politics of Empire, Justice and the Life of Faith*, ed. Allan Boesak and L. D. Hansen (Bloemfontein, South Africa: African Sun Media), 107.

Chapter Eight

Empire 2.0

Land Matters in Jamaica and the Caribbean

Garnett Roper

Empire does the same thing to people all over the world, but in different forms. As it is in Palestine, for instance, so it is in the Caribbean. In *Faith in the Face of Empire*, Mitri Raheb argues that the designation "Middle East" represents a Eurocentric view: Middle of what? and East of where?[1] Similarly, the designation Caribbean is Eurocentric—it is a nickname that shows the contempt of European invaders for the spirit of resistance they encountered in the region. The name Carib (cannibal) was pejorative and meant to stigmatize the Kalinago people that fiercely resisted European invasion.

It is ironic, but intentionally postcolonial, that the independent territories in the region describe themselves as the Caribbean Economic Community (CARICOM). This leaves an open question, whether or not the region has moved away from the clutches of empire. This essay contends that in relation to empire, at its most fundamental level, when it comes to landownership and land use, there is both a residue and a resurgence of empire, hence "Empire 2.0," in the Caribbean region (and elsewhere).

The forces of empire dispossess indigenous peoples of their land in the name of conquest. Those forces distorted the use of the land in the name of economic domination and grew crops that were for the tables of the North Atlantic rather than to serve the needs of the nation-state and its people. Land was distributed in ways that were for the advantage of the economically dominant minority and perpetuated their advantage over against the people of the land. This remains the open question, as to whether or not political priorities and programs ought to include the repossession and redistribution of land for the purposes of causing the people of the land to flourish and prosper. Is there a narrative that can rescue such policies in the name of the people? It also raises a question about theology deployed in the interest of human flourishing by seeking to bring the grace and power of God to bear upon the lived reality of the people in spaces of domination and oppression. Is this a legitimate concern of theology, and does theology offer a response to both the residue and the resurgence of empire?

The small island states of the Caribbean do not have enough land to ensure quality of life comparable to European farmers. The problems of the Caribbean, which does not have enough land to benefit from economies of scale, are made worse because of the unequal distribution of land. This essay explores the land question as historical legacy and challenge for public policy.

Has the history of the Caribbean bequeathed a land situation that perpetuates the agendas of empire rather than facilitates human flourishing in the region? The land situation is one in which a place like Jamaica finds itself with between 20 and 30 percent of its population landless and living in unplanned and unorganized communities called squatter settlements.[2] On the one hand, this landlessness has exacerbated the identity crisis and the situation of inequality and intensified lack of economic and social mobility for the majority of the people at the base of the population, whose lived reality is marked with privation, poverty, and misery.

The situation of landlessness is not unrelated to the numerous incidents of crime, violence, and social dysfunction that have come to characterize parts of Jamaica and the Caribbean. On the other hand, the forces and powers that colonized the Caribbean and imposed the plantation economy and chattel slavery benefit from the economic and social circumstances of the Caribbean. These forces and powers remain in positions that allow them to be in control of the narrative and to determine the public transcript as far as priorities of public policy and national development are concerned.

Has emancipation, nationalism, and political independence succeeded or failed to secure economic, political, and social advantage for the people of the Caribbean? Have they merely tinkered at the edges? Have the powers that were the erstwhile masters and owners of the region merely reconfigured themselves in order to continue to benefit as they have in the past? Put differently, does the Caribbean remain in the periphery or clutches of empire? Is the Caribbean a basin, playground, or stomping ground for the forces of empire, imperialism, and hegemony? How much of what constitutes Caribbean reality is self-inflicted, the result of misgovernance or misrule since political independence, and how much is the result of the technologies of power?

It is important that this analysis does not minimize the progress of the people of the Caribbean as a way of perpetuating self-doubt. This discussion cannot afford to believe that the more things change, the more they remain the same for the people of the region. Despite remarkable inherited disadvantages, the people of the Caribbean have punched above their weight as global players and actors, and in some respects the Caribbean has achieved a quality of life (rates of infant mortality, life expectancy, telecommunications infrastructure, rates of literacy and numeracy, extent of press freedom) that rivals places in the metropoles of the North Atlantic. On the other hand, there are matters arising from the legacy of misrule by its own and by the emissaries of the North Atlantic, from chattel slavery, colonialism, and the since hurriedly abandoned (by the North Atlantic, anyway) globalization.

Empire 2.0 invites us to consider the residue and resurgence of empire, the ways in which the technology and infrastructure of power have reconfigured themselves to do to the people of the Two-Thirds World what they have done before. In this regard we consider the nature of the intersection between people, land, and empire—factors that are at play in the Caribbean.

Land is an important flashpoint. Land is the site through which, in many respects, European hegemony has been asserted in the region. It must be borne in mind that the Caribbean has been the arena in which various European powers sought to assert their hegemony and dominance in relation to each other. Some Caribbean territories changed hands among European countries (England, France, Spain, and Holland) in the period of colonization, and some of the territories in the region were sold from one member of the North Atlantic community to another. Land that is owned publicly (government land) is still referred to as Crown Lands, which is a relic of the colonial past.[3]

When slavery was abolished in Jamaica, there was no attempt to enfranchise the landless African population, who left the hobbles and plantation grounds and fled to the hillsides. Very little has happened since.

BIBLICAL NARRATIVES CONCERNING LAND

The creation account in Genesis 2 depicts interdependence and corelationship between human beings and the land. The human was formed from the dust of the ground, Adam from Adamah. When Adam was formed "The LORD God took the man and put him in the Garden of Eden to work it and take care of it." The separation of Adam from Adamah has created all forms of crises (such as the ecological crisis), but also precipitated the economic, social, and political crises that bedevil modern human society. The separation of Adam from Adamah is the greatest impediment to human flourishing. In Paradise past, there was oneness between Adam and Adamah that resulted in the flourishing of creation and harmony within the human community. The curse in Gen. 3:17–19 means that the land becomes less assured or predictable and it requires more from human beings in order to produce sustainably. Hostility between Adam and Adamah is the consequence of the curse and so also is the rivalry between the partners in the human family. To find remedies for this is the task of salvation, redemption, and liberation.[4]

The provisions made and injunctions given in the books of Deuteronomy and Joshua are instructive in terms of the value placed on land. Land was critical to the self-identity of the fledgling people of Israel. How land was handled and how land issues were settled were pivotal to the progress of social justice in Israel. The Promised Land was a gift from Yahweh to Israel in the quest of a nationalist agenda. Joshua was a significant figure for the land project in which Israel was made to settle on the allotment of land in the broad, spacious, and fertile plain given to the tribes of Yahweh. Whether or not the historicity of the text is established, it is clear that the perspective of the Deuteronomist is that land was critical to the agency and viability of the nation-state.

Having left Egypt, Israel entered the land of the Hittites in order to find space to become a people. The drama of the passing out parade of empires and their relationship to the fledgling Israelite nation-state was also about land. The Assyrians absorbed the northern ten tribes and over time the identity of Israel as a separate and distinct people vanished. Babylon expatriated the best of Judah, laid waste both their agricultural development and their civic, religious, commercial, and political infrastructure. Jeremiah, who looked beyond the exile for a new beginning, bought a parcel of land as a token of hope in the future of the people of the land, the *'am ha 'aretz*. The Persian emperor Cyrus returned Israel to their land and in that sense restored the prospect of an Israelite nation-state. Yahweh was the ultimate landowner, and the land was leased to clans and families, but it could not be sold. This was structured into the Israelite economy by the so-called jubilee principle, in which every fifty years land reverted to the ownership by families to which it was first allotted. The jubilee principle preserved liberty and equality within Israel and was critical to social justice legislation.

The biblical concepts of land as promised, land as divine possession, and land as sacred are related. The project of social justice and the ecological crisis require that the issue of land, made worse for the people by the machinations of empire, be addressed.

COLONIZATION AND IMPERIALISM

The empires of the Greeks and the Romans have chosen to invade and colonize people in their homeland, reducing nation-states in political, social, and economic terms to become vassals (to empires, as suzerain). The empires that have colonized and co-colonized the Caribbean region followed the model of the Greco Roman empires. In the case of Jamaica, major tracts of land in the plains were given to mono-crop agriculture that was destined for exports to the metropolis. The food produced was not part of the diet of the people but was intended for elsewhere. The pattern is true of the entire region that was subjected to slavery, colonization, and the plantation economy. Mono-crop agriculture meant in general that the following three things were features of the lived reality of the people in this region:

1) *Food sufficiency, food safety, and food security could not be guaranteed.* The diet within the region for the broad mass of the people was based on staples imported from elsewhere. The diet afforded from the imported staples has been more akin to forced feeding than to nourishment. The high incidence of lifestyle diseases such as hypertension, diabetes, heart disease, and certain cancers is related to this diet of imported staples that include concentrated fats and sugars.

2) *The returns from the export of mono-crop agriculture, whether sugar cane or banana, have resulted in massive trade deficits between the region and the metropolitan north, the centers of empire.* The export of commodities from the region to the metropolitan north has been the locus of unfair trade. The large plantations or estates that were devoted to growing sugarcane and banana impoverished the region. This systematic impoverishment has continued long after colonization has been dismantled.

3) *The allotment of the largest tracts of land to mono-crop agriculture has been a locus for misrule and misgovernance in the region.* In the first place, the mass of the people has limited access to the most arable land. The percentage of the Jamaican population that continues to live in irregular communities or squatter settlements ranges from 20 percent to 30 percent. As I will argue below, the high incidence of criminal violence is related to this reality. Social dysfunctions such as deteriorating family life and public health challenges have been the antecedent causation for the intergenerational poverty that is the lived reality of the people of African descent at the base of the population.

LAND AS THE SITE OF PERPETUATING OPPRESSION

Jamaica's homicide rate varied from a high of 62 to a low of 38 per 100,000 over the last ten years. The current rate of 47 per 100,000 has held since 2015. When the homicide rate is disaggregated parish by parish (geographical locations in Jamaica), it reveals the relationship between crime and the socioeconomic circumstances. In the parish of Manchester, the homicide rate was 21 per 100,000 of the population, but in St. James the homicide rate was 145 per 100,000 of the population for the same period. The most important differences between Manchester and St. James are their settlement patterns. Landownership in the parish of Manchester, that is home to a fairly large Free Village in Maidstone,[5] is different from the land settlement pattern in the parish of St. James (which has no Free Villages). Manchester has an economy based on bauxite mining and has a number of colleges and universities that are significant employers. The parish offers citizens a higher income; this may explain its relatively low homicide rate.

St. James by contrast has an economy that was founded on mono-crop agriculture of sugarcane and banana. Later, tourism became the largest contributor to GDP for the parish of St James. Tourism and resort development typically fail to make the requisite social investment, especially in worker housing or education. Montego Bay,[6] which is the largest and oldest tourist resort town in Jamaica, is surrounded by eighteen squatter settlements.[7] More than 70 percent of citizens in the Greater Montego Bay area live in informal communities. This is despite the fact that St. James is the parish in which the first successful slave rebellion took place.[8] Land has remained in the hands of the heirs and successors of the plantation economy. St. James is also the parish of the Coral Gardens uprising.[9]

Failure to engage in land redistribution and failure to ensure land tenure for the base of the population in St. James is emblematic of the problems of inequality, a distorted sense of identity, and the lack of economic mobility. St. James has become the headquarters of lotto scamming that has swindled thousands of US senior citizens out of their money and has resulted in extraordinary violence in Jamaica. The violence and crime are directly related to the inadequacy of options available to the base of the Jamaican population for economic and social mobility. Where the redistribution of land is concerned, the hands of the political class appear to have been tied in the period since gaining political independence. And this is despite the fact that the right of private ownership is deeply entrenched in the Jamaican constitution.[10]

The lack of clarity about land tenure has tied the hands of homeowners. They cannot make permanent plans for themselves. Social development has been marked by tentativeness and incompleteness, and many see their best prospects in migrating to the metropolitan centers to the North or elsewhere. The lack of a franchise of land and the lack of tenure on land have also eroded prospects for sustainable economic and financial action because their entrepreneurial dreams are stillborn. This is the environment in the economic options available to people at the base who are of African descent, informal, irregular, or downright criminal. This is the context in which both lotto scamming and the violence it spawns have thrived. This is the social context that has given rise to inner-city violence and gang culture.

Airport Opening in St. Vincent

On February 14, 2017, St. Vincent and the Grenadines (SVG) opened for the first time the Argyle International Airport (AIA). At a cost of EC $700M, it is the largest capital project ever undertaken in the history of SVG. The

Argyle International Airport boasts a nine-thousand foot runway that can accommodate 747 jet airlines and for the first time in its history has created a fully functional and modern international gateway that opens SVG to the world. It simultaneously provides a platform for the economic and social development of SVG. The government anticipates that it will be a spring-board to double the population and exponentially expand the GDP of SVG, because at last there is direct international access to SVG.

The search for a solution to the need for air access to SVG began in 1946. Studies concluded that all the identified sites were unfeasible in economic and financing terms or were engineering nightmares. The previous airport could only accommodate LIAT aircraft and those of that size, and the gate-ways to the international market were through Trinidad and Barbados. But now, the AIA has given SVG direct access for its tourism and agricultural produce to the international markets.

The airport project on this 130-square-mile volcanic island required the lowering of three mountains, the lifting of four valleys, and the spanning of two rivers. This provided 140,000 square feet for terminal space with the expectation of processing 1.5 million passengers annually; the airport has five gates and two terminals and is equipped with two jet bridges.

In addition to the significance for the people of SVG, the opening of the AIA is rich with geopolitical and regional significance. Prime Minister Ralph Gonsalves claimed that the airport "is a metaphor of the fact that what the minds can conceive, the hands can achieve." Gonsalves is one of the last remaining socialists in the region. This project and his political longevity make him one of the most successful socialist politicians in this region. The project was a partnership among socialist friends like Taiwan, Cuba, Vene-zuela, and the Manning administration in Trinidad and Tobago, and the air-port is modeled after the Piarco International airport in Trinidad. Thirty years earlier, the people of Grenada received an airport as a gift, constructed by the Cuban government of Fidel Castro. That project resulted in a violent coup and the assassination of prime minister Maurice Bishop, and precipitated the US invasion of Grenada. In a different geopolitical environment, with the end of the Cold War, SVG was able to design, finance, and complete the project in a sea of love. Conspicuous by their absence was any mention of the North Atlantic emissaries (esp. USA, EU, UR, Canada). Instead, there were the usual villains: Cuba (two hundred Cuban engineers and technicians worked on the project), Venezuela, Iran, Turkey, Austria, Georgia, and Libya among others contributed to the AIA project.

The project also has rich regional significance beyond the ease of access to SVG and a chance for a nation-state to come into its own. There is a testament to the struggle for self-determination in the choice of Argyle as the site. Argyle was part of the four thousand acres that the king declared British ownership of for a sugar estate in SVG. In response supreme chief of the

Garifuna people and national hero of SVG, Joseph Chatoyer, in 1763 inquired, *Quel Roi?* ("What King?") and thus started the thirty years' war, which ended with the conquest of SGV by British colonial rule after the death of Chatoyer. (The Garifuna and Kalinago or Caribs of SVG had resisted for 140 years attempts by France and then England to colonize the archipelago; SGV eventually fell in 1796.) The bones of the Caribs that were interred at Argyle have been exhumed and are preserved awaiting re-interment at a museum to be built at Argyle.

Argyle was also the sugar estate from where more than one hundred Indian indentured laborers marched into Kingstown in protest against their working conditions. It has been a site of resistance and of the indomitability of the people of SVG.[11] It is therefore a site rich with symbolism that encapsulates for SVG the story of the past and their aspirations and possibilities for the future.[12]

University of the West Indies Mona

The University of the West Indies (UWI) Mona is built on the site of a former sugar plantation, the Mona Estate. The site is adjacent to August Town, which is named to commemorate emancipation from chattel slavery.[13] It was from August Town in 1921 that free native Baptist preacher and social agitator Alexander Bedward led a march on the city of Kingston to protest the conditions of social contempt to which formerly enslaved people had been subjected. The police intercepted the march at the gate of Mona Estate, and Bedward and his people were carted off to jail. Bedward was confined to a lunatic asylum, in which he died ten years later. In a show of contempt for the people the ruling elite quelled the protest with a show of police and judicial force. The Rastafari Congress describes him this way:

> Given (Bedward's) prophetic persona and self-description as one of the Book of Revelation's "two witnesses," Bedward could not help being dissatisfied. Low wages and land hunger compounded by natural catastrophes pushed many, like the younger Bedward himself, into the wider Caribbean as migrant laborers. Bedward assailed ministers and physicians as mercenaries for charging fees, and he prophesied the imminent end of the world. Jamaica's privileged class feared Bedward's heated sermons, and in 1895 the press and police framed him, accusing him of advocating insurrection. A white lawyer, Philip Stern (d. 1933) defended him. Bedward was acquitted by reason of insanity and committed to an asylum. Released on a technicality, he continued his ministry.[14]

In the 1940s and 1950s, without any relationship to August Town or to Alexander Bedward, the University of the West Indies Mona Campus was developed on the site of the erstwhile Mona Estate.

The juxtaposition of Bedwards lands (a cooperative experiment pursued by Alexander Bedward that was denied success because the governor and the ruling elite did everything they could to frustrate Bewards' efforts) and the university project at Mona is more than an accident of history. They represent both the people's action to assuage their land hunger and the government's use of land in the national interest. In political terms, Bedward failed and has been discredited, demonized, and dismissed by the public transcript. His focus on the welfare of the ordinary Jamaicans that were excluded from mainstream economic activity provided paradigms that have been developed to good effect in Jamaica since.

UWI Mona on the other hand was a more thoughtful and deliberate action by the state to provide the human resource development that the Caribbean needed to make its way in the modern world. The project has succeeded overwhelmingly and provides a future for nearly twenty-five thousand persons annually, including students, staff, and service providers. Its impact in terms of the generation of new ideas, knowledge, training, models, and paradigms for development for Jamaica and the region cannot be overstated.[15]

Empire used the land to serve its needs without regard for the people. The people resisted the imposition of the empire by various improvisations. When there is neglect of the people's need and social exclusion is perpetrated, there is a rise of social dysfunction including violence and crime. If social investment does not include changing the way land is utilized and increasing access to land for the people at the base of the society, the viability of the nation-state is at risk.

POLICY PRIORITIES

The connections outlined above are not those that public policy makes. Public policy is determined by the interests it serves and protects. In that respect, faith communities have the opportunity to fill the void and indicate their faith in reuniting Adam and Adamah not only as the mandate of creation but as a matter arising for the project of salvation, liberation, and redemption. Faith communities need therefore to take positions of activism that are intentional in respect to redressing the land issues. In the context of Jamaica and the Caribbean, those issues have entrenched patterns of inequality and marginality for the people at the base of the population and contributed to the lack of rootedness in and connectedness with the land of their birth. It is important for churches to articulate policy options to be placed in the public domain and to guide public policy discussion. This will build upon their own history in the postemancipation period of organizing Free Villages and so enfranchise landless former enslaved populations. The church can champion the following policy initiatives to settle outstanding issues where land is concerned and can offer its own resources to play leading roles along these lines.

Rural development and agricultural development should be a primary response to the existing situation. Rural development in a comprehensive manner will include agricultural development. The impact may include sound husbandry practices that prevent erosion of the hillsides. This could be a force of mitigation against emerging ecological problems. Most notably, flooding in the plains is exacerbated by desiltification. Rural development should be intentional and seek to curb the urban drift as well as curb the creeping urbanization. Because of the efficiency of Jamaica's road network and the smallness of Caribbean territories on the whole, the development of rural towns can be achieved while providing optimum access to public goods in urban towns and cities. Rural development that is both economic and social development needs to be pursued, mindful of the legacies of marginalization, inequality, and landlessness.

Rebalance the economic opportunities available to the mass. Both the projects in SVG and the UWI Mona project provide a template for the kind of economic and social expenditure that can catalyze national development while increasing the options for economic and social mobility of the people at the base of the population. Investments in creating universities and colleges located on underutilized lands in rural areas represent promising opportunities. This can stimulate commerce and strengthen rural agriculture, as well as systematically strengthen the development of the professional classes, while creating new knowledge.

Pursue land lease/acquisition schemes combined with a shelter strategy. Jamaica has successfully utilized a social security approach to the provision of shelter over the last four decades. The project of the National Housing Trust (NHT) has been distorted in recent years, made to function merely as a mortgage bank. The NHT Act needs to be tweaked in order to accommodate social housing and to provide on a basis of direct subsidy for housing for the unemployed and disabled. Similar approaches need to be taken toward providing agricultural credit facilities. The government will need to tilt programs to ensure that persons who have occupied lands for generations can be given tenure.

CONCLUSION

This discussion recognizes that an inherited disadvantage of landlessness has remained unaddressed, and it proposes that in these unorganized communities, a systematic land-titling project should be undertaken by the state. It also suggests that the state should aim for some catalytic national development project that can change the narrative of development for the populations excluded from mainstream economic activities. Over time this will lead toward a more just and equal social environment and help the society to leap toward a space for human flourishing.

The residues of past empires remain in many places where entrenched patterns of inequity and landlessness have facilitated social dysfunction and violence. Montego Bay, St. James, Jamaica, is an example of the ways in which the matters arising from empires past have not been addressed. Eighteen squatter settlements around Montego Bay are the legacy of the colonial past and the failure of political independence to go far enough; these are also the places in which the homicide rates are highest in the country. This is a cry for help and is a demand for public policy to take steps in the direction of greater equity.

This essay has offered examples from the distant and recent past of public policy initiatives that have sought successfully to use land as a site of development and catalyst to change the game in the nation-state. Such initiatives have begun with the legacy and the existing situation as their point of departure. Public policy acknowledges that the greatest resources of a nation-state are first its people and then its land. The situation in Jamaica and the Caribbean, insofar as the project of political independence and national development is concerned, has reached the apex without addressing comprehensive land reform. Land reform is the next frontier to mitigate the impact of empire.

NOTES

1. Mitri Raheb, *Faith in the Face of Empire: The Bible through Palestinian Eyes* (Maryknoll, NY: Orbis, 2014), 43.

2. Most recent estimates by public officials, including Jamaica's leader of opposition at his debut political conference, indicate that 700,000 Jamaicans live in squatter settlements. This is approximately 25 percent of the population.

3. Lessons abound about the ways in which empire still factors and figures in the region. The 2017 hurricane season saw two category 5s (sustained winds greater than 160 mph) come ashore. Several Caribbean islands were directly impacted by these hurricanes, including Antigua and Barbuda (independent and CARICOM member state), St. Martin (Dutch and French territories), St. Bartelemy (French territory), Anguilla (British territory), St. Thomas and St. John (US Virgin Islands,) the Dominican Republic (independent CARICOM member state), Haiti (CARICOM member state), and Cuba (CARICOM observer). Even in a disaster the residual effect of empire is determinative of how solutions are pursued and resources are allocated.

4. See further Richard. A. Horsley (ed.), *In the Shadow of Empire: Reclaiming the Bible as a History of Faithful Resistance* (Louisville, KY: Westminster John Knox Press, 2008).

5. Free villages were one of the responses made to chattel slavery within Christian congregations by acquiring large parcels of lands, subdividing and selling them to the former enslaved. The Baptist movement established many Free Villages, with Sligo Ville being the first and most substantial. The Moravian Church also established Free Villages, with Maidstone in Manchester being its largest.

6. Montego Bay is the capital city and main commercial center in the parish of St. James.

7. Squatter settlements are informal communities in which there is lack of planning coupled with inadequate public utilities and road infrastructure due to the absence of land tenure.

8. The Sam Sharp Rebellion took place after a work stoppage on December 27, 1831, and resulted in the burning of 250 estates in the Great River Valley. It began in Southern St. James and spread to Trelawny, Hanover, and Westmoreland.

9. In April 1963 on Good Friday (dubbed Bad Friday by Rastafari) the police took action to kill a Rastafarian man who was farming on his own one and one-half acre of land adjacent to the one thousand acres, on the suggestion that he was trespassing. The prime minister at the time, Sir Alexander Bustamante, ordered all Rastafari to be taken in dead or alive by the police. This resulted in the brutalization, persecution, and unjust detention of more than three hundred Rastafari men and women. See further William Watty, *From Shore to Shore: Sounding in Caribbean Theology* (Kingston, Jamaica: s.p., 1981).

10. See Garnett Roper, *Caribbean Theology as Public Theology* (Kingston, Jamaica: XPRESS LITHO, 2012), 66–69.

11. Cf. Burchell Taylor, *Saying No to Babylon: A Reading of Daniel* (Kingston, Jamaica: XPRESS LITHO, 2006).

12. PM Gonsalves insisted in his address at the opening that the name Argyle should be kept in perpetuity. A woman in the audience responded, "we love you back, but it will be kept as long as you live, but when you are gone we are going to name it the Ralph Gonsalves International Airport."

13. Chattel Slavery of the African people ended on August 1, 1838, in Jamaica.

14. http://www.darcfoundation.org/alexander-bedward.html (accessed May 4, 2017). Bedward had approximately 125 congregations in Jamaica, Cuba, and Central America. Many members were poor, but others earned a good living as dray-cart operators or contractors, and one owned an ice-cream parlor. Bedwardites in August Town worked for neighboring plantations, farmed, and sold firewood, Hope River water, or home-processed foods. Bedward settled labor disputes when they arose. In April 1921 Bedward rebuffed an armed police attempt to evict him from his home, flouted a ban on marching, and led a procession "to show the people of Kingston how strong I was." An armed force surrounded the procession and arrested Bedward and several hundred supporters. Released by the judge, Bedward was rearrested, declared insane, and again committed to a lunatic asylum, where he died in 1930. Under the leadership of George Burke (1873–1939), Bedward's son-in-law, the sect declined.

15. A. A. Brooks, *History of Bedwardism or The Jamaica Native Baptist Free Church, Union Camp August Town, St. Andrew* (Kingston, Jamaica: The Gleaner Co. Ltd., 1917); Veront Satchell, "Jamaica," Africana.com, 1999.

Chapter Nine

Delusions of Empire

On People and Land in Oceania

Nāsili Vaka'uta

Empires[1] are inspired by delusions that come in different shapes and forms. One, for instance, is the delusion (or nostalgia) about a past that never was; another is the delusion of a world that is not rooted in reality.[2] Delusions are, in most cases, activated by misremembering and fantasies.[3] In themselves, delusions are harmless. But when allied with power, delusions (like ignorance) become, to use the words of the American social critic James Baldwin, "the most ferocious enemy justice can have."[4]

Imperial delusions inspired the most violent forms of injustice pertaining to people and land in colonized contexts. Colonized people have been victims of racism (such as suffered by black and colored Africans under the apartheid leadership in South Africa), religious intolerance and violence (like minority religious groups in Asia and the Middle East), and ethnic cleansing and cultural deracination (as with Muslims in the Balkans), because imperialism operated upon the misbelief that some people with certain skin color, belief, ethnicity, and culture, to name a few, are inferior and less human. They therefore do not deserve to own land, to have access to resources, to be free, and/or to have the right of self-determination.

This essay puts a spotlight on various forms of imperial delusions with particular reference to their impact on the people and land in Oceania. Structured into five parts, each part focuses on a particular form of delusion and its impact on people in their own land. I will elucidate each part in general terms with the aim of initiating further discussion on the subject.[5]

EMPTY(ING) OCEANIA

In imperial discourses, the doctrine of *terra nullius* epitomizes the colonial approach to land, especially foreign lands. The term *terra nullius* refers to "land that belongs to nobody" or "empty land."[6] Starting in the seventeenth century, *terra nullius* denoted a legal concept allowing European colonial powers to take control of supposedly "empty" territories that none of the other European colonial powers had claimed. Of course, most of these "empty" territories were inhabited, so the meaning of *terra nullius* grew to include territories considered "devoid of civilized society."[7]

In 1770, Captain James Cook landed in Botany Bay, home of the Eora people, and claimed possession of the East Coast of Australia for Britain under the doctrine of *terra nullius*.[8] According to the international law of Europe in the late eighteenth century, there were three ways that Britain could take possession of another country:

- If the country was uninhabited, Britain could claim and settle that country. In this case, Britain could claim ownership of the (empty) land.
- If the country was already inhabited, Britain could ask for permission from the indigenous people to use some of their land. In this case, Britain could purchase a piece of the land for its own use but it could not steal the land of the indigenous people.
- If the country was inhabited, Britain could take over the country by invasion and conquest. In this case, Britain could defeat that country in war. However, even after winning a war, Britain would have to respect the rights of the indigenous people.[9]

History tells us that Britain rarely observed these conditions. Māori land in Aotearoa New Zealand was affected by this doctrine.[10] In fact, Oceania as a region was, and still is, regarded and treated as empty. This idea sprang forth when explorers failed to discover their imperial fantasy of a great South Sea continent. In his article "Earth's Empty Quarter? The Pacific Islands in a Pacific Century," R. Gerard Ward brings to the fore the European view of Oceania. Oceania, according to Ward, has always seemed empty to European explorers like Vespucci Balboa and Ferdinand Magellan. Even Captain James Cook subscribed to the idea of emptiness during his voyages to the South Seas.[11]

The idea of emptiness proved to be more than just a perception. It affected the indigenous peoples of the region in many ways. In Australia and Aotearoa New Zealand, the concept of *terra nullius* had a disastrous effect.[12] Because the natives "neither practiced agriculture, nor, it was thought, lived in permanent settlements, the land was deemed under laws to be uninhabited. The natives could not own the land on which they lived. Thus, there was no impediment for Europeans to take the land, which was seen, in legal terms, as empty."[13]

The islands in Oceania did not escape the impact of this imperial myth, which spread the delusion that the land was empty and consequently the people were invisible.[14] At the moment of European excursion, many islands were assumed to be empty and therefore became the property of colonial states, for example, Hawai'i, Tutuila (American Samoa), and many Micronesian islands under administration of the USA; Kanaky, and Ma'ohi Nui under French rule; and West Papua, still under the violent rule of Indonesia. For the Australian Aboriginal peoples, New Zealand Maoris, and Pacific islander natives, the consequences of this *legal invisibility* remain.[15]

In the 1940s, recounted Ward, "someone else's war was fought through Oceania, the so-called 'Pacific War'. Island location was of great significance to the combatants—the interests of the islanders were not."[16] Islanders were again *invisible*, because the islands were both considered empty and treated as mere stepping-stones in a "standing" against another people and land.

In the 1950s, the perception of emptiness attracted the attention of imperial states as sites for nuclear tests. In response to this, Ward asked a rhetorical question: Where better to test nukes but in empty islands? In 1954, the Bravo hydrogen bomb was tested at Bikini atoll.[17] The people of Rongelap and nearby islands were blanketed by radioactive dust; the children played in the toxic dust, and they have suffered since then. The delusion of emptiness also served as a justification for using the islands of Oceania for the storage of hazardous waste, as in the leaking "dome" (which the natives call "tomb") that stores US nuclear wastes on Enewetak (Marshall Islands).

The 1980s came with its challenge. Islands like Easter Island (Rapa Nui), because of their remoteness, were used as an emergency landing site for US space shuttles. Viewing Oceania as empty persisted up to the twenty-first century but with a renewed sense of *usefulness*. The region has the world's greatest flow of container traffic. Fishing boats from Asia and other parts of the world roam around the region. About 60 percent of jumbo jets cross over Oceania.[18] Despite the usefulness of the region for outsiders, Oceania is still regarded as a *doughnut*. Everything that matters is on *the rim* (America, Asia, Europe). The middle, where islanders reside, is a *hole*. It is an empty quarter—a space to be crossed.

To Oceanic islanders, Oceania is home. Islands may be 500 km or more from each other, but they are neighbors. Oceania is not empty! Oceania is filled with a sea of islands, spread over a world of water. The idea of emptiness is an imperial delusion, and it exposes the limits of imperial knowledge and the failure of imperial cartographers to account for the gaps and blank spaces on their maps.

DEHUMANIZING OCEANIANS

If Oceania was viewed as empty and belonging to no one, its people were perceived to be absent and less human than their colonial counterparts. Here, I highlight two imperial inventions: "the native (mind)" and the "colonial mind." Stewart Firth, an Australian historian and expert on Pacific history, recounts the colonial attitude to the natives:

> The colonizers' most significant ideological achievement was the invention of the Native, a category embracing all non-Europeans. The Native—singular and masculine—lacked European virtues such as application and foresight. His mind—the Native Mind—worked in mysterious ways.
>
> [. . .] the natives have no expressions for ideas quite unknown to them, such as gratitude, chastity, modesty, humility.[19]

An example of the colonial attitude could be heard in a remark by an Australian woman at a dinner party, with particular reference to Māori, the natives of New Zealand: "Don't you think that the natives [Māori] are just like human beings?"[20] In her mind, Māori natives are *like*, but not fully, human. In a similar frame of mind, a governor of New Guinea in 1919 held this view of the native in defense of corporal punishment:

> The Native is a primitive being, with no well developed sense of duty or responsibility. A full belly and comfortable bed are his two chief desiderata. The native frequently mistakes kindness for weakness. With a native as with an animal—correction must be of deterrent nature.[21]

The portrayal of Oceanic natives did not only come from Europeans.[22] Other imperial powers also played a role. Japanese regarded the Micronesians as a third-class people (under Koreans and Okinawans):

> Micronesians [. . .] had no "concept of progress" and "no sense of industry or diligence. Theirs is a life of dissipation: eating, dancing, and carnal pleasure absorb their waking hours. For these reasons, they have not escaped the common traits of tropic peoples: lewd customs, barbarity, laziness and debauchery.[23]

The depictions of the natives noted above were not mere colonial discourses. On many occasions, the natives became *victims of the words*. In William Howitt's work *Colonization and Christianity*, colonial brutal acts against the natives are documented:

> In these colonies [referring to the Pacific islands], no idea of any right of the natives to the soil, or any consideration of their claims, comforts, or improvements, seem to have been entertained. Colonies were settled, and lands appro-

> priated, just as they were needed; and if the natives did not like it, they were shot at.[24]

A bishop in Sydney speaks of the colonial impact on Australian natives in these words: "They [the natives] are in a state which I consider one of extreme degradation and ignorance; they are, in fact, in a situation much inferior to what I suppose them to have been before they had any communication with Europe."[25]

The construction of the native and the end results of that process put the indigenous inhabitants at risk. In addition to this was the creation of the "colonial mind." This refers to the effect of colonial brainwashing of natives to disregard their own cultures, values, and beliefs, on the one hand, and to internalize colonial values, language, lifestyle, and religion, on the other hand. As a result, natives preferred Western lifestyles over traditional ones, Western cultures over the local, Western religion over indigenous religions, Western values over indigenous values. This program of mental colonization left a psychological mark on the mind of Pacific islanders, which was self-contradictory and self-annihilating. The prevalence of such mentality in Oceanic society hindered any attempt to create a more liberating alternative.

CLONING EMPIRE

Psychological colonization was part of a larger imperial project known within postcolonial circles as "colonial cloning" or "colonial translation." In his *A Very Short Introduction to Postcolonialism,* Robert C. Young sheds some light on this process:

> A colony begins as a translation, a copy of the original located elsewhere on the map. [. . .] No act of translation takes place in an entirely neutral space of absolute equality. Someone is translating something or someone. Someone or something is being translated, transformed from a subject to an object.[26]

This process, according to Young, is "a metaphorical displacement" of realities; the engineering of a "creative lie" whereby colonizers (irreversibly) transformed the geographical, cultural, political, educational, linguistic, religious, ecological, and economic landscapes of many countries and peoples.

In Oceania, regional and national boundaries were redrawn, and new borders created. Samoa was split into Western (islands of Upolu and Savai'i) and American (island of Tutuila) Samoas, each controlled by different empires. Bougainville, which is ethnically a part of the Solomon Islands, came under the control of Papua New Guinea. These new borders created political tensions, and people were geographically and ethnically displaced and even murdered. West Papua, in particular, was fenced off from Papua New Guinea and taken by Indonesia. That created the only land border in the region and led to an ongoing genocide that is largely ignored by the global community.

In most islands, colonial authorities schemed with the most prominent local figures in order to establish a foothold in the decision-making process. New political flavors were introduced and these functioned not to transform but to strengthen the traditional political setup. The best example is the cloning of the Tongan traditional hierarchy into a colonial version of the British monarchy. This political influence brought a concept alien to Tongan culture, a text in the form of a constitution, which proclaimed, on paper, the emancipation of "commoners," on the one hand, but gave more power to chiefs, on the other hand.

Running alongside this political influence was the introduction of a new belief system in the form of Christianity that brought with it its own worldview and social values, based on another "text," the Bible. This strange "text" functioned as the foundational guide for religion and society as the constitution was for politics. Together these two foreign written texts took over the place and assumed the authority of the traditional Tongan cultural "texts" that had shaped the lives of Tongans for millennia. This involved the suppression of many Tongan cultural practices (dances and rituals, for example) and did very little to transform the situation on the ground.[27]

EROTICS OF EMPIRE

Another form of imperial delusion entertains the feminization of lands and sexualization of foreign people.[28] This phenomenon is known as *the porno-tropics of the imperial imagination.*[29] Anne McClintock, in her book *Imperial Leather: Race, Gender and Sexuality in Colonial Test*, coined "porno-tropics" to explain the European tendency to *sexualize* foreign (non-European) women as "a fantastic magic lantern of the mind onto which Europe projected its forbidden sexual desires and fears."[30]

McClintock also speaks of a porno-tropic tradition that goes back to European explorers such as Christopher Columbus. In 1492, Columbus feminized the earth as a cosmic breast to which the epic male hero is a tiny, lost infant, yearning for the Edenic nipple. That image, according to McClintock, is invested with an uneasy sense of male anxiety, infantilization, and longing for the female body. The hallmarks of the porno-tropic tradition are its obsession with *feminization* of foreign lands (*terra incognita*) and *sexualization* of foreign people (as women).

Embedded in these two entwining processes are the following. First, foreign lands are viewed to be *spatially spread for male exploration*, then reassembled and deployed in the interests of imperial power.[31] Feminizing *terra incognita* is an imperial strategy of violent containment.

Second, in foreign lands, *women serve as boundary markers*, and female figures are *situated like fetishes at the ambiguous points of contact.*[32] At the contact zone, on the border, women serve as mediating figures by means of which men orient themselves in space, as agents of power and agents of knowledge.

Third, in patriarchal narratives, to be a virgin is to be empty of desire and void of sexual agency, passively awaiting the thrusting male organ (of its own pleasure and insemination).[33] In imperial narratives, the eroticizing of virgin or empty spaces effects territorial appropriation, for if the land is virgin/empty, colonized peoples cannot claim aboriginal territorial rights, and white patrimony is violently assured.

Fourth, the colonial intrusion into virgin/empty lands reveals a contradiction. On the one hand, it is assumed that in "empty lands" indigenous peoples were not supposed to be there. On the other hand, the colonials faced the dilemma that the empty lands are already peopled and inhabited.[34] In this case, the colonial dream of discovery is delusional; there is nothing to discover. Something or someone has always gone before. Simply put, there is no empty/virgin land.

Fifth, in naming the so-called "new" lands, imperial powers mark those lands as their own, in the embarrassing absence of other guarantees. The imperial act of discovery is likened by McClintock to the male act of baptism.[35] In both cases, men publicly disavow the creative agency of others (the colonized and the women) and arrogate to themselves the power of origins.

Sixth, discovery has no existence, McClintock argues. Discovery exists only in a text, referring to a name on a map, a diary, a lecture, or a travel book. In the act of discovery, imperial men reinvent a moment of pure (male) origin and mark it visibly with fetishes like flags, maps, stones, or a monument.[36]

Seventh, when colonial powers realize that lands are not empty after all, they resort to what I call "empty(ing) (is)lands." This process is activated through the abovementioned process of colonial cloning, but at times "empty(ing) (is)lands" is expressed violently in the form of religious terrorism, cultural annihilation, and/or ethnic cleansing. Perceiving the land as empty leads to a violent attempt to empty the land of its inhabitants.

BAPTIZING EMPIRE

Imperial delusions are not merely political. They are deeply rooted in religious dogma and ideas. In this part, I comment briefly on the collusion between empires and Christianity, a link so strong and violent that it has left permanent scars on both peoples and lands in different parts of the world.

I borrow the phrase "Baptizing Empire" from a recent publication by Wes Howard-Brook entitled *Empire Baptized: How the Church Embraced What Jesus Rejected, 2nd–5th Centuries*. Howard-Brook argues that there are two competing religious visions in the Bible and Christianity. The first vision is "religion of creation" that was embraced by the prophets and Jesus; this is Gospel-based Christianity. The second vision is "religion of empire" which was shaped and promoted by the Roman empire since Constantine (better known as "Constantinian Christianity"); this is the religious vision Christianity embraced, especially Catholic Christianity. Table 9.1 compares the two visions.[37]

These two visions offer a clear view of the kind of religion Christianity has been promoting through the centuries. Whereas the "religion of creation" advocates what Jesus and his early followers lived and died for, the "religion of empire" endorses a brand of Christianity that belongs to a violent past that is disturbing. I am referring specifically in this case to the three papal bulls (an official document or proclamation issued by the pope) from the fifteenth century that authorized European imperialism and colonial expansion.[38]

The first papal bull, *Dum Diversas*, was issued on June 18, 1452 by Pope Nicholas V to Alfonso V of Portugal, instructing the king to reduce any "Saracens (Muslims) and pagans and any other unbelievers" to perpetual slavery. This bull facilitated the Portuguese slave trade from West Africa.

The second papal bull, *Romanus Pontifex*, again written by Pope Nicholas V to Alfonso V as a sequel to *Dum Diversas*, emerged on January 5, 1455.

Table 9.1.

Religion of creation (based on the Gospel)	**Religion of empire (based on Constantinian empire)**
Experience God in relation with creation	Experience God in church buildings and in rituals (sacraments)
Salvation brings people together (on earth) as Body of Christ	Individuals reach salvation after death
Belief in God involves the whole (physical) person	Belief is an intellectual exercise (assent to statements and creeds)
Conversion involves renouncing wealth and status	Conversion involves renouncing sexual desire
Community is open	Community is defined by orthodox rules
Accept women as equals	Reject women (because they tempt men)
Fellowship is egalitarian	Church structures are hierarchical
Reject the patronage system (a loyal patron receives blessing from above)	Church affirms the patronage system
Engage differences in views	Exclude and demonize differences

This bull extended to the Catholic nations of Europe dominion over discovered lands during the age of discovery. Along with sanctifying the seizure of non-Christian lands, it encouraged the enslavement of native, non-Christian peoples in Africa and the New World.

The third papal bull was issued on May 3, 1493, by Pope Alexander VI under the title *Inter Caetera*, "granting" to Spain—at the request of Ferdinand and Isabella—the right to conquer the lands which Columbus had already found, as well as any lands which Spain might "discover" in the future. Pope Alexander VI also stated his desire that the "discovered" people be "subjugated and brought to the faith itself." By this means, according to the pope, the "Christian Empire" would be propagated.

When Portugal protested this concession to Spain, Pope Alexander stipulated in a subsequent bull (issued May 4, 1493) that Spain must not attempt to establish its dominion over lands which had already come into the possession of any Christian lords. Then, to placate the two rival monarchs, the pope drew a line of demarcation between the two poles, giving Spain rights of conquest and dominion over one side of the globe, and Portugal over the other.

Together, these papal bulls serve as the basis and justification for the doctrine of discovery, the global slave trade of the fifteenth and sixteenth centuries, and the age of imperialism. Empire was "baptized" by Christianity, and Christianity in many occasions served as the "running dog of imperialism."[39] The ripple effect of this collusion between Christianity and empires reached far and wide, including Oceania.

IN CLOSING

In closing, I pose two questions: How might we practice mission in contexts that are submitted under imperial delusions? How might we do theology and interpret scriptures so that we avoid subscribing to the delusions of empire? I propose three general suggestions. First, mission activities need to shift from the outdated preoccupation with *conversion* to the more noble task of *transformation*. Second, doing theology must rise above the mere goal of "faith seeking understanding" (Anselm) to the higher call of "faith seeking justice." Third, and finally, biblical interpretation, especially in churches, must acknowledge the situatedness of the task, respect contextual differences, appreciate the plurality of voices and meanings, and read with subjects on the margins of texts and society, particularly with people whose lands have been violently grabbed and occupied because of Christianity's subscription to the delusions of empire.

NOTES

1. "Empire" is defined by the *Merriam-Webster Dictionary* as "a major political unit having a territory of great extent or a number of territories or peoples under a single sovereign authority" or "something resembling a political empire; *especially*: an extensive territory or enterprise under single domination or control." In either form, empire involves "imperial sovereignty, rule, or dominion" (https://www.merriam-webster.com/dictionary/empire, accessed May 25, 2017). See also Robert C. Young, *Empire, Colony, Postcolony* (Chichester, UK: Wiley Blackwell, 2015) and Yale H. Ferguson, "Approaches to Defining 'Empire' and Characterizing United States Influence in the Contemporary World," *International Studies Perspectives* 9 (2008): 272–80.

2. The word "delusion" is broadly understood hereinafter as an idiosyncratic belief, doctrine, or ideology that is invented, maintained, and/or propagated despite being contradicted by reality or rational argument. In psychiatry, delusions are typical symptoms of mental disorder. In that sense, imperial delusion could be defined as imperial disorder. For more information on "delusion" refer to Vaughn Bell, Peter W. Halligan, and Hadyn D. Ellis, "Explaining Delusions: A Cognitive Perspective," *TRENDS in Cognitive Sciences* 10.5 (May 2006): 219–26; and on the political delusion see Eric Hobsbawm, "America's Imperial Delusion: The US Drive for World Domination Has No Historical Precedent," *The Guardian* (June 14, 2003).

3. This is aptly described in an opinion column in *The Guardian* responding to Brexit and the notion of Empire 2.0: "This newfound focus on the Commonwealth feels uncomfortably akin to recent divorcees looking up their former partners on Facebook; and being shocked to discover that they have got married, had kids and moved on. They might have fond memories, they might even want to be on good terms, but don't really miss us. Former colonies, like old flames, build new relationships, based on their own needs and ambitions" (https://www.theguardian.com/commentisfree/2017/mar/19/empire-20-is-dangerous-nostalgia-for-something-that-never-existed; accessed March 2017).

4. James Baldwin, *No Name in the Street* (New York: Vintage Books, 1972), 149.

5. I am here inviting what we call "talanoa" in Oceania. See Nāsili Vaka'uta (ed.), *Talanoa Rhythms: Voices from Oceania* (Albany, New Zealand: Massey University, 2011).

6. Adrian Howkins, "Appropriating Space: Antarctic Imperialism and the Mentality of Settler Colonialism," in *Making Settler Colonial Space: Perspectives on Race, Place and Identity* (Basingstoke, UK: Palgrave Macmillan, 2010), 29; see also Blake A. Watson, "The Impact of the American Doctrine of Discovery on Native Land Rights in Australia, Canada, and New Zealand," *Seattle University Law Review* 34 (2011): 507–51.

7. "Terra Nullius," http://homepages.gac.edu/~lwren/AmericanIdentititesArt%20folder/AmericanIdentititesArt/Terra%20Nullius.html.

8. Paul Carter, *The Road to Botany Bay: An Essay in Spatial History* (London & Boston: Faber & Faber, 1987.

9. "The Myth of Terra Nullius," http://treatyrepublic.net/content/terra-nullius-0.

10. See Judith E. McKinlay, *Troubling Women and Land: Reading Biblical Texts in Aotearoa New Zealand* (Sheffield, UK: Sheffield Phoenix Press, 2014); Stuart Banner, *Possessing the Pacific: Land, Settlers, and Indigenous People from Australia to Alaska* (Cambridge, MA: Harvard University Press Banner, 2007), 47–83.

11. Gerard Ward, "Earth's Empty Quarter? The Pacific Islands in a Pacific Century," *The Geographical Journal* 155.2 (1989): 235.

12. Banner, *Possessing the Pacific*, 13–46.

13. Ward, "Earth's Empty Quarter?," 237.

14. Cf. Banner, *Possessing the Pacific*; Judy Rohrer, *Staking the Claim: Settler Colonialism and Racialization in Hawai'i* (Tucson, AZ: The University of Arizona Press, 2016); Francis X. Hezel, *Strangers in Their Own Land: A Century of Colonial Rule in the Caroline and Marshall Islands* (Honolulu, HI: University of Hawaii Press, 1995).

15. Ward, "Earth's Empty Quarter?," 237.

16. Ward, "Earth's Empty Quarter?," 237.

17. See Jeffrey Sasha Davis, "Representing Place: 'Deserted Isles' and the Reproduction of Bikini Atoll," *Annals of the Association of American Geographers* 95.3 (2005): 607–25.

18. Ward, "Earth's Empty Quarter?," 241.

19. Stewart Firth, "Colonial Administration and the Invention of the Native," in *The Cambridge History of the Pacific Islanders*, ed. Donald Denoon et al. (Cambridge, UK: Cambridge University Press, 1997), 262.

20. Firth, "Colonial Administration and the Invention of the Native."

21. Firth, "Colonial Administration and the Invention of the Native," 263.

22. The native became a homogenized category for all non-Europeans. Indonesian natives were once described as "insensitive to ethics: he represents not only the absence of values but also the negation of values. He is, let us dare to admit, the enemy of values, and in this sense, he is the absolute evil" (Christopher R. Duncan, "Savage Imagery: (Mis)representations of the Forest Tobelo of Indonesia," *The Asia Pacific Journal of Anthropology* 2:1 [2001]), 45.

23. Firth, "Colonial Administration and the Invention of the Native," 263.

24. William Howitt, *Colonization and Christianity: A Popular History of the Treatment of the Natives by the Europeans in All Their Colonies* (London: Longman, Orme, Brown, Green, & Longmans, 1838), 471.

25. Cited in Howitt, *Colonization and Christianity*, 476.

26. Robert C. Young, *Postcolonialism: A Very Short Introduction* (Oxford: Oxford University Press, 2003), 139, 140.

27. Nāsili Vaka'uta, *Reading Ezra 9–10 Tu'a-wise: Rethinking Biblical Interpretation in Oceania* (Atlanta, GA: SBL, 2011).

28. Cf. Nāsili Vaka'uta, "Border Crossing/Body Whoring: Rereading Rahab of Jericho with Native Women," in *Bible, Borders, Belonging: Engaging Readings from Oceania*, ed. Jione Havea, David Neville, and Elaine Wainwright (Atlanta: Society of Biblical Literature, 2014), 143–55.

29. Anne McClintock, "Paranoid Empire: Specters from Guantánamo and Abu Ghraib," *Small Axe* 28 (March 2009): 50–74; Anne McClintock, "The Scandal of the Whorearchy: Prostitution in Colonial Nairobi," *Transition* 52 (1991): 92–99; Daniel Thomas Rothwell Falkiner, "The Erotics of Empire: Love, Power, and Tragedy in Thucydides and Hans Morgenthau," (PhD diss., The London School of Economics and Political Science, 2015); Patricia Grimshaw and Elizabeth Nelson, "Empire, 'the Civilising Mission' and Indigenous Christian Women in Colonial Victoria," *Australian Feminist Studies* 16.36 (2001): 296–308; Greg Thomas, *The Sexual Demon of Colonial Power* (Bloomington, IN: Indiana University Press, 2007).

30. Anne McClintock, *Imperial Leather: Race, Gender and Sexuality in Colonial Contest* (London: Routledge, 1995), 22.

31. Anne McClintock, *Imperial Leather*, 23.

32. Anne McClintock, *Imperial Leather*, 24.

33. Anne McClintock, *Imperial Leather*, 30.

34. Anne McClintock, *Imperial Leather*, 36.

35. Anne McClintock, *Imperial Leather*, 29.

36. Anne McClintock, *Imperial Leather*, 30.

37. This chart is adapted from Wes Howard-Brook, *Empire Baptized: How the Church Embraced What Jesus Rejected, 2nd–5th Centuries* (New York: Orbis, 2016), xx.

38. For more details on the papal bulls, see the working paper written by the Commission for Justice and Peace of the Canadian Conference of Catholic Bishops, "The Doctrine of Discovery, Terra Nullius, and the Catholic Church: An Historical Overview" (2016).

39. Kwok Pui Lan, "Discovering the Bible in the Non-Biblical World," in *Voices from the Margin: Interpreting the Bible from the Third World* (London: SPCK, 1991), 303.

Chapter Ten

People, Land, and Empire in Asia

Geopolitics, Theological Imaginations, and Islands of Peace

Jude Lal Fernando

Blocking the entrance to the naval base in the Gangjeong village in Jeju island, Korea, a group of Christians sings this song as the opening hymn of the Eucharistic celebration:

> You may be the smallest village in the land
> Yet peace across this land will emanate from you (x2)
> We won't forget when you break and shatter
> When you collapse and fall down, we will stand with you
> You may be the smallest village in this land
> Yet peace across this land will emanate from you.[1]

The lead singer is Mun Jeong-hyeon, a Catholic priest, who is more than eighty years old.[2] The song resonates with the hope of peace emanating from a particular land, and people's unbreakable relationship with it. Those who gather revive the memory of massacres in the Korean War.[3] For them, *breaking of bread* has become a protest against militarization and an unwavering commitment to peace.

At another setting: joining the sit-ins in front of a US military base in Henako in Okinawa islands, Japan, opposing its construction, sixty-year-old Kumiko Onaga, a city council woman, states:

> We're a tiny island, and the community and bonds are strong here. . . . Okinawa has the treasure of nature, the ocean and mountains. . . . It's the future generations who will be greatly burdened with all the damage. . . . We have to stop accepting the base as a status quo. We have been protesting every day with the belief our actions will definitely stop them. We're not fighting be-

> cause we think we might be able to block them. We know we will. I won't be beaten up until I collapse, I will keep on going. Even if I do collapse, I'll keep raising my voice. That's how strong my will is.[4]

Her words reflect people's concern for the future generation and the unbreakable commitment to free the land. Okinawans were used as a human shield by the Japanese imperialist army and massacred in thousands in the Pacific Wars. Their US "liberators" occupied their land, using it as a launching pad for wars in the Middle East and East Asia.[5]

At another island setting,[6] sitting with a group of women in front of a Sri Lankan military base in the homeland of displaced Tamils, forty-nine-year-old war widow Saraswathy Alagarasa says, "Even if we die here, our remains will be kept until our village is released for the remains to be buried there."[7] She belongs to thousands of families who voluntarily live in the de facto state of Tamil Eelam as resistance to massacres led by the Sri Lankan state for decades. She survived thousands of others who were massacred in the dismantling of Tamil Eelam during 2007–2009 and she commits to free her land from militarization.

In these words and actions of people who have been deprived of their land due to heavy militarization, one hears a deep yearning for land; their collective homeland; land as shores, paddy fields, forests, rivers, mountains, schools, places of worship, etc. There is a profound commitment to a journey even beyond death in realizing their yearning for land. How do we understand their yearning for land and its connection to peace? It is not possible to answer this question in a proper way without understanding the geopolitics associated with the islands in Asia. The main aim of this essay is to develop a theology of land and peace with the help of hermeneutical tools that capture peoples' collective experiences of massacres and landlessness and the deep yearning for land in the islands of Asia.

Traditional theology and spirituality has held for ages that one's deepest yearning is for God—"My soul thirsts for God." How would churches then understand the yearning for land? How would the churches understand peoples' strong community bonds that are inseparable from land? Denial of such yearnings as "worldly" as opposed to "spiritual," and "divisive" as opposed to "unity," affirm the geopolitics of the empire that condition lives of peoples and lands. Claiming to be nonpolitical in this context is to follow geopolitics and accept the empire as natural. The yearning for land can be understood by adopting the hermeneutical tools of land and people that help develop a theology that envisions a future beyond imperialized relationships. Such a theology has to emerge from sites of concrete resistance to the empire in Asia—rather than general notions of the empire—which is the focus of this chapter. Let us first move to the ways in which the empire is analyzed, empire as the cause of landlessness, and second, theologically reflect on the yearning for land emerging from sites of resistance to empire.

UNDERSTANDING NEOCOLONIAL EMPIRE

In a broad sense, empire is a conglomerate of political powers that are facilitated by military, economic, cultural, religious, and intellectual powers. The geographies, driving powers, and actors of empire change over time. Every empire has a peculiar brand of peace even though it is in a permanent state of war. In the post–Cold War period, there is a tendency to reduce empire to economic and cultural powers and thus ignore the empire's militaristic manifestation, as in the USA's invasion of Afghanistan and Iraq.[8] In fact, the main power that drives the USA as an empire is its military might. It is this military might that has caused large-scale massacres across the world. The three examples of landlessness noted above are associated with the military empire. Moving away from generalized economic analysis of empire, James Petras makes a distinction between the military-driven empire of the USA and the market-driven expansion of China, Europe, and other major powers:

> US empire building in the 21st century is manifested in their strategic decisions, alliances and priorities, each and everyone of which is diametrically opposed to market-based empire building. . . . While the US invests in non-productive and unsuccessful military conquests, profoundly indebting the domestic economy, China, India, Korea, Russia, Europe, the Middle East and even Latin America pile up trade surpluses while expanding their economic empires via private and sovereign investments. . . . Military-driven empire building is manifested not only in the Middle East but throughout the world. . . . While the US spends billions of dollars on endless wars, propaganda campaigns and sanctions, China reaps hundreds of millions in profits.[9]

The military empire builds itself through brute force by means of annihilation, as well as stifles resistance of people to the market-driven empire through extreme securitization of states. The latter (mainly China and EU) shares the globalist security consciousness of the former, but does not utilize and prioritize it as effectively as the former even though both represent the neocolonial empire. These nuances are important to understand the above-mentioned cases of people's yearning for land in Asia. In fact, what the people resist is the USA's military empire in Asia. In the resistance to military occupation we find a vision of peace, which is based on nonexploitative social and ecological relationships that go against market-driven empire. This vision captures glimpses of a liberated future enshrined in the collective memory of religious and ethical traditions. In that sense, resistance to militarization of land can help develop a theology that goes beyond both military-

and market-driven empires. This is why I focus on the military empire as one of the main political contexts of theologizing in Asia.

With the end of formal colonial practice, it was believed that land does not belong to empires but to the postcolonial nation-states. It is this belief that defined one of the features of national sovereignty of decolonized countries. However, the reality is far from what is believed.[10] With the end of the Cold War, a new round of militarization has gained momentum, with the USA's pivot toward Asia leading to landlessness of people in islands like Jeju, Okinawa, and Sri Lanka (mainly among the Eelam Tamils). This move is intended to contain China's growing economic influence as well as to secure the Indian Ocean and South Asia as a safe buffer zone to the Middle East. Furthermore, the inter-Korean conflict, which is part of Cold War politics, is an added justification for this new round of militarization. The yearning of the people for land has to be understood within this geopolitical context in which they live.

The physical control of land and people is not sufficient for the geopolitics of the empire; controlling hearts and minds through manufacturing of consent is pivotal to the justification of the empire. Such consent is reached through forming collective identities that would tally with neocolonial geostrategic complex and destroying other identities that would problematize the empire. Not only land but also the consciousness of people has been altered, causing *memory-cide* of massacres and *empistemi-cide* of liberating identities associated with the oppressed nations. This has been done in the name of imperial peace. Theological imagination that does not take geopolitics seriously ends up critiquing the empire only on the cultural, religious, and social levels while concealing the ways in which the states and identities of people have been constructed by the empire. That is why it is necessary to utilize the hermeneutical tools of land and people in theologizing resistance to empire in Asia.

LAND, PEOPLE, AND THEOLOGICAL IMAGINATIONS

Fundamental to Christian theology is God's covenantal relationship with people in the person of Jesus Christ. The promise of this relationship ushers in the reign of God, seen as God's mighty intervention in history, which is believed to have universal validity. We are aware how the emphasis laid on history, universality, and personhood without recognizing the historical, social, and cultural conditions of peoples can lead to decontextualization of the covenantal relationship. Such a method can lead either to individualistic spiritualism or universalistic Christian supremacy, both of which take empire as a given. Theological imaginations that have emerged from the margins of empire have been sensitive to social and cultural conditions and contributed to the formation of intercultural and interreligious, liberation, feminist,[11] queer, and ecological theologies.[12] One of the missing elements of these promising and critical reflections is the geopolitical contexts or locations that give rise to oppressor and oppressed nations. In that, some nations and states have created as part of the empire while subjugating and destroying other nationalities that resist dominance, discrimination, and oppression.

Without a geopolitical analysis it is not possible to understand the causes of mass atrocities committed against distinct national groups of people (like Eelam Tamils, Palestinians, people of Jeju and Okinawans, islanders of Diego Garcia) by various states, which are strategically connected to military empire. The context is cultural, religious, and social, as well as geopolitical. In that sense, people's yearning for land is not only economic, but also geopolitical. The yearning for land prompts us to include land and people in theological imagination that takes geopolitics seriously. The history of people is not only the history of the poor, but also the history of oppressed communities whose identities have been formed in relation to their land, which problematizes empire-building. If we take the metaphor of the reign of God to refer to fulfillment of people's yearning for land (liberation and peace), such a reign is necessarily geopolitical and challenges the ways in which states have been carved within an imperial strategic complex by an unleashing process of annihilations of distinct groups of people. For centuries Christianity has justified land grab of empire across the world while destroying collective identities of peoples. The three examples above show how some church groups in Asia enter into a process of conversion sharing people's yearning for land with a nonpossessive vision and being part of retrieving and recreating a collective consciousness as opposed to land grabbing dominant identities.[13]

Recognizing the dangers of land theology, Walter Brueggemann, in the preface to the second edition of *The Land: Place as Gift, Promise, and Challenge in Biblical Faith*, shows how the state of Israel has carved a Promised Land as part of a geostrategic imperial complex at the expense of the Palestinian people:

> It is clear on any reading that the modern state of Israel has effectively merged old traditions of land entitlement and the most vigorous military capacity thinkable for a modern state. The outcome of that merger of old traditional claim and contemporary military capacity becomes an intolerable commitment to violence that is justified by reason of state.[14]

As a means of overcoming such dangers in land theology, he proposes a radically dialectical learning which makes us realize that "grasping for home leads to homelessness and risking homelessness yields the gift of home":[15]

> It will not do, as one might be inclined to do with a theology of glory, to say that God's history is simply a story of coming to the land promised. Nor will it do, as one might be tempted in a theology of the cross, to say God's history is a story of homelessness. Either statement misses the main affirmation of the unexpected way in which land and landlessness are linked to each other.[16]

Dangers of land theology are interwoven with the ways in which states and people's national collective consciousness and identities in relation to land have been formed. As lands are carved into states as part of the empire, peoples' collective identities and the ways in which they understand themselves are also forged. States and nations are not formed in a historical vacuum. They are part of a geopolitical process. Referring to the nineteenth-century "rediscovery" of Israel Mitri Raheb shows how "Holy Land" became interesting for the European powers due to geopolitical reasons and how it became an orientalized object to be studied and controlled. The collective consciousness of the Jewish immigrants to the land (who had not shared the biblical experience of the native people of Palestine) was forged according to the image of the colonizing European masters:

> Within this context, a new momentum was building up in Europe regarding the Land of Palestine. On the one hand there was the ancient desire of the Empire to control "Holy Land" again. On the other hand, Christian Europe was struggling with the existence of non-Christians within its boundaries, in this case the Jews. Seemingly presented with two options, ghettoization or assimilation, a third alternative emerged that allowed control of Holy Land by proxy by sending European Jews there. This notion was adopted by the Zionist movement and it became a political program. For it to be successful, a myth had to be developed that the land was abandoned and was waiting for its people to come back, thus recreating an ancient bond between the two. The Jews of European origin were excellent allies: They were Europeans by culture, education and manners, and at the same time they were regarded as exotic enough to fit more in the Orient than in Europe.[17]

Within the empire the ways in which land and peoplehood/nationhood are imagined lead to racialized binaries while denying or/and dehumanizing the existence of the other. In contrast to such dominance Raheb urges Palestinian churches to retrieve their biblical story of collective political aspirations for liberation as a people who yearn for land and resist the empire.[18]

In the above-mentioned islands in Asia, we find similar colonial forging of land and national identities that fits into imperial complexes and leads to subjugation of others. The British colonial masters turned the island of Lanka into a unitary political structure as a strategic location to control the Indian subcontinent while rereading the ancient post-canonical Buddhist Pali texts of dynastic conflicts with a racial and religious lens. The Sinhala numerical majority, who were Buddhists, were led to believe that the entire land belongs to them as opposed to the Tamil people, who were depicted as invaders. The unitary political structure became an essential component of Sinhala Buddhist nationalist consciousness at the expense of the Tamils, who developed a counter-identity in the face of oppression, claiming the north and east of the island as their homeland (Tamil Eelam). In the postcolonial nation-building processes the Sinhala churches embraced the dominant narrative of land and peoplehood associated with the unitary state. The Tamil churches were informed by the Eelam Tamil liberation struggle for land and peoplehood that was emerging particularly from the lower strata of that society, defying not only the unitary state which is part of a geostrategic complex in Asia and its attendant Sinhala Buddhist ideology, but also caste and gender discrimination among the Tamils.

The Eelam Tamil peoplehood problematized the USA's pivot toward Asia. As a result, the de facto state of Tamil Eelam was destroyed by the Sri Lankan security forces with immense political and military support of the UK and USA. Thousands of Okinawa-based US marines were brought to Sri Lanka in 2007 to train its security forces before the final massacre reinforcing the dominant Sinhala Buddhist ideology and the state structure throughout the island. The Sinhala churches embraced this military victory as given by God and blessed the troops, while the Tamil churches shared the plight of thousands of people who were killed and displaced.

In Korea, a collective liberating consciousness developed under Chinese dominance and Japanese imperialism. The biblical message was first read by the people not through the lens of the European colonial masters, but in the native language and alphabet despised by the Japanese rulers. Aloysius Pieris notes:

> For the first time in Asia, the Bible was read and understood directly by the class of people for whom it was primarily meant: *minjung*. The Hebrew expression of *anawin* and the Greek term *ochlos*—which designated the Biblical notion of colonized, marginalized, humiliated and pauperized non-people who struggle to be a people—allowed the Korean minjung to identify as their God the only God that the Bible speaks of: a God who makes a covenant with the "worms" of the earth to be on their side of the struggle against unscrupulous anglers.[19]

However, in the context of the Cold War, with the reinforcement of Americanism to Korea, the imagination of land and people became highly imperialized. Jin Kwan Kwon identifies two theological orientations that conditioned the consciousness of Christians who were mainly led by the Protestant churches. One is the gospel of prosperity that seeks material wealth and individual salvation, which corresponded with the developmentalist economy, and the other is "crusade spirit" based on a rigid and simplistic binary position against communism.[20] The people of Jeju who resisted both Japanese and American imperialism faced one of the worst massacres during the Korean War, which was supported by the churches. The division of Korea is a result of US empire-building in Asia within the politics of the Cold War. Even after the formal end of the Cold War the tensions in the Korean peninsula continued to rise as a result of furtherance of the US empire. Francis Mun-su Park notes:

> The U.S., which was instrumental in getting article 9 put into Japan's "peace constitution," is now urging Japan to increase its military spending and strengthen its alliance with the U.S. to curb China's increasing military power. North Korea, economically unable to compete with the military build-up among its neighbors, has chosen a cheaper way, nuclear weapons. Thus in N. E. Asia the unsettled issues from WWII have combined with unsettled Cold War issues, such as the North-South division of Korea, and the China-Taiwan situation, to make many citizens believe [that] there must be continuing military build-up in the region.[21]

It is in this context that the people of Jeju have revived the memory of massacres, oppose militarization of the island, and propose an island of peace with a strong community bond and a reverence for the ecosystem. This move challenges the growing belief in a geostrategic security complex, which puts Asia in a permanent state of war.

Like the people of Jeju and Eelam Tamils, the Okinawans have been victims of military empire-building in Asia. Christianity in Japan had been part of two processes of empire-building. First it was part of the Western empire. After going through severe suppression it later became part of the Japanese empire-building project. Before and during the Pacific Wars the churches compromised with the government's war policy and accepted the emperor's will as the will of God. The voices of dissent within the churches were silenced through the collusion between the churches and the state. The Okinawans were racially abused by the Japanese imperial state, like the Koreans, Chinese, and others whose countries were invaded. At the end of the war the US security forces acquired large swaths of Okinawan land, including productive rice fields, making the native people dependent on the military bases for their livelihood and reducing many to poverty. The Christian community was dependent on the rich US churches and the military chapels, which separated them from the rest of the Okinawans. This dependency made Okinawan Christians silent and separated from the other Okinawans, despite their common victimhood of war and militarization. However, as a result of Okinawa being increasingly used as a US launching pad for the wars in Vietnam, Korea, and the Gulf, some churches gradually began to reflect critically on their complicity in war and have joined the movement that asserts Riyuku (the older name for the islands) identity as a distinct people who oppose both American and Japanese empire-building while proposing a vision of peace for the island.

In this way, we can see how imperialized structures and imaginations of land and people have been problematized by distinct groups of people who share a common identity and a land that would not fit with the geostrategic complex. Their yearning for land is not simply a demand for a property with an economic value, but an aspiration for a homeland where there is a distinct collective identity associated with a nonexploitative social and ecological relationship. Recognizing, celebrating, and promoting such distinct movements for liberation has to be part of the faith journey of the churches in Asia in the face of the immense military might of the empire. It is in this sense that land and people have to become hermeneutical tools for a new theology of peace in Asia.

EMPIRE VS. ISLANDS OF PEACE

In his masterpiece, *Asian Theology of Liberation*, Aloysius Pieris reinterprets the meaning of the two baptisms as Jordan of Asian Religion and Calvary of Asian Poverty. Jesus's embrace of John the Baptist's spirituality invites Asian churches to plunge into asceticism (voluntary poverty) of Asian religion (first baptism) while linking it to the confrontation of forced poverty in which he embraces the cross (second baptism).[22] Liberation is seen here through the lens of God's covenant with the poor through Jesus Christ, which is seen as unique to biblical tradition. The basic hermeneutical tool here is downtrodden social classes. This has helped immensely to critique colonial and class biases of traditional theology that protect empire. However, empire operates not only through dominant social classes, but also by carving territories and states out of land and forging nations that fit into the geostrategic complexes. In that sense, Pieris's Asian Theology of Liberation needs to be modified by introducing the collective political aspirations for a homeland upheld by Eelam Tamils, Okinawans, national groups in the Northeastern states in India, Burma, Pakistan, Bangladesh, etc. Even in Jeju island the collective political aspiration for peace on the island that has arisen against militarization is interwoven with the people's distinct identity and collective memory of massacres. Without such hermeneutical tools, developing a theology that problematizes empire's new round of militarization in Asia will not be possible.

Resisting the Egyptian empire and leaping toward a land promised led the people to a wilderness of uncertainty, hunger, and death. Brueggemann reflects on two histories as possible options at this crucial juncture of resistance to the empire and leap into wilderness:

> Having rejected safe slavery, Israel found its immediate destiny to be landless. But even in wilderness it discovered that one may be a participant in one of the two histories we have discerned in Genesis. Numbers 14 presents in rapid succession a series of images about facing the competing claims of the two histories. One is driven by a sense of banishment, characterized by mistrust, expressed as quarrelsomeness, and devoted to return to Egypt. The other is the history of hope, trusting in Yahweh's promises, enduring in the face of want and need, sure that history was on its way to the new and good land. Israel discerned what rootless people must each time learn over again, that in such landlessness there may be unexpected sustaining resources. Or one may discern there only darkness and abandonment. In the events of wilderness Israel wrestled like Jacob for its being and for its faith.[23]

In the face of a massacre of thousands of people in the last phase of the war and total dismantling of the Tamil Eelam state, the faith of the Tamil churches has been tested. In the aftermath of the war, while massive structural changes have been put into effect that destroy remaining foundations of the Tamil homeland, empire has channeled millions of dollars for the programs under the rubrics of establishment of law and order (that treats state as natural), security (as state security), and reconciliation (as amnesia of the past) in view of totally destroying the liberated consciousness of the Tamil people and achieving imperial peace on the island. After the massacre there is both physical and psychological pressure mounting on Eelam Tamils to fall into the geostrategic complex as a subjugated people. The metaphor of wilderness is real. The temptation is real. Yet one can see the most dispossessed ones, particularly widows, rising up for a liberated land. Theology of land and peace in Asia has to reflect on the faith in a God who sustains her people in such wilderness and maintains their journey towards a homeland. The language of liberation needs to be adopted in developing a theology of land and peace rather than the language of law and order and security that is the language of the empire.

In their resistance to the naval base in Jeju island, one finds a language of peace rather than security. This notion of peace is intrinsically interwoven with the memory of massacres on the island. The new round of militarization will incorporate the island into a theater of future war. Yearning for land and peace has put the Jeju people into a mode of wilderness on two levels. One is the continuous harassments, arrests, and imprisonments that they have to face. The other is the temptation to return to imperial peace based on the gospel of prosperity that promises economic advantages coming from the naval base. Bishop Peter Kang U-il of Jeju, by using the theological metaphor of the reign of God and the biblical notion of nonpossessive relationship to land, reflects on how militaristic state absolutism is intrinsically interwoven with the claim to ownership of land. Monopoly of land by the state justifies a monopoly of violence by the state. He reminds us that in the biblical tradition, as in many native traditions, land is not something that one can possess.[24] The possessive relationship to land gives the state a divine status that justifies war. Quoting Isaiah's text that "none shall harm or destroy on all my holy mountain says the Lord" (Isa. 65:17–25), the bishop notes that "this prophecy's teaching provides Israel with a completely new vision and understanding of land. The prophets propose to Israel to go beyond the attachment they have to the promised land, a chunk of Palestine, and should exchange it for a new heaven and a new earth, an apocalyptic land."[25] The apocalyptic land is not otherworldly or ahistorical. It is the transformation of land by God's power and action in history that challenges imperial consciousness and its militaristic institutions. A letter written by one Christian activist who was put in jail by the Korean government for his acts of resistance to militarization reflects this faith journey:

> Actually, with the purpose of being with the residents of Gangjeong village in their oppression by the authorities, and acting with the intent of protecting the life and peace of Jeju Island, I have myself become a body oppressed by the authorities. I don't know how long this will last but I accept it as God's will that I live here happily. I look upon this place as a house of prayer and I am praying hard.[26]

His faith sees body, the people, and land as one. In the eyes of faith, Jesus Christ is the corporate body. God's power is experienced through total dependence in the wilderness of persecution for the sake of a new relationship with the land and each other.

Many women in Jeju uphold a cosmic indigenous spirituality, which treats nature as sacred. For them, the naval base destroys the sacred Gurembi Rock. The protesting women have become the most formidable force that combines the memory of massacre ecumenically, interreligiously, and ecologically, forming a vision beyond empire. This vision is not only for the island. It resonates with the faith reflections of churches that work for peace in the Korean Peninsula. North and South Korean animosity has been worsening with the USA's pivot towards Asia. The WCC's continuous efforts in bringing together Christians from both sides for several decades with the National Council of Churches of Korea have provided some of the richest resources for a theology of land and peace in Asia.[27] Theology of land and peace needs to capture the resilience developed by the people through their faith in resisting the empire while harnessing the resistance in Jeju with the demand for peaceful political negotiations for the inter-Korean conflict.

The churches' resistance to empire's land grab in Okinawa reflects a process of conversion from being part of empire to identification with the people's yearning for land and their distinct liberating Okinawa identity. The autobiographical notes of LaSalle Parsons, a Franciscan who has made Okinawa his home for more than fifty years and who joins protests against military bases, employ the word "conversion" in relation to the "Okinawan Heart," referring to the liberation elements in the indigenous culture:

> May be I need to realize that Christ had gotten here before me. That the people in their own way have a deep sense of the living God. . . . My role as a missionary is first of all to work on my own daily conversion. And that means renewing faith each day that the Spirit has been and is now at work in the hearts and minds of the people I encounter each day. Particularly it means being more aware that the peaceful, calm, non-aggressive heart of Okinawa is in many unseen ways a work of the Spirit.[28]

Similarly, Bishop Peter Ichiro Shibusawa of the Anglican Communion of Japan has issued an open letter to the government. It begins with the words "we oppose" and ends with a demand to stop militarization while stating that the church holds "dearly the Okinawan spirit, *Nuchi du Takara* (life is a treasure)":

> We further deem it a calling for the Japanese government and our Church to act against construction of new U.S. military bases and to strive together for life and peace. This is revealed to us in the Gospel of Jesus, the Prince of Peace: "Put your sword back into its place; for all those who take up the sword shall perish by the sword" (Matthew 26:52).[29]

In Japan, in resisting the reinterpretation of Article 9,[30] the two statements issued by the Catholic Bishops' Conference in 2015 and 2016 revive the memory of the Pacific War (Hiroshima, Nagasaki) and reiterate the need for acute awareness of the past. The statements hold onto empathy towards the victims of war, option for the poor, and firm commitment to dialogue as a means for peace, as the vocation of the church.[31]

A joint statement of the National Council of Churches in Japan (NCCP) and Korea (NCCK) makes a firm resolution that reflects the prophetic vocation in the face of military empire.[32] It goes beyond mere academic analysis of memory of war and treats it as a site of existential struggle with particular reference to the memory of sexual enslavement of women during wartime. The words are not addressed to the state, but to the masses who have been afflicted. Hope is built not by depending on the empire, but by the resolution made by the subjects of the empire. Peace cannot dawn from the rulers, but by awakening to the liberating presence of God who walks with and moves ahead of the oppressed peoples. The statement also makes a resolution to join forces to oppose moves to change history books in both countries that would erase the memory of oppression and war. Struggle with memory is the path to develop an alternative consciousness and vision as opposed to the imperial consciousness. The memory of Pacific Wars teaches the deadly effects of land grab by military empires. The vision of peace is intrinsically interwoven with a nonpossessive relationship with land as belonging to God.

CONCLUSION

A theology that does not take geopolitics seriously would not recognize distinct forms of oppression that result in the ways in which the states and their dominant ethno-nationalist identities have been forged within the imperialist complex of nations and states. Distinct identities developed by the peoples (like Jeju, Tamil Eelam, Riyukuku) that have been despised by the empire and its vassal nation-states carry a liberating force that challenges the empire. Contextual theologies developed within a single state structure would not be in a position to capture the history of oppression, massacres, and resistance of these peoples, which form their distinct identity.

A theology of land and peace needs to be based on the stories emerging from the yearning for land and struggle for peace. These stories reflect a long journey of faith which is full of temptations to believe in the false promises of prosperity and security given by the empire as well as uncompromising resilience that is arising from a faith in a God who leads, a crucified God who is with us, and a God who has risen in Jesus Christ and is ahead of us.

God's vision of land is radically different from the imperial vision of land, which objectifies it for militaristic and economic use. It is only by deeply listening to the Gangjeong opening hymn, Kumiko Onaga, and Saraswathy Alagarasa that the churches in Asia can be true to their baptismal calling to commit themselves to a new heaven and earth. Such a commitment will lead the churches to be involved in the peace movement in Asia as a new mission, which has to be the practical goal of a theology of land and peace in Asia.

NOTES

1. U-il Kang, the bishop of Jeju, wrote this song in Korean. Seong-il Gwon composed its music. Its English translation was given to me by the Jesuit priest Sunghwan Kim, one of my doctoral students, who has been persecuted by the South Korean regime for his opposition to the Jeju naval base and his commitment to peace in the island.

2. Jeong-hyeon Mun, "A Priest on the Way"(from an unpublished original manuscript of a speech given in New York, 2016).

3. The island of Jeju as part of the Republic of Korea lies at the crossroads of the seas of China and Japan. It became a strategically pivotal location both for the Japanese and American navies during World War II and subsequently utilized by the US and South Korea as a buffer zone against China and North Korea. During the Korean War many islanders who resisted the US-backed South Korean regime were massacred.

4. Sonia Narang, "In Okinawa, Older Women Are on the Front Lines of the Military Base Protest Movement," *PRI*, February 14, 2017, https://www.pri.org/stories/2017-02-14/okinawa-older-women-are-front-lines-military-base-protest-movement (accessed March 25, 2017).

5. Most of the islands of Okinawa formerly came under the independent Ryukyu kingdom which was annexed to the Japanese empire in the nineteenth century. During World War II it became the most decisive strategic location both for Japan and the USA and continues to be a pivotal location in containing the Chinese sphere of influence in the region.

6. The empire treats the entire island of Sri Lanka as a strategic asset which can be utilized properly as long as it remains a unitary state under the numerically majority Sinhalese, who have been made to believe that they are racially superior to the non-Sinhalese. The Tamils in the north and east consider their region as their homeland, which goes against the imperial geopolitics. They carry the greatest potential to bring about peace on the island by overcoming the imperial design.

7. Tamilnet, "Keappaa-Pulavu Protesters Denounce Compromises, Demand All Their Lands Released," April 24, 2017, http://www.tamilnet.com/art.html?catid=79&artid=38657 (accessed May 23, 2017).

8. See Michael Hardt and Antonio Negri, *Empire* (Cambridge, MA: Harvard University Press, 2000) and Joerg Rieger, *Christ and Empire* (Minneapolis, MN: Fortress Press, 2007) who focus on the economic dimension of globalization led by countries of G8 and transnational cooperation. In developing empire as a hermeneutical category, Reiger sees the USA as "one of the key players" of the empire, arguing that large constellation of power cannot be maintained only by one actor (*Christ and Empire*, 2). Such definitions are not only too general, but also Euro-American-centric and do not help understand many specific sites of people's resistance associated with their yearning for land, particularly in the face of military might. In this definition, the USA's structural military relationships with the states in the Balkans, Middle East, Latin America, Africa, and Asia, as well as a large number of military bases in Asia, particularly on the islands, which have been used as launching pads for the wars in the Middle East, go unnoticed.

9. James Petras, "Military or Market-Driven Empire Building: 1950–2008," April 29, 2008, http://www.globalresearch.ca/military-or-market-driven-empire-building-1950-2008/8841 (accessed May 23, 2017). Donald Trump's imposition of tariffs (trade wars) on the market-driven countries is an attempt to strike a balance between the economic and military might of the USA that has brought to the limelight many contradictions within the US empire.

10. Commenting on Cold War politics the Asian Report issued by the Ecumenical Association of Third World Theologians (EATWOT) in 1990 identifies the extent of the US military presence in Asia by the end of the Cold War. "The Asian region holds a string of US military bases and facilities that extending from northern to the southern portions of the area. From the Pacific Ocean, to the South China Sea, on to the Indian Ocean, these military bases and facilities have been set up to maintain the arc of defense of the 'free world' against the aggression of the 'communist world.'" See K. C. Abraham, *Third World Theologies—Commonalities and Divergences* (Maryknoll, NY: Orbis, 1990), 7.

11. See Keon-joo Christine Pae, "Feminist Activism as Interfaith Dialogue: A Lesson from Gangjeong Village in Jeju Island, Korea," *Journal of Korean Religions* 5 (2014): 55–69.

12. Instead of a universal history (an imperial history) the history of the poor (in an economic sense) has been treated as the history of God's people (Latin American liberation theologies). Asian liberation theologies read this history within the dual realities of poverty of masses and multiplicity of religions. This means that the liberation of the poor has to take place universally and interreligiously.

13. From a biblical perspective it is this geopolitical analysis that can help capture the radical dialectical relationship of landlessness and landedness, yearning for land and land grab, and land promised and Promised Land. For centuries Christianity has justified land grab of empire across the world while destroying collective identities of peoples.

14. Walter Brueggemann, *The Land: Place as Gift, Promise and Challenge in the Bible* (Minneapolis, MN: Fortress, 2002), xv.

15. Brueggemann, *The Land*, 202.

16. Brueggemann, *The Land*, 202.

17. Mitri Raheb, "Land, People, and Empire—The Bible through Palestinian Christian Eyes," *Theologies and Cultures* 11.2 (2014): 28.

18. Raheb, "Land, People, and Empire," 32.

19. Aloysius Pieris, "Buddhists and Christians for Justice—The Korean Connection," *Dialogue* 16 (1989): 1.

20. Jin Kwan Kwon, "Churches in the Divided Nation—An Analysis of the Korean Christianity Structured by the Cold War System, 1945–1990," in *Unfinished History—Christianity and the Cold War in East Asia*, ed. Philip L. Wickeri (Leipzig, Germany: Evangelische Verlagsanstalt, 2016), 224.

21. Francis Mun-su Park,"Conflicts and Peace Movements in N. E. Asia—Focus on Jesuit Involvement" (presentation at the JCAP Social Apostolate Meeting, August 3–7, 2015, Kuala Lumpur), 1.

22. Aloysius Pieris, *Asian Liberation Theology* (Edinburgh, Scotland: T&T Clark, 1988), 45–50.

23. Brueggemann, *The Land*, 33.

24. Peter Kang U-il, "The Gospel and the State" (Gangjeong Peace Conference and Peace Festival, September 26, 2014, Jeju), 4.

25. U-il, "The Gospel and the State," 5.

26. Do-hyun Park, "A Letter from Prison in Jeju," (lower level 2 cell 2, July 18, 2013; received through Kim Sung Hwan, a colleague of Park Do-hyun, 2013).

27. See also Dong Jin Kim, "The Peace-building Role of the Ecumenical Movement in Korea during the 1980s," in *Mining Truths: Festchrift in Honour of Geraldine Smyth OP—Ecumenical Theologian and Peacebuilder*, ed. John O' Grady, Cathy Higgins, and Jude Lal Fernando (Munich: EOS, 2015), 267–285.

28. LaSalle Parsons, "Memories of Fifty Years on Okinawa" (manuscript given to me by the author), 3.

29. Peter Ichiro Shibusawa, "Statement of Opposition to the Deployment of MV-22 Osprey Aircraft at the U.S. Marine Corps Futenma Station," *ACNS*, October 5, 2012, http://www.anglicannews.org/news/2012/10/japanese-primate-tells-prime-minister-no-to-us-military-planes.aspx (accessed March 26, 2017).

30. See Tadakazu Fukase et al., *Let Us Be the Wind to Spread Arcticle 9!—A Record of International Symposium of IFOR Council and The 80th Anniversary of Japan Fellowship of Reconciliation (JFOR)* (Yamagta, Japan: Japan Fellowship of Reconciliation, 2008).

31. Catholic Bishops' Conference of Japan, "70 Years after the War: Blessed Are the Peacemakers—Now Especially, Peace Must Not Depend Upon Weapons," February 25, 2015, https://www.cbcj.catholic.jp/2015/02/25/5182/ (accessed May 25, 2017); Catholic Bishops' Conference of Japan, "Now Especially, Peace Must Not Depend upon Weapons—Regarding the Enforcement of the Security Laws," April 7, 2016, https://www.cbcj.catholic.jp/2016/04/07/5314/ (accessed May 25, 2017).

32. The National Council of Churches in Korea, "Prayer from NCCK for Easter Preparation," *NCCK*, 06 March 2015, http://www.kncc.or.kr/eng/sub03/sub01.php?ptype=view&idx=14158&page=1&code=eng_board_03_1_1, March 6, 2015 (accessed March 27, 2017).

Chapter Eleven

Colonization of the Watersheds and the Green Politics of Hagar

George Zachariah

Colonization of the watershed is a crisis that the community of life confronts today. Reducing this reality to an environmental crisis is problematic because such diagnosis fails to recognize the larger socioeconomic and political causes that lead to the colonization of the watershed and its continued exploitation and plunder. Devoid of deeper political discernment and engagement, responses to the crisis remain apolitical and "feel good" environmentalism, without disrupting the logic and practice of colonization and its conquest of life. This critique applies to various strands of religious environmentalism and initiatives to read scriptures ecologically. Such hermeneutical and theological attempts conceal the systemic and political roots of the crisis. Biblical engagement in the context of the colonization of the watershed is therefore political because it is committed to disrupt and destabilize the regime of truth from locations of power and privilege and to rediscover the Word in the struggles of earth and its children in their creative resilience to flourish in the movement of life.

INTERROGATING DOMINANT TRAJECTORIES OF ENVIRONMENTALISM

In his article entitled "The Historical Roots of our Ecological Crisis," North American historian Lynn White Jr. argued that the worldview of the Industrial Revolution, that the earth was a resource or commodity for human exploitation and consumption, had its roots in the attitudes of medieval Christianity toward nature. He further observed that "what people do about their ecology depends on what they think about themselves in relation to things around them. Human ecology is deeply conditioned by beliefs about our nature and destiny—that is, by religion."[1] Realizing the potential of religions in constructing worldviews and attitudes, White engaged with the Judeo-Christian tradition and its scripture to explore why they bear a "huge burden of guilt" for the contemporary crisis of life. His interrogation led him to two foundational aspects of the Judeo-Christian tradition and scripture which are responsible for the crisis: first, the anthropocentric assertion of the domination of human beings over the rest of creation, and second, the distinction between human beings, the crown of creation created in the image of God, and the "soulless" creatures without intrinsic worth, created with the purpose to serve human beings. "Christianity . . . not only established a dualism of man [sic] and nature, but also insisted that it is God's will that man [sic] exploit nature for his [sic] proper ends."[2] According to White, the Christian (biblical) axiom that nature was meant to serve humanity inspired the conquest of imperial projects in history, including the colonization of the watersheds.

White's critical exposition inspired a host of scholars to engage the Judeo-Christian tradition and scripture using eco-theological lenses. Identifying anthropocentrism as the cause for ecological crisis, faith-based initiatives began to emerge in response to the distress of earth, inspired by Christian tradition and scripture. However, a scrutiny of the politics of eco-theological and biblical reflections exposes the influence of the social location of the interpreters in their theological constructions. Knowledge production is always a social and political activity embedded in particular cultures and worldviews. Knowledge produced in the colonial enterprise reduces reality into a thing or commodity rather than a living organism and legitimizes the domination and abuse of nature. Colonial gaze *thingified* and commodified nature, and in our times this gaze is continued through development, globalization, modern science, and technology. While unleashing a violent regime of technological interventions and social engineering on earth and earth communities, manipulating and desecrating life forms to appease the *ungod* of market, neocolonialism uses the rhetoric of environmentalism to portray its commitment to protect and preserve nature.

The earliest manifestation of colonial environmentalism can be traced back to the emergence of national parks and protected areas, starting as early as 1872 with the Yellowstone National Park in North America. National parks are the products of an environmentalism that considers nature as the "other" of human beings, and hence nature needs to be protected from indigenous communities who have been living in communion with nature from time immemorial. For colonial environmentalism, nature is wilderness, and it should be protected through enclosures from the indigenous communities and exploited sustainably for the common good. The dominant strand of environmentalism advocates wilderness activism and conservationism and critiques anthropocentrism. For them biocentrism is the alternative for anthropocentrism.

Ramachandra Guha, the South Asian environmental historian, nuances the differences between colonial environmentalism and subaltern environmentalism by juxtaposing stories of two anti-dam movements. The Friends of the River organization, in its opposition to the construction of the New Melones dam on the Stanislaus River in California, USA, was motivated by the biocentric perspective. The rationale for their struggle was clear. "All the life of this canyon, its wealth of archaeological and historical roots to our past, and its unique geological grandeur are enough reasons to protect this canyon *just for itself*. But in addition, all spiritual values with which this canyon has filled tens of thousands of folks should prohibit us from committing the unconscionable act of wiping this place off the face of the earth."[3] On the other hand, in the case of the anti-dam movement against the construction of mega dams on the Narmada River in India, the motivation is not just to save the river but also, and more crucially, to benefit the tens of thousands of people—mostly indigenous communities, Dalits, and farmers—to be displaced by the dam. Both are anti-dam movements. The former is in line with the colonial environmentalism which strives toward "the protection of pristine, unspoilt nature: a reservoir of biological diversity and enormous aesthetic appeal which serves as an ideal haven from the urban workday world."[4] But the latter is a movement toward the ultimate goal of a socially just and ecologically sustainable model of development. Differently said, "'No Humanity without Nature!' the epitaph of the colonial environmentalist is here answered by the equally compelling slogan 'No Nature without Social Justice.'"[5]

Colonial environmentalism is also racist and casteist. As James Cone observes, "it is important to ask, however, whose problems define the priorities of the environmental movement? Whose suffering claims attention? . . . If it is important to save the habitats of birds and other species, then it is at least equally important to save black lives in the ghettos and prisons of America."[6] The environmental justice movement came into being in this context to expose the racism of the mainstream environmental movements and to also offer an intersectional approach to engage with the crisis of the earth. Along this line, the first National People of Color Environmental Leadership Summit held in Washington, DC, in 1991 resolved

> to build a national and international movement of all people of color to fight the destruction and taking of our lands and communities, to re-establish our spiritual interdependence to the sacredness of our Mother Earth; to respect and celebrate each of our cultures, languages and beliefs about the natural world and our roles in healing ourselves; to ensure environmental justice; to promote economic alternatives which would contribute to the development of environmentally safe livelihoods; and, to secure our political, economic and cultural

> liberation that has been denied for over 500 years of colonization and oppression, resulting in the poisoning of our communities and land and the genocide of our peoples.[7]

As Cone rightly puts it, the basic question here is not whether we are concerned about the future of the earth, but "whose earth is it, anyway?"

George Tinker extends this critique of colonial environmentalism further to specific issues in biocentrism. According to Tinker, the Native American understanding of creation as sacred and the source of all life goes far beyond the worldview of the Sierra Club or Greenpeace:

> It embraces far more than concern for harp seals or a couple of ice-bound whales. It embraces all of life from trees and rocks to international relations. . . . Respect for creation must result in an ongoing concern for economic balance and resistance to economic injustice that leave many poor and oppressed while their white American and European relatives or even Japanese relatives live in wealth at the expense of others.[8]

The intersectional approach is further affirmed in the writings of some African women:

> Earth-healing praxis requires an understanding of the interconnectedness of the different manifestations of violence. The violence of poverty, racism, sexism and classism, of social dislocation, of militarism, of battering and rape are not unrelated to the violence against the environment. They are all rooted in the abuse of power as domination over the exploitation of the other.[9]

Even though ecological theology and ecological hermeneutics are of recent origin, it is important to evaluate them, informed by the voices from subaltern communities that we have already heard. The dominant tendency within the eco-theological and eco-justice hermeneutical initiatives is to develop interpretations based on the false notion of universality. As a result, concerns such as wilderness conservation, population growth, biocentrism, and sustainable development become the themes of mainstream theological and biblical reflections on ecology. Eco-theologies and eco-justice hermeneutics, in general, continue to remain elitist, colonial, patriarchal, and racist because of the unwillingness to analyze the problem at the interface of race, class, and gender, recognizing the epistemological privilege of the subaltern communities, affirming subaltern social movements as "theological texts."[10]

The ecological bankruptcy of biblical interpretations plays a significant role in developing attitudes toward nature. Ecological awareness and consciousness compel us to reclaim the Bible to transform our communities into earth-honoring communities of cosmic healing, and it has initiated various hermeneutical explorations to make the Bible a resource that inspires and informs faith journeys. The Earth Bible Team has adapted the hermeneutics of suspicion and hermeneutics of retrieval that feminist theology has popularized, in what they christened as "eco-justice hermeneutics:" Hermeneutics of suspicion here invites us to "legitimately suspect that biblical texts, written by human beings, reflect the primary interests of human beings—their human welfare, their human relationship to God and their personal salvation."[11] Norman Habel further explained: "Just as privileged human beings have read the text in biased ways against the most vulnerable human communities, with tragic consequences, so we have read the text with bias against nature herself."[12] The bias of anthropocentrism privileges the interests of human beings over the rest of creation and prevents us from discerning the uniqueness and intrinsic worth of nonhuman creatures. Hermeneutics of suspicion examines whether the biblical texts and our interpretations silence the voices of earth and of nonhuman creatures.

Hermeneutics of retrieval facilitates the retrieval of unnoticed, suppressed, subjugated, and hidden voices of and traditions about earth and earth community in biblical texts. The task here is to "reread the text to discern where earth or members of the earth community may have suffered, resisted or been excluded by attitudes within the text or the history of its interpretation."[13] Hermeneutics of retrieval is hence the breaking of the culture of silence, to listen to the voices of earth and earth community. Retrieval is discerning the creative and restorative powers of earth and nonhuman creatures. The earth through its voices testifies to its God-given creative and restorative powers.[14]

In spite of all these initiatives eco-justice hermeneutics remains a Western, middle class, white enterprise. The absence of people of color and representatives from the Global South and other subaltern communities in the eco-justice hermeneutical initiatives compels us to interrogate the politics of eco-justice hermeneutics. It also calls us to engage in intentional creative explorations to do eco-justice hermeneutics with subaltern perspectives. This essay moves in that direction to reread the story of Hagar and her struggle for survival using the methodology of intersectionality, and to juxtapose Hagar's story with the life story of Soni Sori, an Adivasi woman activist from India who is engaged in a historic struggle to protect the watershed.

HAGAR

Hagar is not a significant character in the biblical narratives. Her name is mentioned in a few places, as part of the story of Abra(ha)m. Biblical authors were not interested in presenting Hagar as an autonomous character, but as a dependent self—the slave-girl of Sarah, the concubine of Abraham, and the mother of Ishmael. The New Testament portrays Hagar and her descendants as alienated outsiders to the promise of new creation that Christ represents

(Gal. 4: 21–5:1). So the biblical representation of Hagar is one of erasing her identity and agency, an act of textual violence. When it comes to biblical interpretation, we see the same attitude and approach. Most commentaries either ignore Hagar's story or strip her identity and agency, and present her story as a less important episode in the patriarchal history. The commentators have done a cognitive injustice by disabling Hagar's speech-ability and blending her story with the meta-narrative of Abraham. In spite of the biblical testimony that Hagar was the first person who named God and the first woman who received the promise of descendants from God, the textual violence and cognitive injustice inflicted upon Hagar are absolved in biblical interpretation. She remains at the margins of biblical faith and spirituality.

Hagar Retold

Hagar's story has been a fascinating source for women theologians in general and women of color theologians in particular. Phyllis Trible in her classic work *Texts of Terror* observes that, "knowledge of her (Hagar) has survived in bits and pieces only, and so our task is precarious; to tell Hagar's story from the fragments that remain."[15] Differently said, the vocation of biblical hermeneutics is to engage in the risky political mission of enabling the silenced voices of women and subaltern characters in the Bible to disrupt the canonized truth and to discover the Word becoming flesh in the subaltern struggles.

Hagar's story begins in Genesis 12, where we read "Egyptian slave-girls" as part of the property of Abraham. Abraham received slave women as part of the bride money that Pharaoh offered him for Sarah, his "sister." We meet her again in Genesis 16, where she is introduced as the "Egyptian slave-girl." Her identity—a slave-girl from a foreign country—reveals her location in the power-relation within the household of Abraham and Sarah. Genesis 16 begins with identifying the problem of this story: the barrenness of Sarah. God's promise of descendants to Abraham remains unfulfilled because of Sarah's barrenness. It is in this context that Abraham and Sarah decide to "use" Hagar's fertility to build their offspring who will occupy the land. The word used in Genesis 16 for Hagar is *sipha*, which means "a virgin, dependent maid who serves the mistress of the house."[16] Hagar was a virgin when Abraham had sex with her. What we find here is the violation of an alien slave woman's sovereignty over her body, sexuality, and reproductive rights, and attaching her fertility for imperial interests—to develop descendants to occupy the land.

From an intersectional point of view, Renita Weems problematizes the story of Hagar as "a story of ethnic prejudice exacerbated by economic and sexual exploitation."[17] For Elsa Tamez, the appearance of Hagar and Ishmael in the patriarchal history has profound implications for all those who are pushed to the peripheries of history. "The marginalized demand their first-born sons to be included in the history of salvation. They break the order of things. They complicate history."[18]

Hagar's decision to flee from the home of her mistress who "dealt harshly with her" was the exodus that she initiated in order to live with dignity and freedom. It is in her sojourn in the wilderness as a liberated person that Hagar speaks for the first time. Speech-ability enables the reclaiming of control over one's life. As Trible observes, "exodus from oppression liberates her voice, though full personhood continues to elude her."[19] It is in her exodus that Hagar encounters God and names God *El Roi*—the God who sees me. In that experience of theophany God promises Hagar a multitude of descendants. However, it is important to ask whether God in this narrative is the God of the oppressed who sojourns with the subalterns or a God who subverts the projects of liberation of the subalterns. For Trevor Dennis, God's command to Hagar to return and submit is problematic because God "seems to be in favor of the *status quo* and on the side of the oppressor, a defender of the interests of the Sarais of this world against its all too vulnerable Hagars."[20]

It is interesting to observe the diverse ways in which women theologians wrestle with this problematic episode. Trible considers this story as a text of terror and observes that "return and submit to suffering bring a divine word of terror to an abused, yet courageous woman."[21] For her "to tell and hear tales of terror is to wrestle demons in the night, without a compassionate God to save us."[22] What we find here is a powerful critique of God who not only protects the interests of the dominant but also betrays the subalterns and their longing for freedom and dignity. Unlike Trible, Elsa Tamez finds the story to signify God's commitment to ensure the survival of the oppressed and to promise them a qualitative life. "What God wants is that she and her child should be saved, and at the moment, the only way to accomplish that is not in the desert, but by returning to the house of Abraham."[23] Delores Williams also supports this position and observes that Hagar "is given hope not only for the survival of her generation but also hope for the possibility of future freedom for her seed. . . . The promise assures survival, and the birth announcement forecasts the strategy that will be necessary for survival and for obtaining a quality of life."[24] Here Tamez and Williams represent the third world and African American women for whom survival in the context of economic, patriarchal, and racial violence is a political battle, and hence it is important to protect life even if it requires strategic retreats from their exodus journeys.

Genesis 16 ends with the seemingly innocent statement that "Hagar bore Abram a son; and Abram named his son, whom Hagar bore, Ishmael." In fact, this statement exposes the power relation within the household of the patriarch, and how a young alien slave woman was stripped of her identity and personhood and used as an instrument to perpetuate the rule of the patriarch. Genesis 21 begins with the story of Sarah's conception and the birth of Isaac and then introduces the problem of the story: "Cast out this slave woman with her son; for the son of this slave woman shall not inherit along with my son Isaac." The presence of Ishmael, the son of the slave woman, in the household was disgusting to Sarah and Abraham, and a threat to their son's exclusive rights over ancestral property and divine promise. Once again God took the side of the oppressor, and Hagar and Ishmael were expelled and sent out to die in the desert. The God who asked Hagar to return from her voluntary exodus and to submit to her mistress now joins the patriarch and the mistress to disinherit and displace them. Hagar's life is a journey from exodus to exile.

Hagar and Ishmael groaning for life in the desert represent millions of single mothers and children in our context who are made refugees thanks to the economic, patriarchal, racial, and ecological injustices perpetrated on them. In their desert experience, God meets them as "God does not leave them to perish in the desert without leaving a trace. They must live to be part of history, and struggle to be subjects of it."[25] It was an experience of annunciation. "Do not be afraid; for God has heard the voice of the boy where he is, Come, lift up the boy and hold him fast with your hand, for I will make a great nation of him" (Gen. 21: 17b–18). The feminist and womanist engagement with this "text of terror" giving voice to the silenced Egyptian slave-girl enables us to recognize the potential of the subalterns to complicate salvation history and to destabilize imperial projects. Hagar is a woman who had to encounter multiple forms of oppression because of her nationality, gender, race, and economic status, and she was subjected to use, abuse, and exclusion. But she lived out the possibility for the subalterns to disrupt the prevailing order. Hagar is an inspiration for all who find their stories in her story.

Rereading Hagar in the Context of the Colonization of the Watersheds

Even though there have been several contextual and postcolonial rereadings of the story of Hagar, the eco-justice significance of the story is yet to be explored, interpreted, and appreciated. Hagar's story has profound implications for our eco-justice theological reimaginations. In this section, I use watershed as the lens to engage with Hagar's story.

Our engagement with the story of Hagar uses the hermeneutical standpoints developed by Dalit women. For Monica Melanchthon, "Dalit biblical interpretation and the material force that grips the Dalits are grounded in a materialistic epistemology that is characterized, among other things, by its location of truth not in a world beyond history but indeed within the crucible of historical struggles."[26] Further, they realize the Bible as "becoming the

'Word' when read in community in the light of the community's experience."[27] Dalit women's hermeneutics "criticize that which is merely theoretical; they validate the experiential, the lived and the ambiguous."[28]

Watershed is generally understood as a geographical space surrounded with water bodies that birth and nurture life. According to John Wesley Powell a watershed is "that area of land, a bounded hydrologic system, within which all living things are inextricably linked by their common water course and where . . . they become part of the community."[29] The mainstream environmental discourses and movements tend to reduce watershed into a pristine ecological space to be conserved and preserved from human defilement through enclosures.

The discourse on watershed in our times oscillates between two dominant arguments: watershed as a resource pile to be exploited or engineered, and watershed as wilderness to be fenced off from the indigenous and subsistence communities. The first argument comes from the logic of neoliberal capitalism, which believes that the trajectory of growth-oriented development is ecologically sustainable. The second argument comes from the same logic, but its proponents are the mainstream environmental movements. For them anthropocentrism is the root cause for the current environmental crisis, and ecological preservation requires the displacement of indigenous and subsistence communities from their traditional abodes. It is in this context that we need to reclaim and redefine watershed.

Brock Dolman's observation of watershed as "basin of relations"[30] is an insightful metaphor for us to reimagine watershed in this "watershed moment." For Dolman, watershed as basin of relations offers us the possibility for "social, local, intentional community with other life forms and inanimate processes." But from a subaltern perspective watershed is also a site of contestation of the dominant socioeconomic power relations. Commenting on this reality of unequal power relations determining the future of the watersheds, Berta Cáceres, the Honduran indigenous rights campaigner who was killed for her historic struggle to protect the watershed, observed that "there is an imposition of a project of domination, of violent oppression, of militarization, of violation of human rights, of trans-nationalization, of the turning over of the riches and sovereignty of the land to corporate capital, for it to privatize energy, the rivers, the land; for mining exploitation; for the creation of development zones."[31] Differently said, colonization of the watersheds is the existential crisis that the movement of life faces in our times, and the hope for life lies in the possibility of transforming our watersheds into "basins of relations" where we combine our struggles for economic, ecological, racial, and gender justice to protect life through resistance and liberation. This re-visioning of watershed is also a critique of misanthropy, through which dominant environmentalism intentionally separates the care of creation from the subaltern struggles for economic, social, racial, and gender justice. Differently said, the alternative vision of watershed is the community of subaltern earth and subaltern communities and their collective struggle to protect, celebrate, and flourish life.

Hagar's story is filled with the images of desert and wilderness. The episodes of theophany take place in the desert and wilderness. Hagar's voluntary exodus and imposed exile are presented as journeys into the desert and wilderness. From a watershed perspective Hagar's story is problematic, as she flees from a seemingly watershed space to the lifeless realities of the desert. She is also leaving the watershed experience of a settled household and its "basin of relations" to be a wanderer in the wilderness with her son. Differently said, Hagar's exodus and exile are her choices to reject the watershed experience offered by Canaan and the patriarchal household in search of an alternative space outside of the dominant watershed. Further, Hagar envisions the annunciation and God's promise of descendants in radical discontinuity with the patriarchal household, and the Promised Land, a watershed filled with milk and honey. Finally, Hagar discovers an alternative watershed in the most unexpected place.

Such a reading invites us to interrogate the dominant perception of the watershed in this story and to discover alternative manifestations of the watershed in the wilderness. The plot in Genesis 16 begins with the statement that Sarah could not bear a child for Abraham. The issue here is more than the barrenness of Sarah; rather it is realizing God's promise to become a nation that will occupy the land. A reading from the perspective of an alien slave woman would problematize the strategy of the patriarch and his wife to have a child through the slave woman without her consent—as a strategy to "build up" their imperial project of occupying the land through descendants. "Because Yahweh has prevented me from bearing children, go to my maid. Perhaps, I shall be built up from her" (Gen. 16:2a). Imperial dreams are projects of conquest and colonization, and the watersheds as well as the subsistence communities who live in communion with the watersheds will experience the violence of colonization on their bodies.

According to the Hammurabi Code, a mistress, in the context of her barrenness, may give slave-girls to her husband to have children. This code presupposes the authority of the master and mistress over the slaves and their bodies, so slaves do not have the right to object. Informed by the materialistic epistemology from the crucible of subaltern struggles, we reread Hagar's surrogacy as the "colonization" of her fertility. In patriarchal history, fertility of women was a means for the imperial project of occupying the land. The fertility of the mistress or the slave-girl has only use value, to bring to life the progeny of the patriarch to invade and conquer the watersheds. In a metaphorical sense, Hagar's fertility can be viewed as a colonized watershed: a watershed which conceives, nourishes, and nurtures life, through its water bodies and fluids, is raped to build up an imperial nation on occupied territory, conquering and displacing its inhabitants. Differently said, Hagar is a figure for all watersheds and watershed communities that are colonized and abused for imperial projects.

How do we read Hagar's willingness to participate in this patriarchal and colonial plot? Even though the Hammurabi Code (146) makes it imperative on slave-girls to obey their masters and mistresses,[32] it is wrong to assume that slave-girls accepted passively such patriarchal, feudal, racist, and imperial aggression on their bodies and sexuality. Materialistic epistemology privileges survival tactics over puritanical virtues. Subaltern women engage in the practice of negotiation even as they confront perennial experiences of abuse and conquest, to survive and to eventually disrupt the culture and rule of patriarchy. We see this skillful survival tactic of negotiation in the story of Hagar.

Hagar now takes control and refuses to allow the fruits of her watershed to be used as a means for occupying the larger watershed called Canaan. In the alternative politics of the subalterns, strategic retreats are essential for survival. But at the *kairos* moment, they reclaim their role as protagonists and thereby complicate the imperial projects. As Delores Williams observes, Hagar thus "becomes the first female in the Bible to liberate herself from oppressive power structures. Though the law prescribes harsh punishment for run-away slaves, she takes the risk rather than endure more brutal treatment by Sarai."[33] A subaltern perspective invites us to go further—it was Hagar's political resolve to detach her "watershed" and its fruits from the project of occupying the land that she decided to take the risk of violating the patriarchal expectation. Watersheds depend on courageous women and men who show the nerve to become seditious to the projects of progress and development.

Hagar's decision to flee from the patriarchal household can also be interpreted as a bold critique of the dominant understanding of watershed. The story takes place in Canaan, the best possible example for watershed in a terrain surrounded with desert and wilderness. Abraham with his family are eagerly waiting for the realization of the divine promise to own the land of Canaan. An etymological study of the name Canaan has profound significance for a watershed hermeneutics. Canaan literally means the "land of purple," which connects it to Phoenicia. However, the root-verb for Canaan is *kana*, and its various meanings include to be humbled, subdued, and brought into subjection. The name Canaan refers to Noah's son Ham, who was cursed by his father. As the Bible testifies, Canaan and his descendants and their land—the watershed and the watershed communities—were conquered by Israel as per the promise of God. Further, the verb *kana* signifies the process of synchronicity, which brings "elements from a wild, feral state into a state of common order and mutual benefit,"[34] and it requires the loss of one's free state, thus stripping one of identity and freedom.

A watershed hermeneutics would interpret the flight of Hagar from Canaan as a rejection of the paradigm of watershed that Canaan represents; namely, it is tamed and engineered by colonial forces to perpetuate the colonial mission of plunder, exploitation, and exclusion. It presupposes subjugation and humiliation of the subsistence communities. The watershed of Canaan has to sacrifice its identity, differences, and distinctiveness, and to undergo modification (read: manipulation) according to the profit-mongering neoliberal market. Natural parks, lush green golf courses, monoculture cash-crop plantations, biofuel plantations, genetically modified crops, and mega dams are contemporary manifestations of the paradigm of the Canaan watershed. The market-driven paradigm of watershed intensifies the economic and social marginalization of subaltern communities. In a context where national governments impose the paradigm of the Canaan watershed as the symbol of ecologically sustainable progress and development, questioning such paradigms is considered a crime. Hagar is thus inspiration for subaltern women and men and their movements to engage in the subversive politics of our times to nurture, protect, and celebrate alternative watersheds.

The biblical narratives of Hagar present the desert-wilderness, a terrain without vegetation and water, as the "other" to Canaan. Canaan invites people to occupy it and settle down, whereas in the wilderness people wander in search of life. Reading from the perspective of the subalterns invites us to sojourn in the desert and wilderness to discover the alternative manifestations of watershed. As Phyllis Trible opines, "wilderness signifies escape from oppression, nourishment of life, and revelation of the divine."[35] This observation defines the vision of an alternative watershed. A watershed should essentially be a safe space that celebrates freedom and differences, as well as offers refuge to those who flee from systems and practices of oppression. It is not a marketplace to satisfy the greed of those who have purchasing power; rather, it is a sacred space where the nourishment of life is assured without price. Finally, wilderness is the abode of God where the community experiences God as a sensual being who sees, hears, and feels the pain, suffering, struggles, pleasures, and joys of the creation.

Hagar's exodus/exile in the wilderness was her expression of independence from bondage to the patriarchal household and the power relations of the watershed called Canaan. The wilderness offered Hagar a home in her journey toward freedom. The same wilderness will be the home for the tribes of Yahweh during their exodus from Egypt. Providing asylum and offering hospitality to communities who are engaged in the struggle to create a world less contaminated with evil and injustice redefines the meaning of community and solidarity in the alternative model of watershed. Here "basin of relations" signifies our unwavering commitment to celebrate diversity and strive together to help life flourish. Further, the wilderness was not a landscape without meaning and ethics. Nomadic communities developed ethical principles and practices to make wilderness a watershed experience for Hagars and Ishmaels. Nomadic life, according to Roland de Vaux,

> gives rise . . . to a law of asylum. In this type of society it is impossible and inconceivable that an individual could live isolated, unattached to any tribe. Hence, if a man [sic] is expelled from his [sic] tribe . . . for any reason . . . or he [sic] leaves it . . . he [sic] has to seek the protection of another tribe. There he [sic] becomes . . . a *dahil*, "he [sic] who has come in." . . . The tribe undertakes to protect him [sic], to defend him [sic] against his [sic] enemies and to avenge his [sic] blood, if necessary."[36]

What we find here is a type of watershed experience where the stranger is welcomed and respected as guest. Hospitality to the other and celebration of community are the basic characteristics of such a watershed; hospitality was "a necessity of life in the desert, but among the nomads this necessity became a virtue, and a most highly esteemed one. The guest is sacred."[37] What we find in the communal practices of nomadic communities in the wilderness is their ethical and spiritual commitment to enable the subalterns to experience watersheds in the most unexpected places.

Hagar and Ishmael were expelled from the patriarchal household. The patriarch offered them only a skin of water and bread. But the alternative watershed in the wilderness nourished their life with springs and wells of water. Those who defy the logic of the watershed of Canaan are disinherited and expelled from the household. On the other hand, the alternative watershed is a "basin of relations" where life is nurtured and flourishes in the solidarity between the members of the community of creation. The final verse of the Hagar story portrays how the wilderness was a watershed. "God was with the boy, and he grew up; he lived in the wilderness, and became an expert with the bow. He lived in the wilderness of Paran; and his mother got a wife for him from the land of Egypt" (Gen. 21:20–21).

The alternative watershed in the wilderness is a God-indwelling space. In the Hagar story we come across diverse God-talks. The vision of God in the patriarchal narratives is a God who blesses and perpetuates the status quo. The perpetuation of the prevailing order is understood as the will of God. Patriarchal faith is based on the promise of God that the descendants of Abraham would inherit the watershed of Canaan. Conquest and displacement of the native watershed communities are theological projects. Hagar's courageous attempt to complicate the colonial project of the patriarch was sabotaged by God commanding her to return and submit to the mistress. God further endorsed the decision of the patriarchal household to disinherit Ishmael and his mother and to expel them from the household. What we find in this dominant God-talk is the understanding of a powerful, transcendent God who is indifferent to the systemic violence and injustice inflicted upon the subalterns.

In the alternative watershed of the wilderness we see a different God-talk. The watershed in the wilderness is symbolized by bushes and shrubs where the subalterns initiated an alternative God-talk. In Genesis 21 and Exodus 3, God is revealed as the vulnerable one who experiences the pain and pathos of the subalterns. We meet here a God who hears, sees, knows, and intervenes—a God who acts in favor of the subalterns, informed by organic, body-mediated experiences. This is not a God who commands the conquest and destruction of watersheds and watershed communities. This is not a God who legitimizes and perpetuates unjust and sinful practices of oppression and exclusion. Rather the God of the wilderness is a God who makes watersheds that nourish life.

Hagar appears in this story as an alternative theologian who articulates the vision of God by radically challenging the God-talk of the patriarchs. She is the only person in the Bible who named God. In her naming, she avoids the names of God used by the patriarchs. Through her naming, Hagar rejects the deity of the patriarchs and their projects of conquest and invasion of the watersheds. The God of the wilderness watersheds, who appears in the bushes and shrubs, with visions of burning bush and wells of water in the desert, provides an alternative vision of watersheds. For the dispossessed and the displaced that go through desert experiences, God is present as watershed in their struggles for survival, dignity, and liberation. In our contemporary context of growing desertification and dispossession due to climate injustice, we re-vision God as springs of life that kindle our hope to engage in creating alternative watersheds to protect and celebrate life.

The vision of springs and wells of water in the desert empowers the subalterns to believe that life-nourishing watersheds are possible outside the logic and projects of conquest and control. From being the protectors of the colonized watersheds, Hagar invites us to create and be part of alternative watersheds that nourish life and disrupt the colonial projects of our times.

THE GREEN POLITICS OF SONI SORI

Hagar's story is not isolated. We witness a host of Hagars in our times. Soni Sori is one among them, and she too invites us to join the watershed politics to destabilize the colonial dreams and projects of the elitist and casteist state and corporations.

Soni Sori is an Adivasi[38] schoolteacher from the state of Chhattisgarh in India. Chhattisgarh is a resource-rich region, and most of the mines are located on Adivasi land. Extreme deprivation and desertification of the watersheds thanks to corporate plunder and state indifference affect the food sovereignty of the Adivasis and their sovereign right over their land and life. Adivasi identity is closely connected with the watersheds. Their identity, culture, religiosity, moral practices, and livelihood depend on *jal, jungle*, and *jamin* (water, forest, and land). Adivasi alienation from their watersheds and commons is a reality all over the country due to land acquisition for industrial and development projects. In the name of national interest, any protest against corporate plunder or state policies is viewed as seditious, and people are attacked, sexually abused, imprisoned, and killed in the name of progress, patriotism, and development.

Soni Sori and her nephew were arrested in September 2011, accused of conspiring to "wage war" against the government through an unlawful organization. Sori narrates her ordeal at the police station:

> The superintendent asked me to sign documents that would confirm I was involved with the Maoists (left-wing militants). I refused. The police officials stripped me naked, made me stand in an "attention" position and gave me electric shocks on various parts of my body. I still didn't relent. They then shoved red chili powder inside my vagina. By now, I was losing consciousness, but I refused to sign the documents. The cops started inserting stones into my private parts. I finally collapsed.[39]

In the era of neoliberal globalization, protecting watersheds and watershed communities is treated as a crime. More recently, Soni Sori was attacked by unknown assailants with an acid-like substance on her face. Responding to the media, she said, "My face today is the face of the fight in Bastar." Yes, her face resembles the face of the watersheds: colonized and disfigured by greedy corporations.

As Priti Gulati Cox rightly observes,

> The democracy-like substance being rubbed here and there on the Indian countryside, its peoples, birds, animals, is slowly morphing into a giant, dark ash-pile, sinking right in the heart of mineral rich Mother India. But she's not giving up. This mother India is never still. She is always moving. Fearless. The coward state and its cronies will stop at nothing in their efforts to crush Mother India and her fearless mothers and daughters. But she still moves protecting her soil, her forests, her endangered wild Buffalo, her Hill Mynah, and all the living creatures. This is her Memorandum of Understanding with our dying planet.[40]

Through these daring women, Hagar continues to live, protecting watersheds from the imperial projects, to help the movement of life flourish.

NOTES

1. Lynn White Jr., "The Historical Roots of our Ecological Crisis," *Science* 155.3767 (1967): 1204.
2. White, "Historical Roots."

3. Cited in Ramachandra Guha and Juan Martinez-Alier, *Varieties of Environmentalism: Essays North and South* (Delhi, India: Oxford University Press, 1997), 20 (emphasis added).
4. Guha and Martinez-Alier, *Varieties of Environmentalism*.
5. Guha and Martinez-Alier, *Varieties of Environmentalism*, 21.
6. James H. Cone, "Whose Earth Is It, Anyway?" in *Earth Habitat: Eco-Injustice and the Church's Response*, ed. Dieter Hessel and Larry Rasmussen (Minneapolis, MN: Fortress, 2001), 30, 32.
7. "Principles of Environmental Justice," http://www.ejnet.org/ej/principles.html (accessed on June 20, 2017).
8. George E. Tinker, "Spirituality, Native American Personhood, Sovereignty and Solidarity," *Ecumenical Review* 44.3 (1992): 14.
9. Denis Ackermann and Tahira Joyner, "Earth-Healing in South Africa: Challenges to Church and Mosque," in *Women Healing Earth: Third World Women on Ecology, Feminism, and Religion*, ed. Rosemary Radford Ruether (New York: Orbis Books, 1996), 125.
10. See also George Zachariah, *Alternatives Unincorporated: Earth Ethics from the Grassroots* (London: Equinox, 2011).
11. The Earth Bible Team, "Guiding Ecojustice Principles," in *Readings from the Perspective of Earth,* ed. Norman Habel (Cleveland, OH: Pilgrim Press, 2000), 39.
12. Norman Habel, "Engaging the Bible in a New Key: Reading and Preaching with Creation," in *The Season of Creation: A Preaching Commentary*, ed. Norman Habel, 54–68 (Minneapolis, MN: Fortress Press, 2011).
13. The Earth Bible Team, "Guiding Ecojustice Principles," 39.
14. Based on the hermeneutical engagements of suspicion and retrieval, the Earth Bible Team identified six eco-justice principles to develop eco-justice hermeneutics (see The Earth Bible Team, "Guiding Ecojustice Principles," 42–53).
15. Phyllis Trible, *Texts of Terror: Literary-Feminist Readings of Biblical Narratives* (Minneapolis, MN: Fortress Press, 1984), 9.
16. Trible, *Texts of Terror*, 30.
17. Renita J. Weems, *Just a Sister Away: A Womanist Vision of Women's Relationships in the Bible* (San Diego, CA: Lura Media, 1988), 2.
18. Elsa Tamez, "The Woman Who Complicated the History of Salvation," *Cross Currents* 36.2 (1986): 14
19. Trible, *Texts of Terror*, 15.
20. Trevor Dennis, *Sarah Laughed: Women's Voices in the Old Testament* (London: SPCK, 2010), 66,
21. Trible, *Texts of Terror*, 16.
22. Trible, *Texts of Terror*, 4.
23. Tamez, "The Woman Who Complicated the History of Salvation," 14.
24. Delores Williams, *Sisters in the Wilderness: The Challenge of Womanist God-Talk* (Maryknoll, NY: Orbis Books, 1996), 22.
25. Tamez, "The Woman Who Complicated the History of Salvation," 13.
26. Monica Jyotsna Melanchthon, "Unleashing the Power Within: The Bible and Dalits," in *The Future of the Biblical Past: Envisioning Biblical Studies on a Global Key*, ed. Roland Boer and Fernando F. Segovia (Atlanta: Society of Biblical Literature, 2012), 60.
27. Melanchthon, "Unleashing the Power Within."
28. Melanchthon, "Unleashing the Power Within."
29. "What Is a Watershed?" *Watershed Discipleship Blog*. http://watersheddiscipleship.org/what-is-a-watershed/ (accessed July 12, 2017.).
30. "What Is a Watershed?"
31. Jonathan Watts, "Honduran Indigenous Rights Campaigner Wins Goldman Prize," *The Guardian*, April 20, 2015, http://www.theguardian.com/world/2015/apr/20/honduran-indigenous-rights-campaigner-wins-goldman-prize (accessed July 1, 2017).
32. Tamez, "The Woman Who Complicated the History of Salvation," 10.
33. Williams, *Sisters in the Wilderness*, 19.
34. http://www.abarim-publications.com/Meaning/Canaan.html#.Vut6Z-J95dg.
35. Trible, *Texts of Terror*, 15.

36. Roland de Vaux, *Ancient Israel: Its Life and Institutions* (London: Darton, Longman & Todd, 1961), 10.
37. De Vaux, *Ancient Israel*.
38. Indigenous people who are socially ostracized and economically marginalized.
39. Priyali Sur, "Q & A with Indian Tribal Rights Activist Soni Sori," http://www.kractivist.org/tag/maoist/ (accessed June 18, 2017).
40. Priti Gulati Cox, "Soni Sori as Mother India: A Painting Dedicated to Resilience and Resistance," http://www.indiaresists.com/soni-sori-mother-india-painting-dedicated-resilience-resistance/?fb_action_ids=10207575279632876&fb_action_types=og.shares (accessed June 18, 2017).

Chapter Twelve

Lost Land

Visualizing Deforestation and Eschatology in the Apocalypse of John and the Column of Trajan in Rome

Barbara Rossing

"Trajan's column is . . . a Roman narrative of national identity and destiny that is characterized by aggression and violence toward both people and land."[1]

"On either side of the river is the tree of life . . . and the leaves of the tree are for the healing of the nations." (Rev. 22:2)

The economic critique of Rome in Revelation 18 opposes the Roman narrative with Hebrew prophets' critiques of ancient imperial economic injustices.[2] In terms of visual exegesis, the Emperor Trajan's column, erected in Rome after the violent conquest of Romania in 106 CE, exemplifies the Roman narrative of conquest that John is critiquing in Revelation. This essay argues that the iconography of Trajan's column—including the conquest of Romania's forests—furnishes visual insights on how John constructed his counternarrative against Rome's idolatrous economy. The column's upward spiraling sculptural narrative of Trajan's military campaigns, culminating in the huge statue of the triumphant emperor at the top, embodies Rome's eschatology of eternal empire—the very eschatology Revelation opposes. Visual reimagining of the tree of life (Rev. 22:2) can help us envision world-healing today.

CONQUEST OF FORESTS AND THE ROLE OF DEFORESTATION IN TODAY'S CLIMATE CRISIS

Destruction of peoples' forests by private industry and multinational corporations constitutes a global justice crisis today, especially for indigenous communities. On the reverse of this claim is the point made by the poet Wendell Berry, that to save the (indigenous) people we must also save the land to which they belong.[3]

In a 2014 sermon Indonesian bishop Rev. Willem Simarmata hauntingly decried the crisis of deforestation of Indonesia's once-verdant landscape.[4] Prior to the 1980s, in his village on the island of Samosir in North Sumatra, "you could hear the gigantic sound of the water of rivers." But now, "there are no streams of water anymore, because the indigenous trees have disappeared." Multinational companies have replaced Indonesia's rain forests with palm oil and eucalyptus pulp plantations, taking advantage of economic incentives to produce biofuel.[5] Because the plantations require so much water, rivers dry up. "My heart longs to hear the same voice (of the rivers)," laments Rev. Simarmata. "But it is no longer there . . . . It is now history."

For Rev. Simarmata, the environmental justice question becomes also a biblical hermeneutical question: "Is it not against God to take away the reality of the imagery of a tree planted by streams of water from the Scripture?" If scripture teaches people to visualize their relationship to God in terms of a tree planted beside a river (Ps. 1:3), then is scripture's witness diminished when the reality of rivers and trees disappears from people's lives?

The massive scale of the plunder and deforestation of Indonesia's rain forests is staggering. The 2016 film *Before the Flood* takes viewers on an aerial flyover tour of Indonesia's burning forests and palm plantations. "I've never seen anything like this," host Leonardo DeCaprio says of the smoke-choked landscape. "Welcome to Sumatra," says activist Farwiza Farhan. "In Indonesia we're seeing fires deliberately set to grow palm oil plantations, the cheapest vegetable oil in the world. This cheap commodity is making companies tremendous profits." The expansion of the palm oil industry in Indonesia "has taken over about 80 percent of our forests. . . . Companies bribe government officials to issue a permit to them to start burning the land."[6]

Deforestation destroys communities and livelihoods. In Borneo, brutal ethnic cleansing of the Madurese people in 2001 prepared the way for palm oil companies to burn the forests and replace them with plantations.[7] The rain forests of the Amazon and the Congo River Basin, like those of Indonesia, are all under assault. When villages and indigenous communities try to assert their rights to their land, their leaders are often killed. In Honduras, renowned environmental activist and indigenous leader Berta Cacercas was murdered after organizing protests and campaigns to prevent oppressive logging and to keep a dam from displacing indigenous people.[8] In Brazil, indigenous environmental activist Chico Mendes, as well as Sister Dorothy Stang and other defenders of forests, have been murdered for their work. In the Philippines, Father Nerilito Satur, a young priest, was murdered for his opposition to illegal logging. In Guatemala in 2015, after the government suspended operations of the largest palm oil plantation, three community leaders were abducted and one murdered. Mexican indigenous environmental activist Isidro Baldenegro Lopez and many others have all been killed for their work of protecting forest ecosystems and communities.[9]

Assaults on forests, lands, and rivers for short-term private profits at the expense of the public good pose an urgent justice crisis, as Rev. Simarmata notes. Moreover, cutting down forests also accelerates climate change, contributing 15 percent of annual global carbon emissions. Forests provide vital, living carbon storehouses. Trees breathe in carbon, sequestering it in the leaves and trunks. Rain forests serve as the "lungs of our planet," as Pope Francis describes in his 2015 encyclical *Laudato Si.*[10] Tropical peat swamp forests such as those in Borneo function as enormous "carbon sinks," safely sequestering huge amounts of carbon in the peat soil itself as well as in the trees. Deliberate burning of forests on the scale happening in Indonesia acts "like a carbon bomb," says Lynsey Allen, executive director of Rainforest Action Network.[11] The burning of Borneo's forests constitutes the largest single global increase in carbon emissions in two millennia. Globally, more than 15 billion trees are cut down or burned each year.[12] Deforestation adds more carbon to the atmosphere than the total of all the world's cars and trucks on the roads.

Scientists assure us that a large-scale reversal or "drawdown" of carbon from the atmosphere is still possible, in order to prevent the worst effects of global warming and to stabilize global temperatures. But the world's nations must reverse deforestation and act to preserve indigenous communities' forests. Economic incentives must also support traditional and innovative forest and soil practices such as biochar, agroforestry, and other practices that return carbon to the soil, rather than incentivizing forest clearing for biofuel production. Forests and agriculture will play key roles in drawing down carbon: "Stopping all deforestation and restoring forest resources could offset up to one-third of all carbon emissions worldwide," according to scientific analyses.[13]

How do we speak theologically of rampant deforestation and assault on peoples' lands, in the context of climate change? How does scripture's imaging of those who trust the Lord as trees beside the river speak to people and communities whose life depends on forests, if rivers and trees have disappeared?

This essay applies empire-critical scholarship to interpret deforestation and devastation of peoples' lands not only as an ecological justice crisis, but also as a crisis of eschatology. Eschatology—especially for women, and for enslaved and colonized peoples—is grounded in "struggle and resistance."[14] Eschatology recognizes that things are not how they are meant to be. For earliest Christians, resistance was an important dimension of eschatology. The current situation—what they called "the present age"—is a system in which unjust structures of power have temporarily taken over the world and its life—but this system will not last forever. Biblical critiques of ancient imperial injustice by prophets such as John of Patmos in Revelation 18 can give an eschatological frame for interpreting the crisis of climate injustice and assault against Earth and its communities.

DEFORESTATION AND PROPHETIC CRITIQUES IN THE HEBREW BIBLE: CEDARS OF LEBANON

We begin with the ancient problem of deforestation in the Mediterranean. Hebrew prophets' critiques of ancient empires' economic injustice, including deforestation, provide the biblical background to Revelation's critique of Rome and its idolatrous economy in chapter 18.

Deforestation is not a recent problem, although the scale on which it is practiced today is unprecedented. As environmental historian J. Donald Hughes observes, "Mediterranean environmental history is in large part a history of deforestation and its consequences."[15] Destruction of the forests of the Mediterranean began as early as the Neolithic period.[16] The most prized timber in the ancient Near East was cut from the cedar forests in the mountains of Lebanon—huge logs valuable as load-bearing beams both for building construction and ship masts. Deforestation of the cedars of Lebanon was already underway as early as 2800 BCE. Lebanese cities of Tyre, Sidon, and Byblos exported cedars to Egypt and Mesopotamia for shipbuilding, in exchange for metals. Logging of the cedars powered the fearsome Phoenician (Lebanese) shipping economy.

Solomon's temple, built through the conscripted labor of more than 30,000 people, accelerated the imperial deforestation of Lebanon's cedar forests. As chronicled in 1 Kings 5, King Solomon's shrewd "wisdom" forged a treaty with the king of Lebanon for large-scale logging of cedars for construction of his temple in Jerusalem, in exchange for Judah's food and agricultural crops. King Hiram of Lebanon's message to King Solomon lays out the terms of this transnational contract:

> "I will fulfill all your needs in the matter of cedar and cypress timber. My servants shall bring it down to the sea from the Lebanon; I will make it into rafts to go by sea to the place you indicate. . . . And you shall meet my needs by providing food for my household." So Hiram supplied Solomon's every need for timber of cedar and cypress. Solomon in turn gave Hiram twenty

> thousand cors of wheat as food for his household, and twenty cors of fine oil. Solomon gave this to Hiram year by year. So the Lord gave Solomon wisdom. . . . King Solomon conscripted forced labor out of all Israel; the levy numbered thirty thousand men. He sent them to the Lebanon, ten thousand a month in shifts (1 Kings 5:9–14 RSV)

Isaiah and other prophets denounced the denuding of cedar forests as part of their critiques of Israel's and Judah's unjust alliances with foreign powers (Isa. 37:24). As Ched Myers notes, it is striking that Isaiah portrays the trees themselves as rejoicing at the fall of the Babylonian Empire: "How the oppressor has ceased! . . . The whole earth is at rest and quiet; they break forth into singing. The cypresses exult over you, and the cedars of Lebanon, saying, 'Since you were laid low, no one comes to cut us down!'" (Isa. 14:4).[17]

The prophet Ezekiel gives the most devastating critique of Tyre's (Lebanon's) exploitative trade and deforestation, in the oracles against foreign nations in Ezekiel 26–28—from which Revelation 18 draws some six centuries later for the prophetic critique of Rome's predatory economic system. Tyre boasts of its power and invincibility, "the merchant of the peoples on many coastlands" (Ezek. 27:1), sitting at the entrance to the sea. In a brilliant metaphor, Ezekiel images Tyre as a beautiful merchant ship constructed of materials from all its global trading partners: fir trees from Lebanon for the mast, oak from Bashan for oars, and luxury goods from three continents. Below deck, the ship's hold contains trade goods taken from all over the world, even at the cost of murdered human lives (Ezek. 27:13, *nephesh adam*). Dealers, traders, and import and export nations are all named in this cargo list. Ezekiel portrays the shipwreck of the merchant ship Tyre, as it sails out on the water to sink. Princes who watch sit in deep mourning, appalled that the ship Tyre has perished, lamenting the disappearance of the global mercantile system (Ezek. 26:16–18).

DEFORESTATION, CONQUEST, AND ANCIENT SIEGE WARFARE

Destroying forests served not only for building construction and shipping, but also for ancient warfare and military siege. Besieging villagers' fruit trees and orchards was standard Assyrian conquest practice. Sandra Richter cites Sargon II's boasts over the city of Ursal after his conquest: "I entered triumphantly. . . . His great trees, the adornment of his palace, I cut down like millet. . . . The trunks of all those trees which I had cut down I gathered together, heaped them in a pile and burned them with fire."[18] Assyrians communicated this strategy visually, in sculptural images as well as texts. Richter suggests that scenes of Assyrian troops cutting down date palms in the siege of Dilbat, as depicted at the Palace of Sinacherib, may help make sense of Deuteronomy's prohibition of annihilation of orchards, "When you besiege a city for many days, to make war against it in order to capture it, you shall not destroy its trees" (Deut. 20:19), a verse echoed in Revelation 7:3.

The Romans intensified the use of environmental destruction in conquest and warfare, continuing the precedent of the Hellenistic, Ptolemaic, and Seleucid empires.[19] Romans deliberately salted fields after the conquest of Carthage so no crops could grow. Roman legions felled large quantities of trees for siege works, battering rams, catapults, camps, and forts. In his description of the siege of Jerusalem by the Romans in 70 CE, the Jewish author Josephus laments the clear-cutting of Jerusalem's forests and countryside by Roman legions for construction of earthworks, describing the former forests as "stripped naked" (*gegymnōto*). "Pitiful too was the aspect of the country, sites formerly beautiful with trees . . . now reduced to an utter desert and stripped bare of timber."[20]

Rome also expanded the strategic use of visual propaganda to celebrate its military conquests. Along with parading enslaved captive people and spoils of wars, Roman victory processions displayed placards of lands and trees taken captive. Pliny the Elder describes the parading of Judea's balsam trees captured by the Romans:

> Ever since the time of Pompey the Great even trees have figured among the captives in our triumphal processions. The balsam-tree is now a subject of Rome, and pays tribute together with the race to which it belongs.[21]

Tacitus's famous quotation attributed to the British chieftain Calgacus, lamenting the Roman conquest of Britain, could apply to many other conquered lands:

> These plunderers of the world [the Romans], after exhausting the land by their devastations, are rifling the ocean: stimulated by avarice, if their enemy be rich; by ambition, if poor; unsatiated by the East and by the West: the only people who behold wealth and indigence with equal avidity. To ravage, to slaughter, to usurp under false titles, they call empire; and where they make a desert, they call it peace.[22]

VISUAL EXEGESIS: IMPERIAL ESCHATOLOGY, ROME'S "GOSPEL," AND THE COLUMN OF EMPEROR TRAJAN

The most vivid monument to Rome's never-ending wars of conquest is the column of Emperor Trajan. This spectacular visual monument narrates not only violent Roman military victory, but also Roman eschatology—the idea of empire and conquest without end, spiraling upwards to the heavens: *Roma Aeterna*.[23]

The column of Trajan was dedicated in 113 CE to celebrate Emperor Trajan's conquest of Dacia (Romania) in two back-to-back wars. Trajan and tens of thousands of troops crossed the Danube River on two of the longest bridges ever built in antiquity and then defeated the Dacian "barbarian" army in its forested mountain terrain. The quantity of loot Trajan and his troops brought back from Dacia was "staggering," notes Andrew Curry. "One contemporary chronicler boasted that the conquest yielded a half million pounds of gold and a million pounds of silver, not to mention a fertile new province."[24]

Trajan's column served as a "propaganda piece intended to be noticed and 'read' by the public," notes Arthur Dewey.[25] A kind of Tower of Babel, the column of Trajan makes a claim for Rome's rule extending upward toward the heavens, a vision of an eternal empire, without end. Intricately carved, like a scroll unrolling a succession of narrative scenes, the 190-meter frieze of 153 spiraling panels graphically chronicles the conquest and cutting of forests, assaults on rivers, building of bridges and siege works, mining of resources, looting of treasure, and overall conquest of the Dacian landscape as part of the sequence of battles against the Dacian (Romanian) peoples. The narrative spirals twenty-three times around the shaft of the column, reading "like a modern-day comic strip."[26] The upward spiraling of the sculptural narrative of conquest "presents a public location and structure for viewers to take these scenes to heart and to keep the momentum going until they reach the imperial figure on top"—namely, the colossal bronze statue of Trajan.

The "gospel of Rome" is what Trajan's column functions to advance visually, similar to Emperor Augustus's *Res Gestae* in the first century. Whereas Augustus had announced his "gospel" or *euangelion* textually, through inscriptions listing his accomplishments on bronze pillars in Rome and copied throughout the empire, Trajan used his towering column to announce the same Roman gospel. "We do not have a *Res Gestae* of the Emperor Trajan," says Dewey, but "Trajan's column represents a significant turn in the advancement of the gospel of Rome.[27]

Trajan's gospel also makes an eschatological claim: Rome's conquest of the whole world is never-ending. The gods are shown intervening in key scenes, to give Trajan's victory a divine stamp. Eternal Rome, as visually suggested by the upward spiral, is "conquest without end." Images of military strategy and victory dominate the column. Trajan appears in fifty-eight scenes. Graphic violence shows Dacian houses in flames, Roman soldiers with cutoff heads in their mouths, looting and pillaging while villagers flee. As Davina Lopez notes, the column is a "penetrating example of an attempt to stabilize a Roman narrative of national identity and destiny that is characterized by aggression and violence toward both people and land."[28]

Key to Trajan's conquest of Dacia was first to conquer the Danube River. At the beginning of the campaign, at the bottom of Trajan's column, we see the Danube River personified as a male figure. Harris suggests that proximity to water-transport—whether by river or sea—often determined whether or not a conquered area became deforested. "Being close to water-borne transport under the Roman Empire meant economic opportunity and also ecological trouble."[29] Trees appear in a striking number of the column's 153 sculptural panels, usually in the process of being chopped down by soldiers wielding axes. At the beginning of the campaign near the bottom of the column, we see Roman troops logging the forests to build bridges to cross the Danube. As Roman legions undertake huge campaigns to build forts and other structures, more trees are chopped down. Further up the column, the Dacian king hides in a tree. Over the course of multiple scenes of violence and beheading, spiraling upward through two wars, Trajan's military forces conquer the Dacian people and also their lands, forests, and trees.

With the exception of Dewey and Lopez, the column of Trajan has received little attention from biblical scholars—perhaps because of its late date. One methodological challenge is how to draw on a later second-century monument to interpret a first-century biblical text. Here I take my cue from Brigitte Kahl's 2015 chapter on "visual exegesis"[30] arguing that a later second-century statue of Emperor Hadrian can be "compatible" with a reimagination of Revelation. In developing criteria for visual exegesis Kahl focuses not strictly on contemporaneous dates but on the "imperial imagination." Historical context "does not need to be confined to an all-too-narrow chronological framework," Kahl argues. Rather, we can look for "communalities" that "bridge considerable time gaps." James Harrison likewise argues that there is a "ubiquity of certain visual elements" that allow one to call some monuments "a typical Roman monument"—that is, it could predate or postdate a text by some years and still be usable. Even though second-century imperial statue or monument may postdate a text, it forms "part of a shared symbolic and imaginary universe."[31]

I will make a similar claim for Trajan's column, erected in Rome a decade after Revelation and at a geographical distance thousands of miles away from John's location in Asia Minor. Despite the distance of time and space, using Kahl's method, we can reference the column as part of a "shared symbolic and imaginary universe" that John critiques in Revelation. I suggest that the overtly eschatological and ecological iconography of Trajan's column can help furnish important insights for how John constructed his critique of Rome in Revelation 18, including the economic critique of Rome's endless extractive conquests of lands and enslavement of peoples—countering Babylon's/Rome's eschatological boast that it would "never" see mourning (Rev. 18:7).

APOCALYPSES AND END-TIMES AS THE END OF EMPIRE

The eschatological book of Revelation takes up the tradition of Jewish apocalyptic and prophetic resistance literature, opposing unjust imperial conquest. The characterization of Revelation as "prophecy" (1:3) situates it in the tradition of Hebrew prophets. Prophecy is not about predicting the future so much as about diagnosing and unmasking the present.

Like other apocalypses, the book of Revelation employs a narrative framework. It tells the story of the Lamb Jesus who defeats evil and leads the community on a great exodus out of the unjust empire, personified both as a dragon and as "Babylon." The narrative journey ends in a utopic new city, the New Jerusalem, with a river of life and a healing tree in a renewed world. Although the plagues of ecological catastrophe can give the impression that Revelation is anti-ecological, what the book describes is not Earth's destruction but rather its liberation, with the proclamation that "the time (*kairos*) has come . . . for destroying those who destroy the Earth" (Rev. 11:18). Earth plays a central role in the narrative's dramatic conflict. In one of the most spectacular scenes, Earth herself becomes a hero in Revelation 12:16—coming to the help of a mythic woman who represents God's people, about to be killed by the dragon (empire).

Revelation locates the audience in a brief "in-between," symbolically portrayed as the time and space after the expulsion of the dragon ("Satan, the Deceiver of the whole empire," *oikoumenē*; Rev. 12:9) from heaven, but before God finally locks Satan down in the abyss (Rev. 20:3, 10).[32] This location is important for reading our situation today in light of Revelation. Oppression will get worse on Earth, John says. But Jesus the Lamb has already conquered. Ours is a finite, short time (*kairos*), symbolically identified as 1,260 days (Rev. 11:3, 12:6), before God's final judgment against the Roman Empire. The in-between place and time in which we live may seem hopeless, but it is the turning of the ages. It is a space of new birth, in which God's people are "nourished" (*trephetai*; Rev. 12:6, 14), and in which God's people play an important role in the struggle. Satan has already been defeated by Jesus and by the courageous witness and testimony of God's people (Rev. 12:11). "The kingdom of this world has become the kingdom of our Lord and of his Christ" (Rev. 11:15), an event that has already happened!

Liberation scholars Allan Boesak, Elisabeth Schüssler Fiorenza, Pablo Richard, Brian Blount, and others underscore Revelation's eschatological critique of the Roman imperial system.[33] As Anathea Portier Young and Richard Horsley have demonstrated, earlier Jewish apocalyptic literature such as Daniel and 1 Enoch emerged as a literature of resistance to empire during the Seleucid and Ptolemaic regimes, when persecution became at times so totalizing that the regimes "de-created" the world.[34] Their most important insight is that the discourse of apocalyptic is not escapist, otherworldly, or despairing of the world, as some formerly interpreted apocalyptic. It is resistance discourse. The "end" (*eschaton*) that these apocalyptic texts envision is not the end of the created world but rather the end of unjust empire (*oikoumenē*).[35]

Apocalypses rebuild people's imaginations and mythic consciousness, as Chilean Pablo Richard underscores.[36] In the face of empire and its totalizing narrative of conquest, biblical apocalypses provide a counternarrative that includes renewal for Earth and its communities. A "revolution of the imagination" is how John Collins describes the apocalyptic worldview.[37] Apocalypses teach the community that empires are temporary, and that true reality is an alternative reality.

REVELATION 18: CRITIQUE OF DEFORESTATION AS SYMPTOMATIC OF ROME'S UNJUST ECONOMY

The Roman imperial economy wreaked ecological havoc upon its territories, leaving "ruined cities surrounded by ruined land" across the Mediterranean world.[38] Deforestation, erosion, siltation, and extinctions of animals and habitats were consequences of the Roman extractive economy. Environmental historian J. Donald Hughes references Pliny the Elder's *Natural History* and other ancient texts to document the ecological consequences of the Roman Empire's plunder of lands and peoples. While forests recovered sustainably in some places, there is little question that Mediterranean forests were largely denuded by the time of the New Testament's writing.

Revelation 18 may be the most daring anti-Roman polemic ever written during the empire's rule. It brilliantly and poetically combines the lament and cargo list of Ezekiel's anti-Tyre oracle with the proleptic funeral for the king of Babylon in Isaiah 14, as well as other anti-Babylon oracles, in order to critique Rome's insatiable lust for resources. John portrays the fall of Rome's unbridled economic system through a series of funeral dirges voiced by three groups who profited from Babylon's wealth: kings, merchants, and seafarers. Each group cries "Alas! Alas!" ("Woe," *ouai*; Rev. 18:9, 16, 19), lamenting their fallen city. The central dirge is that of the merchants, lamenting the loss of shipments of cargo they can no longer buy and sell (Rev. 18:11–17).

Rome's crimes extended beyond crimes against humanity to crimes against creation. With the cargo list of Rev. 18:12–13 John connects the over-consumption of the empire with ecological devastation of lands and peoples. The cargo list of Rev. 18:12–13 encompasses the span of Rome's extractions from the land and sea: gold, precious stones, pearls, exotic hardwoods and wooden products, ivory, metals, marble, luxury spices, food, armaments and war horses, and even "slaves, that is, human souls" (*sōmatōn, kai psychas anthrōpōn*; Rev. 18:13):

> The merchants of the earth weep and mourn for her, since no one buys their cargo any more, cargo of gold, silver, jewels and pearls, fine linen, purple, silk and scarlet, all kinds of scented wood (*pan xylon thyinon*), all articles of ivory, all articles of costly wood (*pan skyos ek xylou timiōtatou*), bronze, iron and marble, cinnamon, spice, incense, myrrh, frankincense, wine, oil, fine flour and wheat, cattle and sheep, horses and chariots, and slaves, that is, human souls. (Rev. 18:11–13 RSV)

The model of the cargo list draws from Ezekiel's critique of the merchant empire Tyre (Ezek. 27:12–22), updated to specifically indict Rome's economy. The final two items in the cargo list—"slaves, even human lives" (18:13)—furnish the most explicit critique of slavery and slave trade anywhere in the New Testament. John denounces the lucrative slave trade that served as the economic backbone of the Roman system.[39] Slaves are not just "bodies" (*sōmatōn*), he insists, but living people, "human souls" (*psychai*).

Richard Bauckham's economic analysis of the cargo list of Rev. 18:12–13 traces the origins of the twenty-eight items of merchandise to their sources in North Africa and other locations.[40] I follow Bauckham and extend his economic analysis also ecologically. Using Pliny the Elder and other ancient sources cited by Bauckham, in conversation with J. Donald Hughes's *Environmental Problems of the Greeks and Romans*, Meiggs's *Trees and Timber in the Ancient World*, and recent archaeological survey work on deforestation in Asia Minor by Nic Rauh, we can interpret John's economic critique of Rome also as an ecological critique of Rome's deforestation and devastation.[41]

John shows a remarkable understanding of the damage Rome has done to the environment. Two items in the cargo list of Revelation 18:12–13 are forest products: "all kinds of scented woods (*xylon thyinon*)," likely rare citrus or "thyine" tree imported from North Africa, especially for table tops favored by the rich; and "objects made of ivory and of expensive wood," possibly ebony or cypress from Lebanon. Both were specialty imported woods.[42] North Africa's thyine (citrus) forests had suffered ecological damage and were being depleted.[43] Whereas citrus/thyine forests had once been widespread across North Africa, by the time of the first century the citrus trees' range had shrunk to only a small part of Morocco. In addition, "cinnamon" (Rev. 18:13) is a tree spice whose harvest sometimes necessitated killing the entire tree.

Roman authors applaud Rome's deforestation of conquered lands. Aelius Aristides's *Roman Oration* celebrates Rome's stripping of forests "naked" (*gymnos*), as evidenced by the huge logs he sees arriving in Rome's harbor from Asia and Africa:

> So many merchants' ships arrive here, conveying every kind of goods from every people every hour and every day, so that the city is like a factory

> common to the whole earth. It is possible to see so many cargoes from India and even from Arabia Felix, if you wish, that one imagines that for the future *the trees are left bare (gymna)* for the people there and that they must come here to beg for their own produce.[44]

Could it be that John, like Aelius Aristides, had watched so many ships unload logs from the forests of conquered nations that he would agree with Aristides's diagnosis: "One imagines that for the future the trees there are left bare"? John's Apocalypse pronounces a bold verdict of "no" against the whole Roman system.

John portrays the final defeat of Babylon/Rome not as a military siege but in a legal class-action court trial scene.[45] The plaintiffs are the saints, representing all Rome's victims who have been killed on earth. The charge is murder: "In you was found the blood of prophets and of saints, and of all who have been slaughtered on earth" (Rev. 18:24). The cargo list of Rev. 18:12–13 serves as the "list of exhibits in the lawsuit," notes Allen Callahan.[46] The judge is God. An angelic voice pronounces Babylon guilty on all charges and sentences the empire to receive a like measure of its own unjust medicine at the hands of its victims (Rev. 18:6–8).

The vision culminates with a dramatization of Babylon's fall (Rev. 18:21), modeled on a similar scene from Jeremiah 51:63–64. An angel takes up a large millstone and throws it into the sea, proclaiming Babylon's/Rome's final end.

CONCLUSION: DUELING ESCHATOLOGIES, EMPIRE AND ECOLOGY

The first century was a time of dueling eschatologies—Roman boasts of its imperial eternity ("Roma Aeterna") versus Christian and Jewish hope for an end to oppression and a future in God's renewed world. Rome viewed itself as endless and eternal, politically and geographically as well as temporally. I have argued that the upward spiraling sculptural narrative of Trajan's column proclaims Rome's eternal "gospel" of conquest—embodying the very Roman eschatology John condemns as idolatrous. John called on communities of Jesus's followers to "come out" (Rev. 18:4) from participation in the unjust economic system, lest they share in its sins. He advocated exodus from an empire that harmed peoples and also Earth.

This perspective of dueling eschatologies can help us today, as we draw on the Bible to discern and resist injustice against peoples and lands. As Jürgen Moltmann reminds us, eschatology announces not the end of the world but "the end of the system of this world."[47] In order to reclaim the subversive and hopeful power of New Testament eschatologies today, we must reimagine eschatology not as the end of the created world, but rather as the end of empire. We can learn from New Testament authors' critique of Rome's eschatological propaganda. The stunning iconography of the Roman "gospel" of conquest, proclaimed on Trajan's column in Rome, can help us diagnose and respond to idolatrous gospels and eschatologies today—including to claims of endless fossil fuels, endless conquest, endless GDP growth, and other lies. The endlessly spiraling narrative of the "system of this world" that leads to deforestation and death must come to an end.

Climate scientists use the term "irreversible"—an eschatological term—to warn of the consequences of inaction. Rev. Simarmata likewise frames the question of the tree planted by water and Indonesia's deforestation in eschatological terms. He asks, "Can we still maintain this imagery of a tree planted by a river, of a tree planted by streams of water in our time? Is the imagery still there? Is the imagery not being threatened by a constant destruction of the jungle and forest in our world, which has caused the disappearance of streams of water from many lands?"[48]

It is not too late. Kenyan Wangari Maathai, founder of the Green Belt Movement, interprets Revelation's world-healing vision as an invitation to "prophets" today, in the tradition of John of Patmos, to work for world-healing. Trees and forests have amazing biological power for healing. Revelation's New Jerusalem vision of the "tree of life" on either side of the river of life, promising "leaves of the tree for the healing of the nations" (Rev. 22:2), coheres with scientific and biological understandings of the tree of life and forests of life as a community of relationships. As Maathai writes of Revelation, the call to us as prophets is to dream of "an alternative to the degradation of the environment that has turned waters of life here and earth that were 'bright as crystal' into mud and silt, and the 'tree of life with its twelve kinds of fruit' into stumps and charcoal."[49]

Biblical hermeneutics must engage evidence from scientists who underscore the urgency of our present moment, while also assuring us it is not too late to act. Revelation embodies a strong call for repentance. The call of Revelation is to cease trafficking with the systems of Babylon/Rome before it is too late and to dare to reimagine alternatives. Revelation calls on us to ally ourselves as citizens of God's alternative political economy, the New Jerusalem, whose open gates welcome all, especially the poor and those "without money" (Rev. 21:6, 22:17). The invitation to "Come" (Rev. 22:14) invites everyone to God's healing tree of life, planted beside the river of life.

NOTES

1. Davina Lopez, "Visualizing Significant Otherness: Reimagining Pauline Studies Through Hybrid Lenses," in *The Colonized Apostle: Paul Through Post-Colonial Eyes*, ed. Joseph Marchal (Minneapolis, MN: Fortress, 2011), 88.

2. For the ancient Roman Empire, the credo of "Roma Aeterna" ("eternal Rome") was the dominant totalizing narrative. For us today, the credo of what Naomi Klein calls "winner take

all capitalism" is our world's dominant totalizing narrative. See Sam Mowe, "Capitalism vs. the Climate: Naomi Klein On Why Only a Mass Movement Can Save Us from Ourselves," *Tricycle* 25 (Fall 2015), https://tricycle.org/magazine/capitalism-vs-climate; Naomi Klein, *This Changes Everything: Capitalism vs. the Climate* (London: Penguin, 2014).

3. Wendell Berry, *Our Only World* (Berkley, CA: Counterpoint, 2015), 58.

4. Willem T. P. Simarmata, "Like a Tree Planted by Streams of Water" (manuscript from the 2014 Lutheran World Federation Council meeting in Medan, Indonesia). Pastor Simarmata is bishop (ephorus) in the HKPB, the largest Protestant church in Indonesia, with membership of 3.5 million in thirty-five hundred congregations.

5. See Abrahm Lustgarten, "Palm Oil Was Supposed to Help Save the Planet: Instead It Unleashed a Catastrophe," *New York Times Magazine,* (November 24, 2018).

6. *Before the Flood*, directed by Fisher Stevens (RatPac Dosumentary Films and Appian Way, 2016).

7. Lustgarten, "Palm Oil."

8. John Dear, *They Will Inherit the Earth: Peace & Nonviolence in a Time of Climate Change* (Maryknoll, NY: Orbis, 2018), 61.

9. See interactive essay by Monica Ulmanu, Alan Evans, and Georgia Brown, "The Defenders: 207 Environmental Defenders Have Been Killed in 2017 While Protecting Their Community's Land or Natural Resources," *The Guardian* (July 13, 2017), www.theguardian.com/environment/ng-interactive/2017/jul/13/the-defenders-tracker.

10. Pope Francis, *Laudato Si: On Care for Our Common Home* (New York: Paulist, 2015), sec. 38.

11. *Before the Flood*, directed by Fisher Stevens (RatPac Dosumentary Films and Appian Way, 2016).

12. Justin Worland, "Here's How Many Trees Humans Cut Down Each Year," *Time Magazine* (September 2, 2015).

13. Paul Hawken and Tom Steyer, eds., *Drawdown: The Most Comprehensive Plan Ever to Reverse Global Warming* (New York: Penguin, 2017), 110. Project Drawdown is an effort of scientists, engineers, entrepreneurs, and advocates to "describe a realistic future in which the world achieves drawdown by collecting and analyzing the best available research on one hundred carefully vetted technological, social, and ecological solutions," proposing the one hundred most effective ways to "draw down" carbon dioxide out of the atmosphere in order to reverse the increase in global temperatures.

14. Kwok Pui-lan, "Mending of Creation: Women, Nature, and Eschatological Hope," in *Liberating Eschatology: Essays in Honor of Letty M. Russell*, ed. Margaret A. Farley and Serene Jones (Louisville, KY: Westminster John Knox, 1999), 152.

15. J. Donald Hughes, *Environmental Problems of the Greeks and Romans*, 2nd ed. (Baltimore, MD: Johns Hopkins University Press, 2014), ix.

16. W. V. Harris, "Defining and Detecting Ancient Mediterranean Deforestation, 800 BCE to 700 CE," in *The Ancient Mediterranean Environment between Science and History*, ed. W. V. Harris (Leiden: Brill, 2013). For deforestation in the Epic of Gilgamesh and other ancient Near East texts and images, including Trajan's column, see also K. Jan Oosthoek, "The Role of Wood in World History," October 15, 1998, www.eh-resources.org/the-role-of-wood-in-world-history (Accessed May 20, 2017).

17. Ched Myers, "'The Cedar Has Fallen!' The Prophetic Word vs. Imperial Clear-Cutting," in *Earth and Word: Classic Sermons on Saving the Planet*, ed. David Rhoads (New York: Continuum, 2007), 220.

18. Sandra Richter, "Environmental Law in Deuteronomy: One Lens on a Biblical Theology of Creation Care," *Bulletin for Biblical Research* 20.3 (2010): 367.

19. For the Hellenistic siege of Tyre and deforestation of Tyre's environs, see Micah Kiel, *Apocalyptic Ecology: The Book of Revelation, the Earth and the Future* (Collegeville, MN: Liturgical Press, 2017), 43–45; citing Russell Meiggs, *Trees and Timber in the Ancient Mediterranean World* (Oxford: Clarendon, 1982), 162.

20. Flavius Josephus, *The Jewish War*, 2 vols., trans. H. St. J. Thackeray, Loeb Classical Library (Cambridge, MA: Harvard University Press, 1943), 5.264, 6.6–7.

21. Pliny, *Natural History*, trans. H. Rackham, Loeb Classical Library (Cambridge, MA: Harvard University Press, 1945), 12.111–12.

22. Tacitus, *Agricola*, trans. John Jackson, Loeb Classical Library (Cambridge, MA: Harvard University Press, 1945), 30.

23. See Andrew Curry, "Trajan's Amazing Column," with photographs by Kenneth Garrett and interactive graphics, *National Geographic Magazine* (April 2015), www.nationalgeographic.com/trajan-column. This website shows each of the 153 sculpture panel images: www.trajans-column.org.

24. Curry, "Trajan's Amazing Column."

25. Arthur J. Dewey, "The Gospel of Trajan," in *Jesus, The Voice, and the Text: Beyond the Oral and the Written Gospel*, ed. Tom Thatcher (Waco, TX: Baylor University Press, 2008), 188.

26. Curry, "Trajan's Amazing Column."

27. Dewey, "Gospel of Trajan," 185.

28. Lopez, "Visualizing Significant Otherness," 74–94.

29. Harris, "Defining and Detecting," 186.

30. Brigitte Kahl, "Gaia, Polis, and Ekklesia at the Miletus Market Gate: An Eco-Critical Reimagination of Revelation 12:16," in *The First Urban Churches 1: Methodological Foundations*, ed. James R. Harrison and L. L. Welborn (Atlanta, GA: Society of Biblical Literature Press, 2015), 111–50.

31. James R. Harrison, "'More Than Conquerors' (Rom 8:37): Paul's Gospel and the Augustan Triumphal Arches of the Greek East and Latin West," *Buried History* 47 (2011): 3.

32. For the theme of deception, see Wiriya Tipvarakankoon, *The Theme of Deception in the Book of Revelation: Bringing Early Christian and Thai Cultures into Dialogue* (Claremont, GA: Claremont Press, 2017).

33. Allan Boesak, *Comfort and Protest: The Apocalypse from a South African Perspective* (Philadelphia, PA: Westminster, 1987); Elisabeth Schüssler Fiorenza, *Revelation: Vision of a Just World* (Minneapolis, MN: Fortress, 1991); Pablo Richard, *Apocalypse: A People's Commentary on the Book of Revelation* (Maryknoll, NY: Orbis, 1995); Brian Blount, *Can I Get A Witness? Reading Revelation Through African American Culture* (Louisville, KY: Westminster, 2005).

34. Anathea Portier Young, *Apocalypse Against Empire: Theologies of Resistance in Early Judaism* (Grand Rapids, MI: Eerdmans, 2011); Richard Horsley, *Revolt of the Scribes: Resistance and Apocalyptic Origins* (Minneapolis, MN: Fortress, 2009).

35. For the translation of *oikoumenē* as "empire," see Barbara Rossing, "(Re)Claiming *Oikoumenē*: Empire, Ecumenism and the Discipleship of Equals," in *Walk in the Ways of Wisdom: Essays in Honor of Elisabeth Schüssler Fiorenza*, ed. Shelly Matthews, Cynthia Briggs Kittredge, and Melanie Johnson-DeBaufre (Harrisburg, PA: Trinity Press International, 2005), 73–87.

36. Richard, *Apocalypse*, 30–31

37. John Collins, *The Apocalyptic Imagination: An Introduction to Jewish Apocalyptic Literature*, 2nd ed. (Grand Rapids, MI: Eerdmans, 1998), 283.

38. Hughes, *Environmental Problems*, 2.

39. Clarice Martin, "Polishing the Unclouded Mirror: A Womanist Reading of Revelation 18:13," in *From Every People and Nation: The Book of Revelation in Intercultural Perspective*, ed. David Rhoads (Minneapolis, MN: Fortress, 2005), 82–109.

40. Richard Bauckham, "The Economic Critique of Rome in Revelation 18," in *Images of Empire*, ed. Loveday Alexander, JSOTS 122 (Sheffield, UK: Sheffield Academic, 1991), 47–86.

41. Nicholas Rauh et al., "The Archaeology of Deforestation in South Coastal Turkey," *International Journal of Sustainable Development & World Ecology* 19 (2012): 395–405.

42. Bauckham, "Economic Critique," 65, 67.

43. J. Donald Hughes, "Ancient Deforestation Revisited," *Journal of the History of Biology* 44.1 (February 2011): 43–57.

44. Aelius Aristides, "Roman Oration," in *P. Aelius Aristides. The Complete Works*, ed. Charles A. Gehr, 2 vols. (Leiden: Brill, 1981), 26.12.

45. Schüssler Fiorenza, *Revelation*, 99; Richard, *Apocalypse*, 134.
46. Allen Callahan, "Apocalypse as Critique of Political Economy: Some Notes on Revelation 18," *Horizons in Biblical Theology* 21, no. 1 (1999): 60.
47. Jürgen Moltmann, "Liberating and Anticipating the Future," in *Liberating Eschatology: Essays in Honor of Letty M. Russell*, ed. Margaret A. Farley and Serene Jones (Louisville, KY: Westminster John Knox, 1999), 189.
48. Simarmata, "Like a Tree."
49. Wangari Maathai, *Replenishing the Earth: Spiritual Values for Healing Ourselves and The World* (New York: Doubleday, 2010), 125.

Bibliography

Abesamis, Carlos. 1991. *Exploring Biblical Faith*. Quezon City, Philippines: Claretian Publications.

Abraham, K.C., ed. 1990. *Third World Theologies—Commonalities and Divergences*. Maryknoll, NY: Orbis.

Ackermann, Denis and Tahira Joyner. 1996. "Earth-Healing in South Africa: Challenges to Church and Mosque." In *Women Healing Earth: Third World Women on Ecology, Feminism, and Religion*, edited by Rosemary Radford Ruether, 121–34. Maryknoll, NY: Orbis Books.

Aelius Aristides. 1981. *P. Aelius Aristides: The Complete Works*. Edited by Charles A. Behr. 2 vols. Leiden: Brill.

Allen, John. 2009. *The Future Church: Ten Trends Revolutionizing the Catholic Church*. New York: Doubleday.

Amjad-Ali, Charles. 2009. "Christian Ethics in the Context of Globalism, the Clash of Civilisations and the American Empire." In *Globalisation*, Volume 1, *The Politics of Empire, Justice and the Life of Faith*, edited by Allan Boesak and L.D. Hansen, 83–114. Bloemfontein, South Africa: African Sun Media.

Anzaldua, Gloria. 1987. *Borderlands/La Frontera: The New Mestiza*. San Francisco, CA: Spinsters/Aunt Lute.

Asamoah-Gyadu, J. Kwabena. 2012. "To The Ends of the Earth: Mission, Migration and the Impact of African-Led Pentecostal Churches in the European Diaspora." *Mission Studies* 29.1: 23–44.

Asante, Emmanuel. 1985. "Ecology: Untapped Resource of Pan-Vitalism in Africa." *AFER: African Ecclesial Review* 27: 289–293.

Auffarth, Christoph. 1999. "Paradise Now—But for the Wall Between: Some Remarks on Paradise in the Middle Ages." In *Paradise Interpreted: Representations of Biblical Paradise in Judaism and Christianity*, edited by Gerard P. Luttikhuizen, 168–79. Leiden: Brill.

Avineri, Shlomo. 1991. *The Making of Modern Zionism*. New York: Basic Books.

Bacon, David. 2008. *Illegal People: How Globalization Creates Migration and Criminalizes Immigrants*. Boston: Beacon Press.

Bakare, S. 1993. *My Right to Land—in The Bible and in Zimbabwe*. Mutare, Zimbabwe: Delsink Publishers.

Baldwin, James. 1972. *No Name in the Street*. New York: Vintage Books.

Bales, Kevin. 2012. *Disposable People: New Slavery in the Global Economy*. Berkeley, CA: University of California Press.

Bambara, Toni Cade. 1981. *The Salt-Eaters*. New York: Vintage Books.

Banana, C. S. 1989. *Turmoil and Tenacity: Zimbabwe 1890—1990*. Harare, Zimbabwe: College Press.

Banner, Stuart. 2007. *Possessing the Pacific: Land, Settlers, and Indigenous People from Australia to Alaska*. Cambridge, MA: Harvard University Press.

Battistela, Graziano. 1995. *For a More Abundant Life: Migrant Workers in Asia*. Background Paper for the Sixth FABC Plenary Assembly. Hong Kong: FABC.

Bauckham, Richard. 1991. "The Economic Critique of Rome in Revelation 18." In *Images of Empire*, edited by Loveday Alexander, 47–90. Journal for the Study of the Old Testament Supplement Series 122. Sheffield, UK: Sheffield Academic.

Bazian, Hatem. 2016. *Palestine, It is Something Colonial*. The Hague: Amrit Publishers.

Before the Flood. 2016. Directed by Fisher Stevens. RatPac Documentary Films and Appian Way.

Bell, Vaughn, Peter W. Halligan, and Hadyn D. Ellis. 2006. "Explaining Delusions: A Cognitive Perspective." *TRENDS in Cognitive Sciences* 10.5 (May): 219–26.

Berry, Wendell. 2015. *Our Only World*. Berkley, CA: Counterpoint.

Blount, Brian. 2005. *Can I Get A Witness? Reading Revelation Through African American Culture*. Louisville, KY: Westminster.

Blyth, Caroline, and Nāsili Vaka'uta, eds. 2017. *Bible & Art, Perspectives from Oceania*. London: Bloomsbury.

Boesak, Allan. 1987. *Comfort and Protest: The Apocalypse from a South African Perspective*. Philadelphia, PA: Westminster.

Bonk, Jonathan. 2012. "Whose Head is This and Whose Title?" Presidential address delivered at the International Association for Mission Studies 13th Quadrennial Conference, Toronto, August 15, 2012. https://sites.google.com/a/iams2012.org/toronto-2012/ (accessed March 11, 2017).

Bremmer, Jan N. 1999. "Paradise: From Persia, via Greece, into the Septuagint." In *Paradise Interpreted: Representations of Biblical Paradise in Judaism and Christianity*, edited by Gerard P. Luttikhuizen, 1–20. Leiden: Brill.

Brooks, A. A. 1917. *History of Bedwardism or The Jamaica Native Baptist Free Church, Union Camp August Town, St Andrew*. Kingston, Jamaica: The Gleaner Co. Ltd.

Brueggemann, Walter. 2002. *The Land: Place as Gift, Promise and Challenge in the Bible*. Minneapolis, MN: Fortress Press.

Callahan, Allen. 1999. "Apocalypse as Critique of Political Economy: Some Notes on Revelation 18." *Horizons in Biblical Theology* 21.1: 46–65.

Campese, Gioacchino. 2008. "Cuantos Más?: The Crucified People at the U.S.-Mexico Border." In *A Promised Land, A Perilous Journey: Theological Perspectives On Migration*, edited by Daniel Groody and Gioacchino Campese, 271–98. Notre Dame, IN: University of Notre Dame Press.

Carrigan, Anthony. 2011. *Postcolonial Tourism: Literature, Culture, and Environment*. New York: Routledge.

Carter, Paul. 1987. *The Road to Botany Bay: An Essay in Spatial History*. London & Boston: Faber & Faber.

Castles, Stephen, and Mark Miller. 2009. *The Age of Migration: International Population Movements in the Modern World*. 4th ed. Basingstoke, UK: Palgrave MacMillan.

Catholic Bishops' Conference of Japan. 2016. "Now Especially, Peace Must Not Depend upon Weapons—Regarding the Enforcement of the Security Laws," April 7, 2016, https://www.cbcj.catholic.jp/2016/04/07/5314/ (accessed May 25, 2017).

———. 2015. "70 Years after the War: Blessed are the Peacemakers—Now Especially, Peace Must Not Depend upon Weapons," February 25, 2015, https://www.cbcj.catholic.jp/2015/02/25/5182/ (accessed May 25, 2017).

Central Land Council. "Kinship and Skin Names." https://www.clc.org.au/index.php?/articles/info/aboriginal-kinship (accessed October 10, 2018).

Césaire, Aimé. 1955. *Discours sur le colonialism*. Paris: Présence Africaine

———. 2001. *Discourse on Colonialism*. Translated by John Pinkham. New York: Monthly Review Press.

Clarke, Sathianathan, Deenabandhu Manchala, and Philip Peacock, eds. 2010. *Dalit Theology in the Twenty-first Century: Discordant Voices, Discerning Pathways*. Oxford: Oxford University Press.

Collins, John. 1998. *The Apocalyptic Imagination: An Introduction to Jewish Apocalyptic Literature*. 2nd ed. Grand Rapids: Eerdmans.

Columbus, Christopher. 1847. *Select Letters of Christopher Columbus, With Other Original Documents, Relating to His Four Voyages to the New World*. Translated by R. H. Major. London: Hakluyt Society.

Commission for Justice and Peace of the Canadian Conference of Catholic Bishops. 2016. "The Doctrine of Discovery, Terra Nullius, and the Catholic Church: An Historical Overview." http://saltandlighttv.org/blogfeed/getpost.php?id=69373.

Commission, Southern African Anglican Theological. 1998. "The Land and Its Use in Southern Africa: Report of the Southern African Anglican Theological Commission, 26th January 1995." *The Bulletin for Contextual Theology on Church and Land* 5 (3): 6–16.

Cone, James H. 2001. "Whose Earth Is It, Anyway?" In *Earth Habitat: Eco-Injustice and the Church's Response*, edited by Dieter Hessel and Larry Rasmussen, 23–32. Minneapolis, MN: Fortress Press.

Cruz, Gemma Tulud. 2012. "I Was a Stranger and You Welcomed Me: Hospitality in the Context of Migration." *CTC Bulletin* 28.1: 96–118.

———. 2016. "Light of the World?: Christianity and Immigrants from the Global South." In *World Christianity and Global Theologizing: Perspectives and Insights*, edited by Jonathan Tan and Anh Tran, 85–107. New York: Orbis Books.

———. 2014. "The Moral Economy of Labor Mobility: Migration and the Global Workforce." In *Religious and Ethical Perspectives on Global Migration*, edited by Charles R. Strain and Elizabeth W. Collier, 35–51. Lanham, MD: Lexington Books.

———. 2004. "The Power of Resistance: An Inquiry into the Power of the Power-less." *CTC Bulletin* (December 2004): 131–37.

Curry, Andrew. 2015. "Trajan's Amazing Column." With photographs by Kenneth Garrett and interactive graphics. *National Geographic Magazine* (April) www.nationalgeographic.com/trajan-column.

Danesi, P. Giacomo. 1981. "Towards a Theology of Migration." In World Council of Churches, *Church and Migration: WCC Fifth Assembly Dossier No. 13*, 10–41. Geneva: WCC Migration Secretariat.

Davis, Jeffrey Sasha. 2005. "Representing Place: 'Deserted Isles' and the Reproduction of Bikini Atoll." *Annals of the Association of American Geographers* 95.3: 607–25.

de las Casas, Bartolomé. 2005. *Brevísima relación de la destrucción de las Indias*. Madrid: Alianza Editorial.

de Sepúlveda, Juan Ginés. 1951. *Democrates Segundo: O De Las Justas causas de la Guerra contra los indios*. Madrid: CSIC.

de Vaux, Roland. 1961. *Ancient Israel: Its Life and Institutions*. London: Darton, Longman & Todd.

Dear, John. 2018. *They Will Inherit the Earth: Peace & Nonviolence in a Time of Climate Change*. Maryknoll, NY: Orbis.

Deloria Jr., Vine. 2003. *God is Red: A Native View of Religion*. New York: Putman, 2003.

DeLoughrey, Elizabeth M. 2007. *Routes and Roots: Navigating Caribbean and Pacific Island Literatures*. Honolulu: University of Hawai'i Press.

Delumeau, Jean. 1995. *History of Paradise: The Garden of Eden in Myth and Tradition*. Translated by Matthew O'Connell. New York: Continuum.

Dennis, Trevor. 2010. *Sarah Laughed: Women's Voices in the Old Testament*. London: SPCK.

Dewey, Arthur J. 2008."The Gospel of Trajan." In *Jesus, The Voice, and the Text: Beyond the Oral and the Written Gospel*, edited by Tom Thatcher, 181–196. Waco, TX: Baylor University Press.

"The Doctrines of Discovery, 'Terra Nullius' and the Legal Marginalisation of Indigenous Peoples in Contemporary Africa: Statement by the Indigenous Peoples of Africa Coordinating Committee to the 11th Session of the UN Permanent Forum on Indigenous Issues (UNPFII)." May 7, 2012.

Donnan, Hastings, and Fiona Magowan. 2010. *The Anthropology of Sex*. Oxford: Berg.
Duncan, Christopher R. 2001. "Savage Imagery: (Mis)representations of the Forest Tobelo of Indonesia." *The Asia Pacific Journal of Anthropology* 2:1:45–62.
Dussel, Enrique. 1995. *The Invention of the Americas: Eclipse of "the other" and the Myth of Modernity*. Translated by Michael D. Barber. New York: Continuum.
———. 1994. *1492: El encubrimiento del otro: Hhacia el origen del "mito de la modernidad": conferencias de Frankfurt, octubre de 1992*. La Paz, Bolivia: Plural Editores.
The Earth Bible Team. 2000. "Guiding Ecojustice Principles." In *Readings from the Perspective of Earth,* edited by Norman Habel, 38–53. Cleveland, OH: Pilgrim Press.
Elizondo, Virgilio. 1998. '"Transformation of Borders': Border Separation or New Identity." In *Theology: Expanding the Borders*, edited by Maria Pilar Aquino and Roberto S. Goizueta, 22–39. Mystic, CT: Twenty-Third Publications.
Ellefson, Benjamin. 2016. *The Land Without Color*. Edina, MN: Beaver's Pond.
Falkiner, Daniel Thomas Rothwell. 2015."The Erotics of Empire: Love, Power, and Tragedy in Thucydides and Hans Morgenthau." PhD, The London School of Economics and Political Science.
Fanon, Frantz. 2008. *Black Skin, White Masks*. New York: Grove.
Federation of Asian Bishops' Conferences-Office of Human Development. 1994. *Pilgrims of Progress??? A Primer of Filipino Migrant Workers in Asia*. Manila, Philippines: FABC-OHD.
Fejo, Wali. 2000. "The Voice of the Earth: An Indigenous Reading of Genesis 9." In *The Earth Story in Genesis*, edited Norman Habel, 140–46. Sheffield, UK: Sheffield Academic Press.
Ferguson, Yale H. 2008. "Approaches to Defining '"Empire"' and Characterizing United States Influence in the Contemporary World." *International Studies Perspectives* 9: 272–80.
Fewell, Danna Nolan, and David M. Gunn. 1992. *Gender, Power and Promise: The Subject of the Bible's First Story*. Nashville, TN: Abingdon.
Firth, Stewart. 1997. "Colonial Administration and the Invention of the Native." In *The Cambridge History of the Pacific Islanders*, edited by Donald Denooni et al., 253–88. Cambridge, UK: Cambridge University Press.
Foley, Michael, and Dean Hoge. 2007. *Religion and the New Immigrants: How Faith Communities Form Our Newest Citizens*. New York: Oxford University Press.
Francis (Pope). 2015. *Laudato Si: On Care for Our Common Home*. New York: Paulist.
Fukase, Tadakazu et al. 2008. *Let Us Be the Wind to Spread Arcticle 9!—A Record of International Symposium of IFOR Council and The 80th Anniversary of Japan Fellowship of Reconciliation (JFOR)*. Yamagta, Japan: Fellowship of Reconciliation.
Gill, Jerry. 2003. *Borderland Theology*. Washington, DC: EPICA.
Gorski, Mike. 2012. "Karl Jaspers on Delusion: Definition by Genus and Specific Difference." *Philosophy, Psychiatry, & Psychology* 19.2 (June): 79–86.
Grimshaw, Patricia, and Elizabeth Nelson. 2001. "Empire, 'the Civilising Mission' and Indigenous Christian Women in Colonial Victoria." *Australian Feminist Studies* 16.36: 296–308.
Groody, Daniel D. 2013. "The Church on the Move: Mission in an Age of Migration." *Mission Studies* 30: 27–42.
———. "Jesus and the Undocumented Immigrant: A Spiritual Geography of a Crucified People." *Theological Studies* 70: 307–16.
Grosfoguel, Ramon. 2013. "The Structure of Knowledge in Westernized Universities: Epistemic Racism/Sexism and the Four Genocides/Epistemecides on the Long 16th Century." *Human Architecture: Journal of Sociology of Self-Knowledge* 11.1: 8.
Grove, Richard H. 1995. *Green Imperialism: Colonial Expansions, Tropical Island Edens and the Origins of Environmentalism, 1600–1860*. Cambridge, UK: Cambridge University Press.
Guha, Ramachandra, and Juan Martinez-Alier. 1997. *Varieties of Environmentalism: Essays North and South*. Delhi, India: Oxford University Press.
Gutierrez, Gustavo. 2008. "Poverty, Migration, and the Option for the Poor." In *A Promised Land, A Perilous Journey: Theological Perspectives On Migration*, edited by Daniel Groody and Gioacchino Campese, 76–86. Notre Dame, IN: University of Notre Dame Press.

Habel, Norman. 2011. "Engaging the Bible in a New Key: Reading and Preaching with Creation." In *The Season of Creation: A Preaching Commentary*, edited by Norman Habel, 54–68. Minneapolis, MN: Fortress Press.

Hall, C. Michael, and Hazel Tucker. 2004. "Tourism and Postcolonialism: An Introduction." In *Tourism and Postcolonialism: Contested Discourses, Identities and Representations*, edited by C. Michael Hall and Hazel Tucker, 1–24. London: Routledge.

Hardt, Michael, and Antonio Negri. 2000. *Empire*. Cambridge, MA: Harvard University Press.

Harris, W. V. 2013. "Defining and Detecting Ancient Mediterranean Deforestation, 800 BCE to 700 CE." In *The Ancient Mediterranean Environment between Science and History*, edited by W. V. Harris. Leiden: Brill.

Harrison, James R. 2011. "'More Than Conquerors' (Rom 8:37): Paul's Gospel and the Augustan Triumphal Arches of the Greek East and Latin West." *Buried History* 47: 3–20.

Hau'ofa, 'Epeli et al. eds. 1993. *A New Oceania: Rediscovering Our Sea of Islands*. Suva, Fiji: Institute of Pacific Studies, USP.

Hawken, Paul, and Tom Steyer, eds. 2017. *Drawdown: The Most Comprehensive Plan Ever to Reverse Global Warming*. New York: Penguin.

Haywood, John. 2009. *The Great Migrations: From the Earliest Humans to the Age of Globalization*. London: Quercus.

Herzl, Theodor. 1900. *Altneuland: Roman*. Berlin: H. Seeman.

———. 1920. *Der Judenstaat*. Berlin: Jüdischer Verlag.

———. 1988. *The Jewish State*. Translated by Jacob Alkow. New York: Dover Publications.

———. 1960. "Letter 6/12/1985." In *The Complete Diaries of Theodor Herzl*, edited by Raphael Patai and translated by Harry Zohn. New York: Herzl Press.

———. 1941. *The Old-New-Land*. Translated by Lotta Levenshon. New York: Bloch Pub.

Hezel, Francis X. 1995. *Strangers in Their Own Land: A Century of Colonial in the Caroline and Marshall Islands*. Honolulu, HI: University of Hawaii Press.

Himmerlfarb, Martha. 1991. "The Temple and the Garden of Eden in Ezekiel, the Book of the Watchers, and the Wisdom of Ben Sira." In *Sacred Places and Profane Spaces: Essays in the Geographics of Judaism, Christianity, and Islam*, edited by Jamie Scott and Paul Simpson-Housley, 63–78. New York: Greenwood.

Hobsbawm, Eric. 2003. "America's Imperial Delusion: The US Drive for World Domination Has No Historical Precedent." *The Guardian* (June 14).

Hollenbach, David, ed. 2010. *Driven from Home: Protecting the Rights of Forced Migrants*. Washington, DC: Georgetown University Press.

Horsley, Richard. 2009. *Revolt of the Scribes: Resistance and Apocalyptic Origins*. Minneapolis, MN: Fortress.

———. ed. 2008. *In the Shadow of Empire: Reclaiming the Bible as a History of Faithful Resistance*. Louisville, KY: Westminster John Knox Press.

Howard-Brook, Wes. 2016. *Empire Baptized: How the Church Embraced What Jesus Rejected, 2nd–5th Centuries*. New York: Orbis.

Howitt, William. 1838. *Colonization and Christianity: A Popular History of the Treatment of the Natives by the Europeans in all their Colonies*. London: Longman, Orme, Brown, Green, & Longmans.

Howkins, Adrian. 2010. "Appropriating Space: Antarctic Imperialism and the Mentality of Settler Colonialism." In *Making Settler Colonial Space: Perspectives on Race, Place and Identity*, edited by Tracey Banivanua Mar and Penelope Edmonds, 29–52. New York: Palgrave Macmillan.

Hughes, J. Donald. 2011. "Ancient Deforestation Revisited." *Journal of the History of Biology* 44.1 (February): 43–57.

———. 2014. *Environmental Problems of the Greeks and Romans*. 2nd ed. Baltimore, MD: Johns Hopkins University Press.

International Organization for Migration. 2010. *World Migration Report 2010: The Future of Migration: Building Capacities for Change*. Geneva: IOM.

———. 2018. *World Migration Report 2018*. Geneva: IOM. https://publications.iom.int/system/files/pdf/wmr_2018_en_chapter2.pdf (accessed May 20, 2018).

Jeong-hyeon, Mun. 2016. "A Priest on the Way" (from the original manuscript of a speech given in New York, unpublished).

Josephus, Flavius. 1943. *The Jewish War*. Translated by H. St. J. Thackeray. 2 vols. Loeb Classical Library. Cambridge, MA: Harvard University Press.

Kahl, Brigitte. 2015. "Gaia, Polis, and Ekklesia at the Miletus Market Gate: An Eco-Critical Reimagination of Revelation 12:16." In *The First Urban Churches 1: Methodological Foundations*, edited by James R. Harrison and L. L. Welborn, 111–50. Atlanta, GA: Society of Biblical Literature Press.

Kane, Ousmane Oumar. 2011. *The Homeland Is the Arena: Religion, Transnationalism and the Integration of Senegalese Immigrants in America*. New York: Oxford University Press.

Kang U-il, Peter. 2014. "The Gospel and the State." Gangjeong Peace Conference and Peace Festival, September 26, 2014, Jeju. Unpublished.

Kaoma, John Kapya. 2013. *God's Family, God's Earth: Christian Ecological Ethics of Ubuntu*. Zomba, Malawi: Kachere Series.

Karanga, Shoko T. 2007. *Indigenous Religion in Zimbabwe: Health and Well-Being*. Oxford: Routledge Books.

Katerere, Y. et al. 1991. "Zimbabwe: An Environmental Profile." ZERO Working Paper, No. 27.

Kiel, Micah. 2017. *Apocalyptic Ecology: The Book of Revelation, the Earth and the Future*. Collegeville, MN: Liturgical Press.

Kim, Dong Jin. 2015. "The Peace-building Role of the Ecumenical Movement in Korea during the 1980s." In *Mining Truths: Festchrift in Honour of Geraldine Smyth OP—Ecumenical Theologian and Peacebuilder*, edited by John O' Grady, Cathy Higgins, and Jude Lal Fernando, 267–285. Munich: EOS.

Kincaid, Jamaica. 1988. *A Small Place*. New York: Farrar, Straus and Giroux.

Klein, Naomi. 2014. *This Changes Everything: Capitalism vs. the Climate*. London: Penguin.

Kristeva, Julia. 1991. *Strangers to Ourselves*. Translated by Leon S. Roudiez. New York: Columbia University Press.

Kwok, Pui Lan. 1991. "Discovering the Bible in the Non-Biblical World." In *Voices from the Margin: Interpreting the Bible from the Third World*, edited by R.S. Sugirtharajah, 299–315. London: SPCK.

———. 1999. "Mending of Creation: Women, Nature, and Eschatological Hope." In *Liberating Eschatology: Essays in Honor of Letty M. Russell*, edited by Margaret A. Farley and Serene Jones, 144–55. Louisville, KY: Westminster John Knox.

Kwon, Jin Kwan. 2016. "Churches in the Divided Nation—An Analysis of the Korean Christianity Structured by the Cold War System, 1945–1990." In *Unfinished History—Christianity and the Cold War in East Asia*, edited by Philip L. Wickeri, 215–30. Leipzig, Germany: Evangelische Verlagsanstalt.

Laishley, Roy. 2014. "Is Africa's Land Up for Grabs." *Africa Renewal: Special Edition on Agriculture* 2014. http://www.un.org/africarenewal/magazine/special-edition-agriculture-2014/africa%E2%80%99s-land-grabs (accessed September 21, 2017).

Lancaster House Agreement. https://sas-space.sas.ac.uk/5847/5/1979_Lancaster_House_Agreement.pdf (accessed October 25, 2019).

Land issues in Zimbabwe. https://www.colonialrelic.com/appendixes/appendix-vi-the-land-tenure-act-1969-and-the-land-apportionment-act-1930/ (October 25, 2019).

Land reform in Zimbabwe. https://en.wikipedia.org/wiki/Land_reform_in_Zimbabwe#cite_note-Security-4 (accessed October 25, 2019).

Landolt, Patricia. 2008. "The Transnational Geographies of Immigrant Politics: Insights from a Comparative Study of Migrant Grassroots Organizing." *The Sociological Quarterly* 49: 53–77.

Lanfer, Peter T. 2009. "Allusion to and Expansion of the Tree of Life and Garden of Eden in Biblical and Pseudepigraphical Literature." In *Early Christian Literature and Intertextuality*, edited by Craig A. Evans and H. Daniel Zacharias, 96–108. London: T&T Clark.

Langmead, Ross. 2014. "Refugees as Guests and Hosts: Towards a Theology of Mission Among Refugees and Asylum Seekers." *Exchange* 43: 29–47.

Lewis, Martin W. 1994. "Environmental History Challenges the Myth of a Primordial Eden." *Journal of Geological Education* 42: 474–75.

Lopez, Davina. 2011. "Visualizing Significant Otherness: Reimagining Pauline Studies Through Hybrid Lenses." In *The Colonized Apostle: Paul Through Post-Colonial Eyes*, edited by Joseph Marchal, 74–289. Minneapolis, MN: Fortress.

Lustgarten, Abrahm. 2018. "Palm Oil Was Supposed to Help Save the Planet. Instead It Unleashed a Catastrophe." *New York Times Magazine* (November 24).

Maathai, Wangari. 2010. *Replenishing the Earth: Spiritual Values for Healing Ourselves and The World*. New York: Doubleday.

Madigan. Patricia. 2016. "Graced by Migration: An Australian Perspective." In *Christianities in Migration: The Global Perspective*, edited by Elaine Padilla and Peter Phan, 135–52. New York: Palgrave.

Maduro, Otto. 2014. "2012 Presidential Address: Migrants' Religions under Imperial Duress: Reflections on Epistemology, Ethics and Politics in the Study of the Religious 'Stranger'." *Journal of the American Academy of Religion* 82: 35–46.

Makura-Paradza, G. G. 2010. "Single Women, Land and Livelihood Vulnerability in a Communal area in Zimbabwe." Wageningen, Netherlands: Wageningen University and Research Centre.

Maluleke, Tinyiko. 1998. "The Land of the Church of the Land: A Response to the Whole Issue." *The Bulletin for Contextual Theology on Church and Land* 5.3: 61–64.

Mares, Peter. 2002. *Borderline*. Sydney: University of New South Wales Press.

Martin, Clarice. 2005. "Polishing the Unclouded Mirror: A Womanist Reading of Revelation 18:13." In *From Every People and Nation: The Book of Revelation in Intercultural Perspective*, edited by David Rhoads, 82–109. Minneapolis, MN: Fortress.

Marx, Karl. 1967. "Toward a Critique of Hegel's Philosophy of Law." In *Writings of the Young Marx on Philosophy and Society*, translated by Lloyd D. Easton and Kurt H. Guddat. New York: Anchor Books.

———. "Zur kritik der hegelschen rechtsphilosophie." In *Ökonomische-philosophische Manuskripte* in *Marx/Engels Gesamtausgabe*. Berlin: Dietz Verlag.

Massad, Joseph. 2000. "The "Post-Colonial: Time, Space, and Bodies in Israel/Palestine." In *The Pre-occupation of Postcolonial Studies*, edited by Fawzia Afzal-Khan et al. Durham, NC: Duke University Press.

McClintock, Anne. 1995. *Imperial Leather: Race, Gender and Sexuality in Colonial Contest*. London: Routledge.

———. 2009. "Paranoid Empire: Specters from Guantánamo and Abu Ghraib." *Small Axe* 28 (March): 50–74.

———. 1991. "The Scandal of the Whorearchy: Prostitution in Colonial Nairobi." *Transition* 52: 92–99.

McFague, Sally. 2008. *A New Climate for Theology: God, the World, and Global Warming*. Minneapolis, MN: Fortress Press.

McKinlay, Judith E. 2014. *Troubling Women and Land: Reading Biblical Texts in Aotearoa New Zealand*. Sheffield, UK: Sheffield Phoenix Press.

Meiggs, Russell. 1982. *Trees and Timber in the Ancient Mediterranean World*. Oxford: Clarendon.

Melanchthon, Monica Jyotsna. 2012. "Unleashing the Power Within: The Bible and Dalits." In *The Future of the Biblical Past: Envisioning Biblical Studies on a Global Key*, edited by Roland Boer and Fernando F. Segovia, 47–66. Atlanta, GA: Society of Biblical Literature.

Merrill, Dennis. 2009. *Negotiating Paradise: U.S. Tourism and Empire in Twentieth-Century Latin America*. Chapel Hill, NC: University of North Carolina Press.

Mignolo, Walter. 1995. *The Darker Side of the Renaissance*. Ann Arbor, MI: Michigan University Press.

———. 2000. *Local Histories/Global Designs: Coloniality, Subaltern Knowledges and Border Thinking*. Princeton, NJ: Princeton University Press.

Milton, John. 2005. *Paradise Lost*. Edited by Gordon Teskey. New York: Norton.

Min, Anselm. 2008. "Migration and Christian Hope." In *Faith on the Move: Towards a Theology of Migration in Asia*, edited by Fabio Baggio and Agnes Brazal, 177–202. Quezon City, Philippines: Ateneo de Manila University Press.

Moltmann, Jürgen. 1999. "Liberating and Anticipating the Future." In *Liberating Eschatology: Essays in Honor of Letty M. Russell*, edited by Margaret A. Farley and Serene Jones, 189–208. Louisville, KY: Westminster John Knox.

Morris, Henry M. 1976. *The Genesis Record: A Scientific and Devotional Commentary on the Book of Beginnings*. Grand Rapids, MI: Baker.

Morton, Nelle. 1985. *The Journey Is Home* Boston: Beacon Press.

Mosley, P. 2009. "The Settler Economies: Studies." In *Economic History of Kenya and Southern Rhodesia 1900–1963*. Cambridge, UK: Cambridge University Press.

Mowe, Sam. 2015. "Capitalism vs. the Climate: Naomi Klein On Why Only a Mass Movement Can Save Us from Ourselves." *Tricycle* 25 (Fall). https://tricycle.org/magazine/capitalism-vs-climate.

Murray, Melanie A. 2009. *Island Paradise: The Myth: An Examination of Contemporary Caribbean and Sri Lankan Writing*. Amsterdam: Rodopi.

Myers, Ched. 2007. "'The Cedar Has Fallen!' The Prophetic Word vs. Imperial Clear-Cutting." In *Earth and Word: Classic Sermons on Saving the Planet*, edited by David Rhoads, 211–23. New York: Continuum.

Narang, Sonia. 2017. "In Okinawa, Older Women Are on the Front Lines of the Military Base Protest Movement." *PRI*, February 14, 2017. https://www.pri.org/stories/2017-02-14/okinawa-older-women-are-front-lines-military-base-protest-movement (accessed March 25, 2017).

Nel, Philip J. 2008. "Morality and Religion in African Thought." *Acta Theologica* 2: 33–47.

Nelson, H. 1998. "Zimbabwe: A Country Study." In *Zimbabwean Realities and Christian Responses*, edited by F. J. Verstraelen, 137–53. Gweru, Zimbabwe: Mambo Press.

Noort, Ed. 1999. "Gan-Eden in the Context of the Mythology of the Hebrew Bible." In *Paradise Interpreted: Representations of Biblical Paradise in Judaism and Christianity*, edited by Gerard P. Luttikhuizen, 21–36. Leiden: Brill.

Okome, Mojubaolu Olufunke. 2012. "African Immigrant Relationships with Homeland Countries." In *Africans in Global Migration: Searching for Promised Lands*, edited by John Arthur et al., 199–224. Lanham, MD: Lexington Books.

Oosthoek, K. Jan. 1998. "The Role of Wood in World History." October 15. www.eh-resources.org/the-role-of-wood-in-world-history (accessed May 20, 2017).

Opiniano, Jeremiah. 2005. "Filipinos Doing Diaspora Philanthropy: The Development Potential of Transnational Migration." *Asian and Pacific Migration Journal* 14.1–2: 225–41.

Owusu, Thomas. 2012. "The Role of Ghanian Immigrant Associations in Canada." In *Africans in Global Migration: Searching for Promised Lands*, edited by John Arthur et al., 19–44. Lanham, MD: Lexington Books.

Pae, Keon-joo Christine. 2014. "Feminist Activism as Interfaith Dialogue: A Lesson from Gangjeong Village in Jeju Island, Korea." *Journal of Korean Religions* 5: 55–69.

Park, Do-hyun. 2013. *A Letter from Prison in Jeju* (lower level 2 cell 2, 18 July 2013; received through Kim Sung Hwan, a colleague of Park Do-hyun, unpublished).

Park, Francis Mun-su, S.J. 2015. "Conflicts and Peace Movements in N. E. Asia—Focus on Jesuit Involvement." Presentation at the JCAP Social Apostolate Meeting, August 3–7, 2015, Kuala Lumpur: unpublished.

Parra, Aritz. "Almost 500 Migrants Smash into Border Fence with Spain," https://www.yahoo.com/news/red-cross-assists-hundreds-migrants-entered-spain-084555096.html (accessed February 19, 2017).

Parsons, LaSalle. n.d. "Memories of Fifty Years on Okinawa" (original manuscript provided by the author).

Pasura, Dominic. 2012. "Religious Transnationalism: The Case of Zimbabwean Catholics in Britain." *Journal of Religion in Africa* 42: 26–53.

Pelikan, Jaroslav, ed. 1958. *Luther's Works: Lectures on Genesis Chapters 1–5*. Vol. 1. St. Louis, MO: Concordia.

Petras, James. 2008. "Military or Market-Driven Empire Building: 1950–2008," April 29, 2008, http://www.globalresearch.ca/military-or-market-driven-empire-building-1950-2008/8841 (accessed May 23, 2017).

Philpott, Graham and Zondi, Phumani. 1998. "Church Land: A Strategic Resource in the War against Poverty." *Bulleting for Contextual Theology on Church and Land* 5.3: 17–39.

Pieris, Aloysius. 1988. *Asian Liberation Theology*. Edinburgh: T&T Clark.

———. 1989. "Buddhists and Christians for Justice—The Korean Connection," *Dialogue* 16.1–2–3: 1–3.

Pliny. 1945. *Natural History*. Translated by H. Rackham. Loeb Classical Library. Cambridge, MA: Harvard University Press.

Polinska, Wioleta. 2000. "Dangerous Bodies: Women's Nakedness and Theology." *Journal of Feminist Studies in Religion* 16: 45–62.

Pontifical Council Cor Unum and Pontifical Council for the Pastoral Care of Migrants and Itinerant People. *Welcoming Christ in Refugees and Forcibly Displaced Persons: Pastoral Guidelines*. http://www.pcmigrants.org/documento%20rifugiati%202013/927-INGL.pdf (accessed March 20, 2017).

Portier Young, Anathea. 2011. *Apocalypse Against Empire: Theologies of Resistance in Early Judaism*. Grand Rapids, MI: Eerdmans.

Quijano, Anibal. 2000. "Coloniality of Power, Eurocentrism, and Latin America." *Nepantla: Views from the South* 1.3: 533–80.

Raheb, Mitri, and Suzanne Watts Henderson. 2017. *The Cross in Contexts: Suffering and Redemption in Palestine*. Maryknoll, NY: Orbis.

Raheb, Mitri. 2014. *Faith in the Face of Empire: The Bible through Palestinian Eyes*. Maryknoll, NY: Orbis.

———. 2014. "Land, People, and Empire—The Bible through Palestinian Christian Eyes," *Theologies and Cultures* 11.2: 17–32.

Rauh, Nicholas et al. 2012. "The Archaeology of Deforestation in South Coastal Turkey." *International Journal of Sustainable Development & World Ecology* 19: 395–405.

Reddie, Anthony G. 2011. *Is God Colour-blind? Insights from Black Theology for Christian Ministry*. London: SPCK.

Richard, Pablo. 1995. *Apocalypse: A People's Commentary on the Book of Revelation*. Maryknoll, NY: Orbis.

Richter, Sandra. 2010. "Environmental Law in Deuteronomy: One Lens on a Biblical Theology of Creation Care." *Bulletin for Biblical Research* 20.3: 355–76.

Rieger, Joerg. 2007. *Christ and Empire: From Paul to Postcolonial Times*. Minneapolis, MN: Fortress Press.

Rivera-Pagan, Luis. 1992. *A Violent Evangelism*. Louisville, KY: Westminster/John Knox Press.

Rohrer, Judy. 2016. *Staking the Claim: Settler Colonialism and Racialization in Hawai'i*. Tucson, AZ: The University of Arizona Press.

Roper, Garnett. 2012. *Caribbean Theology as Public Theology*. Kingston, Jamaica: XPRESS LITHO.

Rossing, Barbara. 2005. "(Re)Claiming *Oikoumenē*: Empire, Ecumenism and the Discipleship of Equals." In *Walk in the Ways of Wisdom: Essays in Honor of Elisabeth Schüssler Fiorenza*, edited by Shelly Matthews, Cynthia Briggs Kittredge, and Melanie Johnson-DeBaufre, 73–87. Harrisburg, PA: Trinity Press International.

Rundquist, Kristina. 2016. "Sandals Eyes Tobago for New Resort." *Travel Pulse*, November 24. http://www.travelpulse.com/news/hotels-and-resorts/sandals-eyes-tobago-for-new-resort.html.

Russell, Letty. 1987. *Household of Freedom: Authority in Feminist Theology*. Philadelphia, PA: The Westminster Press.

Said, Edward W. 1979. *The Question of Palestine*. New York: Vintage.

Salazar, Noel B. 2010. *Envisioning Eden: Mobilizing Imaginaries in Tourism and Beyond*. New York: Berghahn.

Salevao, Iutisone. 2000. "'Burning the Land': An Ecojustice Reading of Hebrews 6:7–8." In *Readings from the Perspectives of Earth*, edited by Norman C. Habel, 221–31. Sheffield, UK: Sheffield Academic Press.

Satchell, Veront. 1999. "Jamaica." Africana.com.

Schüssler Fiorenza, Elisabeth. 1991. *Revelation: Vision of a Just World*. Minneapolis, MN: Fortress.

Scott, James. 1990. *Domination and the Arts of Resistance*. New Haven, CT: Yale University Press.

———. 1995. *Weapons of the Weak: Everyday Forms of Peasant Resistance*. New Haven, CT: Yale University Press.

Sheller, Mimi. 2003. *Consuming the Caribbean: From Arawaks to Zombies*. London: Routledge.

Shibusawa, Bishop Peter Ichiro. 2012. "Statement of Opposition to the Deployment of MV-22 Osprey Aircraft at the U.S. Marine Corps Futenma Station," *ACNS*, October 5, 2012, http://www.anglicannews.org/news/2012/10/japanese-primate-tells-prime-minister-no-to-us-military-planes.aspx (accessed March 26, 2017).

Simarmata, Willem T. P. 2014. "Like a Tree Planted by Streams of Water." Manuscript from the 2014 Lutheran World Federation Council meeting in Medan, Indonesia.

Sindima, Harvey. 1989. "Community of Life." *The Ecumenical Review* 41.4: 537–51.

———. 1990. "Community of Life: Ecological Theology in African Perspective." In *Liberating Life: Contemporary Approaches in Ecological theology*, edited by Charles Birch, William Eaken, and Jay B. McDaniel, 137–47. Maryknoll, NY: Orbis Books.

Skwiot, Christine. 2010. *The Purpose of Paradise: U.S. Tourism and Empire in Cuba and Hawai'i*. Philadelphia, PA: University of Pennsylvania Press.

Slabodsky, Santiago. 2015."The Narrative of Barbarism: Westerns Designs for a Globalized North" in *Decolonial Judaism: Triumphal Failures of Barbaric Thinking*, 39–66. New York: Palgrave Macmillian.

Smith, Andrea. 1998. "Walking in Balance: The Spirituality/Liberation Praxis of Native Women." In *Lift Every Voice: Constructing Christian Theologies from the Underside*, edited by Susan Brooks Thislethwaite and Mary Potter Engel, 53–68. New York: Orbis.

Smith, Robert O. 2013. *More Desired Than Our Owne Salvation: The Roots of Christian Zionism*. New York: Oxford University Press.

———. 2015. Jerusalem World Council of Churches. https://www.youtube.com/watch?v=etTBIHHYq6M.

Sobrino, Jon. 2003. *Witnesses of the Kingdom: The Martyrs of El Salvador and the Crucified Peoples*. Maryknoll, NY: Orbis.

Sternhell, Zeev. 1988. *The Founding Myths of Israel: Nationalism, Socialism and the Making of the Jewish State*. Princeton, NJ: Princeton University Press.

Strachan, Ian Gregory. 2002. *Paradise and Plantation: Tourism and Culture in the Anglophone Caribbean*. Charlottesville, VA: University of Virginia Press.

Sullivan, Kathleen. 2000. "St. Mary's Catholic Church: Celebrating Domestic Religion." In *Religion and the New Immigrants: Continuities and Adaptations in Immigrant Congregations*, edited by Helen Rose Ebaugh and Janet Saltman Chafetz, 125–40. Walnut Creek, CA: Altamira Press.

Tacitus. 1931. *Agricola*. Translated by John Jackson. Loeb Classical Library. Cambridge, MA: Harvard University Press.

Tahhan, Zena. 2018. "More Than a Century Later: The Balfour Declaration Explained," *Al Jazeera* (November 2, 2018), https://www.aljazeera.com/indepth/features/2017/10/100-years-balfour-declaration-explained-171028055805843.html (accessed November 5, 2018).

Tamez, Elsa. 1986. "The Woman who Complicated the History of Salvation." *Cross Currents* 36.2: 129–39.

Tamilnet. 2017. "Keappaa-pulavu Protesters Denounce Compromises, Demand All Their Lands Released," April 24, 2017, http://www.tamilnet.com/art.html?catid=79&artid=38657 (accessed May 23, 2017).

Taylor, Burchell. 2006. *Saying No to Babylon: A Reading of Daniel*. Kingston, Jamaica: XPRESS LITHO.

The National Council of Churches in Korea. 2015. "Prayer from NCCK for Easter Preparation," *NCCK*, March 6, 2015, http://www.kncc.or.kr/eng/sub03/sub01.php?ptype=view&idx=14158&page=1&code=eng_board_03_1_1 (accessed March 27, 2017).

———. 2015. "Swords into Plowshares, and Spears into Pruning Hooks," *Joint Statement of the 9th Consultation of the NCCJ and NCCK*, December 12, 2015, http://www.kncc.or.kr/eng/sub04/sub03.php?ptype=view&code=eng_board_04_2&idx=15150 (accessed March 25, 2017).

Theology of Empire. http://pauldouglaswalker.blogspot.com/2013/06/loving-your-enemy-part-4-what-did-jesus.html (accessed October 25, 2019).

Theology of Land Covenant. http://www.churchofscotland.org.uk/__data/assets/pdf_file/0009/13230/Theology_of_Land_and_Covenant.pdf (accessed October 25, 2019).

Thomas, Greg. 2007. *The Sexual Demon of Colonial Power*. Bloomington, IN: Indiana University Press.

Tigchelaar, Eibert J.C. 1999. "Eden and Paradise: The Garden Motif in Some Early Jewish Texts (1 Enoch and Other Texts Found at Qumran)." In *Paradise Interpreted: Representations of Biblical Paradise in Judaism and Christianity*, edited by Gerard P. Luttikhuizen, 37–57. Leiden: Brill.

Tinker, George E. 1992. "Spirituality, Native American Personhood, Sovereignty and Solidarity" *Ecumenical Review* 44.3: 312–24.

Tipvarakankoon, Wiriya. 2017. *The Theme of Deception in the Book of Revelation: Bringing Early Christian and Thai Cultures into Dialogue*. Claremont, GA: Claremont Press.

Tomasi, Silvano. 1996. "The Prophetic Mission of the Churches: Theological Perspectives." In *The Prophetic Mission of the Churches in Response to Forced Displacement of Peoples, Report of a Global Ecumenical Consultation, Addis Ababa* (November 6–11, 1995), 36–43. Geneva: World Council of Churches.

Tran, Peter. 1998. "Migrant Workers in Asia: The Call by the Synod for Asia to Assist Migrants." *Migration World Magazine* 26.5: 32–35.

Trible, Phyllis. 1984. *Texts of Terror: Literary-Feminist Readings of Biblical Narratives*. Minneapolis, MN: Fortress Press.

Ulmanu, Monica, Alan Evans, and Georgia Brown. 2017. "The Defenders: 207 Environmental Defenders Have Been Killed in 2017 While Protecting Their Community's Land or Natural Resources." *The Guardian* (July 13).www.theguardian.com/environment/ng-interactive/2017/jul/13/the-defenders-tracker.

United Nations Department of Economic and Social Affairs. 2013. *International Migration Report 2013*. New York: United Nations.

Vaka'uta, Nāsili. 2014. "Border Crossing/Body Whoring: Rereading Rahab of Jericho with Native Women." In *Bible, Borders, Belonging(s): Engaging Readings from Oceania*, ed. Jione Havea, David Neville, and Elaine Wainwright, 143–55. Atlanta, GA: Society of Biblical Literature.

———. 2011. *Reading Ezra 9–10 Tu'a-wise: Rethinking Biblical Interpretation in Oceania*. Atlanta, GA: SBL.

———, ed. 2011. *Talanoa Rhythms: Voices from Oceania*. Albany, NZ: Massey University.

Valtonen, Kathleen. 1996. "East Meets North: The Finnish-Vietnamese Community." *Asian and Pacific Migration Journal* 5.4: 471–89.

Verstraelen, F. J. 1998. *Zimbabwean Realities and Christian Responses: Contemporary Aspects of Christianity in Zimbabwe*. Gweru, Zimbabwe: Mambo Press.

Walcott, Derek. 1990. *Omeros*. London: Faber and Faber.

Wallerstein, Immanuel. 2006. *European Universalism: The Rhetoric of Power*. New York: The New Press.

Ward, Gerard. 1989. "Earth's Empty Quarter? The Pacific Islands in a Pacific Century." *The Geographical Journal* 155.2: 235–46.

Watson, Blake A. 2011. "The Impact of the American Doctrine of Discovery on Native Land Rights in Australia, Canada, and New Zealand." *Seattle University Law Review* 34: 507–51.

Watty, William. 1981. *From Shore to Shore: Sounding in Caribbean Theology*. Kingston, Jamaica.

Weems, Renita J. 1988. *Just a Sister Away: A Womanist Vision of Women's Relationships in the Bible*. San Diego: Lura Media.

Welch, Sharon. 2000. *A Feminist Ethic of Risk*. Minneapolis, MN: Fortress Press.

Westermann, Claus. 1994. *Genesis 1–11: A Continental Commentary*. Minneapolis, MN: Fortress.

White, Lynn, Jr. 1967. "The Historical Roots of Our Ecological Crisis." *Science* 155.3767: 1203–7.

Wilensky-Lanford, Brook. 2011. *Paradise Lust: Searching for the Garden of Eden*. New York: Grove.

Williams, Delores. 1996. *Sisters in the Wilderness: The Challenge of Womanist God-Talk*. Maryknoll, NY: Orbis Books.

Williams, Jr., Robert A. 1990. *The American Indian in Western Legal Thought: The Discourses of Conquest*. New York: Oxford University Press.

Witte, Griff. 2015. "Hungarian Bishop Says Pope is Wrong about Refugees." https://www.washingtonpost.com/world/hungarian-bishop-says-pope-is-wrong-about-refugees/2015/09/07/fcba72e6-558a-11e5-9f54-1ea23f6e02f3_story.html (accessed March 20, 2017).

Worland, Justin. 2015. "Here's How Many Trees Humans Cut Down Each Year." *Time Magazine* (September 2).

Wyatt, Nicolas. 2014. "A Royal Garden: The Ideology of Eden." *SJOT* 28: 1–35.

Yothu Yindi. 2007. *Garma*. Phantom 1091333 compact disc.

Young, Robert C. 2015. *Empire, Colony, Postcolony*. Malden, MA: Wiley Blackwell.

———. 2003. *Postcolonialism: A Very Short Introduction*. Oxford: Oxford University Press.

Zachariah, George. 2011. *Alternatives Unincorporated: Earth Ethics from the Grassroots*. London: Equinox.

Index

Contributors

Gemma Tulud Cruz, a native of the Philippines, has lived in the Netherlands and the United States prior to moving to Australia, where she works as Senior Lecturer in Theology at Australian Catholic University in Melbourne. Cruz is the author of *Toward a Theology of Migration: Social Justice and Religious Experience* (Palgrave Macmillan, 2014), *An Intercultural Theology of Migration: Pilgrims in the Wilderness* (Brill, 2010) and a number of book chapters and journal articles on migration, women and gender issues, urbanization, transnationalism, missiology, contextual theologies, liberation theologies, and Asian and Filipino theologies. Cruz is currently working on a book tentatively titled *Sacrament of Solidarity, A House for All Peoples: The Mission of the Churches in the Age of Migration.*

Steed Vernyl Davidson is associate professor of Hebrew Bible/Old Testament, dean of the faculty, and vice president of academic affairs at McCormick Theological Seminary (Chicago). He previously taught at the Pacific Lutheran Theological Seminary and the Graduate Theological Union in Berkeley, California, as well as Luther College in Iowa. Davidson, an ordained Methodist clergyman, has served churches in the Caribbean and New York. He is the author of *Empire and Exile: Postcolonial Readings in the Book of Jeremiah* and *Writing/Reading Jeremiah in Postcolonial Perspective*, and coeditor of *Islands, Islanders and the Bible: Ruminations*. He provides ways in his academic work to make the Bible more relevant and liberating to the lives of people.

Jude Lal Fernando is assistant professor in Irish School of Ecumenics, Trinity College Dublin. He teaches on the postgraduate programs of international peace studies, and intercultural theology and interreligious studies. He has written widely on religion, conflict, and peace as well as geopolitics and human rights. He is the director of Trinity Centre for Post-Conflict Justice and was visiting professor at Tampere University, Finland, Uppsala University, Sweden, and Ritsumeikan and Sophia Universities, Japan.

Jione Havea is a native Methodist pastor from Tonga who is research fellow with Trinity Theological College (Aotearoa New Zealand) and the Public and Contextual Theology research centre of Charles Sturt University (Australia). Jione has taught at institutions in Tonga, USA, Australia, and Aotearoa New Zealand, and edited *Sea of Readings: The Bible and the South Pacific* (SBL 2018) and *Religion and Power* and *Scripture and Resistance*, both from Lexington Books/Fortress Academic.

Sifiso Mpofu is a Zimbabwean scholar and theologian. Mpofu studied marketing, education, and religious studies, and has been a lecturer at the University of Zimbabwe, United Theological College, Holy Trinity College, and Christian College of Southern Africa, and was a visiting Scholar at Emmanuel College of the University of Toronto in Canada. In 2000, Mpofu was awarded a young theologian accolade by the World Alliance of Reformed Churches.

Kuzipa Nalwamba is an ordained minister of the United Church of Zambia (UCZ). Her primary research background is in dogmatics and Christian ethics, with a focus on eco-theology. Her research interests include themes in eco-theology, science-theology dialogue, history of Christianity and mission, coloniality of power, church-state relations, and human sexuality.

Mitri Raheb is the founder and president of Dar al-Kalima University College of Arts and Culture in Bethlehem. Raheb is the author of eighteen books, including *The Cross in Contexts: Suffering and Redemption in Palestine* and *Faith in the Face of Empire: The Bible through Palestinian Eyes*. Raheb served as the senior pastor of the Christmas Lutheran Church in Bethlehem from June 1987 to May 2017 and as the president of the Synod of the Evangelical Lutheran Church in Jordan and the Holy Land from 2011 to 2016. Raheb founded several NGOs, including Dar annadwa Cultural and Conference Center, the Christian Academic Forum for Citizenship in the Arab World (CAFCAW), in addition to other civic initiatives on national, regional, and international levels.

Garnett Roper is the president of the Jamaica Theological Seminary in Kingston Jamaica. He has served as pastor of local congregations in the Missionary Church in Jamaica for more than thirty-five years. Roper has also served as chairman of the board of a number of public agencies, including the

Social Development Commission, the Jamaica Urban Transit Company, and the National Energy Solutions Ltd. He served as the executive director for the National Youth Service in its formative years. Roper has also been a radio talk show host, radio preacher, and newspaper columnist, and has published works including *Caribbean Theology as Public Theology* (2012).

Barbara Rossing is professor of New Testament at the Lutheran School of Theology at Chicago. She chairs the Society of Biblical Literature Ecological Hermeneutics section and is a board member of the Center for Advanced Study in Religion and Science (CASIRAS). Her publications include *The Rapture Exposed: The Message of Hope in the Book of Revelation* (Basic Books, 2004); *The Choice Between Two Cities: Whore, Bride and Empire in the Apocalypse* (Trinity Press, 1999); *Journeys Through Revelation: Apocalyptic Hope for Today* (PCUSA, 2010); and articles and book chapters on the apocalypse and ecology. As an ordained Lutheran pastor and public theologian, her media appearances included CBS's *Sixty Minutes*, The History Channel, National Geographic, Living the Questions, and many others.

Santiago Slabodsky is the Florence and Robert Kaufman Chair in Jewish studies and associate director of the Center for Race, Culture and Social Justice at Hofstra University in New York. Previously he directed the graduate program of religion, ethics, and society and was assistant professor of global ethics at Claremont School of Theology. His book *Decolonial Judaism* was awarded the 2017 Frantz Fanon Outstanding Book Award by the Caribbean Philosophical Association. He cochairs the Liberation Theologies unit at the American Academy of Religion and codirects the trilingual journal *Decolonial Horizons*. He has also served as visiting professor at institutions in Spain, The Netherlands, South Africa, Argentina, Costa Rica, and Macedonia.

Nāsili Vaka'uta is Principal and Ranston Lecturer in Biblical Studies, Trinity Theological College, Auckland, New Zealand. He is the author of *Reading Ezra 9–10 Tu'a-wise: Rethinking Biblical Interpretation in Oceania* (SBL, 2011), editor of *Talanoa Rhythms: Voices from Oceania* (Massey University, 2011), and coeditor of *Bible and Art, Perspectives from Oceania* (Bloomsbury, 2017), and contributed to various academic journals and book volumes such as *Bible, Borders, Belonging(s): Engaging Readings from Oceania* (Atlanta: SBL, 2015), *Islands, Islanders and the Bible: RumInations* (SBL, 2015), and *Voices from the Margin* (Orbis, 2016).

George Zachariah joins the faculty of Trinity Theological College (Aotearoa New Zealand) after serving the United Theological College, Bangalore, India, as professor and chairperson of the department of theology and ethics.

His publications include *Alternatives Unincorporated: Earth Ethics from the Grassroots* (Equinox, 2011), *Disruptive Faith Inclusive Communities: Church and Homophobia* (ed.)(ISPCK, 2015), and *The Life, Legacy and Theology of M.M. Thomas* (ed.)(Routledge, 2016).